THE OLD TESTAMENT AS LIVING LITERATURE

RUTH H. BLACKBURN
ASSOCIATE PROFESSOR OF ENGLISH
UNIVERSITY COLLEGE
RUTGERS UNIVERSITY

MONARCH
PRESS

Published by
MONARCH PRESS
a Simon & Schuster division of
Gulf & Western Corporation
Simon & Schuster Building
1230 Avenue of the Americas
New York, N.Y. 10020

MONARCH PRESS and colophon are trademarks of Simon &
Schuster, registered in the U.S. Patent and Trademark Office.

Standard Book Number: 0-671-00964-8

Printed in the United States of America

CONTENTS

PREFACE

The aim of this book is to provide an elementary guide to the Old Testament. As anyone knows who has tried to read it without help, the Bible is not an easy book to read. It comes to us from a remote world, one very different from our own. It knows nothing of science or philosophy as we understand them. It assumes the existence of angels, demons, devils, and other supernatural beings. It assumes, as many people today do not, the existence of the living God, who cares for his chosen people, the Jews, and who enters dynamically into history to guide them and all mankind.

Another obstacle for the reader is the sheer size and variety of the Old Testament. It contains thirty-nine books, and a single book may be an elaborate composite, such as the book of Isaiah, which includes the work of many authors and periods. The Old Testament and the Apocrypha contain literary and historical material from a period of well over a thousand years. Within this great library is contained a great variety of literary forms, myths, legends, epics, law codes, hymns, love poems, battle songs, prophetic oracles, allegories and history. Each of these forms has its own problems and fascinations,

and each requires — and repays — careful study.

Another seeming obstacle, which must be turned to advantage, is the quantity and complexity of recent Biblical scholarship, including archaeology.

This guide is intended to help the reader clear these obstacles. It contains articles on the historical background of the Bible, on its various literary forms, as well as on the making of the Canon and on the most important English translations. The chronology has been revised in accord with recent findings. The summaries of the books contain commentary in as much detail as the beginner should be expected to handle. When he has mastered its contents, he can go on to some of the books recommended in the bibliography.

All quotations unless otherwise indicated are from the King James Version (KJV). The Revised Standard Version (RSV), the American Translation (AT), and the New English Bible (NEB) have been used where the KJV is inaccurate. LXX stands for the Septuagint, the Greek translation of the Bible made in the third century A.D. The other abbreviations are standard. Details about works cited in the text are given in the bibliography.

DATE CHARTS

Israel and Her Neighbors
2000 — 800 B.C.

	EGYPT	HEBREWS	MESOPOTAMIA
2000	XII Dynasty	Abraham	Hurrians Amorites
1900			
1800	Hyksos Invasion		Hammurabi
1700	XV — XVII Dynasties (Hyksos)	Joseph and Family to Egypt	
1600	XVIII Dynasty		Babylonian Decline Hittite Empire
1500	Hyksos Expelled Thutmose III c. 1490-1435 Amenhotep III c. 1406-1370		New Hittite Empire
1400	Akhnaton c. 1370-1353		Rise of Assyria
1300	XIX Dynasty Seti c. 1308-1290 Rameses II c. 1290-1224 Merneptah c. 1224-1216	The Exodus The Judges c. 1250	
1200	XX Dynasty		
1100		Fall of Shiloh c. 1050 Samuel	
1000	Decline of Egypt XXI Dynasty XXII Dynasty	Saul 1020-1009 David 1009, King of Judah	Tiglath-Pileser I

THE DIVIDED KINGDOM

	ISRAEL		JUDAH		ASSYRIA
	SAMUEL				
	Saul, 1020-				
1000	David 1009/8				Tiglath-Pileser I revives Assyrian Empire
	NATHAN				
950	Solomon 970/69				Decline of Assyria
	Jeroboam I	931	Rehoboam	931	Revival of Assyria
			Abijam	913	
			Asa	911	
900	Nadab	910			Adad-ninari II
	Baasha	909			Ashur-nasir-pal II
	Elah	886			
	Zimri	885			
	Omri	880			
	Ahab	870	Jehoshaphat	873	Shalmaneser III
	ELIJAH				
850	Ahaziah	853	Jehoram	854	Battle of Qarqar
	Jehoram	852	Ahaziah	853	
	ELISHA		Athaliah	841	
	Jehu	841	Joash	835	Shamshi-Adah V
	Jehoahaz	814			Adad-nirari III
	Jehoash	798	Amaziah	796	
800					

Kings and Prophets
From 800 B.C. to the Exile

	ISRAEL	PROPHETS	JUDAH		ASSYRIA	
800	Jeroboam II 793			792	(Period of Assyrian weakness)	
750			Uzziah			
			(Jotham co-regent)			
	Zechariah 753	AMOS	Jotham	750	Tiglath-Pileser III	
	Shallum 752					
	Menahem 752	HOSEA				
	Pekahiah 748	ISAIAH	Ahaz (co-regent)	735	Shalmaneser V	
	Pekah 740	MICAH			Sargon II	
	Hoshea 732					
	Fall of Samaria 723					
700			Hezekiah	716	Sennacherib	
			Sennacherib invades	701		
			Manasseh	697		
			(co-regent)			
650					Esarhaddon	
			Amon	643	Asshurabanapal	
			Josiah	641		
					Asshur-etil-ilani	
		JEREMIAH	Deuteronomic		Sin-shan-ish-Kun	
		ZEPHANIAH	Reform c. 623			
		NAHUM				
600		HABAKKUK	Jehoahaz	609	Fall of Nineveh 612	
			Jehoiakim	609	BABYLONIAN EMPIRE	
		EZEKIEL	Jehoiachin	598	Nebuchadrezzar 605/4-562	
			Zedekiah	597	Battle of Carchemish 605	
			Fall of Jerusalem	587		
			Capture of Jerusalem	597		

Events and Prophets From After the Exile to 400 B.C.

	THE HEBREW PROPHETS	BABYLON		PERSIA / MEDIA	
				MEDIA	
				Cyaxares	625-585
		Nebuchadrezzar 605/4-562		Astyages	595-550
600	1st deportation 597				
	2nd deportation 586				
		Nebuchadrezzar invades			
	II ISAIAH	Egypt	568		
		Amel-marduk	562-560		
	Zerubbabel	Neriglissar	560-556		
	Rebuilding of Temple 520-515	Nabonidus	556-539		
	HAGGAI, ZECHARIAH			Cyrus overthrows Astyages 550	
				PERSIAN EMPIRE	
550		Cyrus takes Babylon	539	Cyrus	550-530
		Edict of Cyrus	538	Cambyses	530-522
				Darius I	522-486
				Marathon	490
				Xerxes	496-465
500	OBADIAH			Thermopylae, Salamis	480
				Artaxerxes I	465-424
	MALACHI			Peace of Gallias	449
450	Nehemiah gov. 445-			Xerxes II	423
	Ezra's mission 397?			Darius II	423-404
				Artaxerxes II	404-438

THE HISTORY OF ISRAEL

The Age of the Patriarchs

Between 3000-2000 B.C., the first great civilizations arose in the Fertile Crescent, which runs from the valleys of the Tigris and the Euphrates, through Syria and Canaan to the mouth of the Nile. Thus Canaan and Syria spanned the gap between the two great power centers, Mesopotamia and Egypt. About 2000 B.C., Semitic nomads, in the Bible called Amorites, began to move into the Fertile Crescent. Babylon for a time became an Amorite state, ruled about 1750 by the great King Hammurabi. There is evidence of many Semitic names in documents of the period, among them Abram, Jacob, Levi, and Ishmael. According to the Bible tradition, Abraham and his family moved north from Ur to Haran, certainly a Semitic settlement. Some of his relatives bear the names of places in that area, e.g., Haran and Nahor, suggestive that they settled there and put down roots. Both Isaac and Jacob are represented as returning to this area to seek wives. Abraham, Isaac, and Jacob seem to have belonged to the Aramaean subgroup of the Amorites: Jacob claims, "A wandering Aramaean was my father" (Deut 26:5). Another group constantly referred to in this period are the "Habiru." "Habiru" seems to be a general term for "outsiders" or "wanderers," who might include slaves, mercenaries, raiders, and other low-class people. The word could cover the "wandering Aramaeans" and was later more specifically applied to them; Abraham is called a "Hebrew" in Gen. 14.

Eventually (called by God according to Gen. 12), Abraham

moved on to Canaan where he was associated with Mamre, Isaac with Beersheba, and Jacob with Bethel, Shechem, and Dothan. (There is archaeological evidence for the existence of these three towns in this period.) These sites were in all probability holy places, where sacred pillars may have been set up, as we hear of Jacob doing (Gen. 28:18ff.). In such hill sites as these, the ancestors of Israel led a pastoral life with their flocks. If the correct date for Abraham is c. 1900 B.C., there were large Canaanite settlements at Gezer, Megiddo, and in the Jordan Valley at this time.[1]

In Egypt, the other great center of power, the Twelfth Dynasty ruled in the early years of the second millennium and had some control over Canaan and Syria. It was a period of great prosperity for Egypt and her satellites, and there is evidence that nomadic bands of Amorites wandered freely from Syria to Egypt. For example, the Tale of Sinuhe, composed about 1900, describes the prosperous seminomadic life of the Amorites in Syria, which was similar to the lives of the patriarchs. An Egyptian painting of the same period shows a group, probably of Amorites, entering Egypt, wearing many-colored garments and shoes or sandals and carrying water-bottles, javelins, bows, and a lyre (see Wright page 23); we remember the visit of Abraham to

---

1 See G. Ernest Wright, **Biblical Archaeology,** Abridged Edition, p. 30, for fuller details. Most of the facts in the present account come from this excellent and readable book. Details on this and other works referred to will be found in the bibliography.

Egypt and later the emigration of the Jacob tribe. (It is important to remember that several tribes remained in Canaan.) The story of Joseph, Gen. 37-50, the traditional account of this emigration, was certainly told by someone who had a thorough knowledge of Egyptian life. The importance of dreams and magicians, the customs of mummification, the titles of the "chief of the butlers" and the "chief of the barbers," and Joseph's own title and position are all in accordance with what we know of Egypt at that time (Wright, pp. 34-35). Joseph and his family probably arrived in Egypt in the seventeenth century, when the Hyksos, a foreign dynasty, ruled the country. The tribe remained there for about 400 years.

What Was the Religion of the Patriarchs? This is a very controversial subject, but it seems that they had a family deity, "the God of Abraham, Isaac, and Jacob," with whom they had a personal covenant, renewed in each generation. Such a covenant is described in Gen. 15. Their god was later identified with Yahweh (Ex. 3). One of his names was the Mesopotamian word "Shaddai" or "mountaineer," which suggests his power and grandeur. The patriarchs were certainly not monotheistic, as is attested, for instance, by Abraham's worship of El Elyon in Jerusalem, an Amorite and later a Canaanite chief deity (Wright, p. 32). It was to be some centuries before absolute monotheism was accepted.

How historically accurate are the stories of the patriarchs? We must remember that the stories about them were handed down orally for hundreds of years, that generations may have been telescoped, accounts simplified, and meanings seen (e.g., in the call of Abraham) which were not apparent to the original actors in the scenes. In the past scholars often surmised that we

had only the pictures of their personalities painted by later writers; or that the patriarchs were personifications of their tribes. There may be something in these hypotheses. We may never be able to prove that Abraham or Jacob existed or that they said and did certain things. On the other hand, we know that oral tradition is often surprisingly accurate and that the personalities of these men stand out with remarkable vividness and conviction in the pages of Genesis. *What we can be very certain of, what archaeology has demonstrated, is that the narratives reflect the background, the mores, the laws, not of the time in which they were written, but of the early centuries of the second millennium B.C.* (See "Archaeology of the Bible.")

Moses and the Exodus (probably 13th century B.C.)

Sometime between three and four centuries after Joseph's death, "there arose a new King over Egypt" (Ex. 1:8) who used forced labor by the Israelites to build the store-cities of Pithon and Raamses, probably in the reign of Rameses II. It was in revolt against this exploitation that the Exodus occurred. The Exodus, the freeing of the Israelites from bondage, and their covenant with their god, Yahweh, is the dominating event in their history, still celebrated in the festival of Passover.

The account of Moses is probably not historical in every detail, but it reflects the magnitude of his personality and accomplishment. His name was Egyptian in form, and it may be that he was really educated in the Egyptian court. His flight to the land of Midian led to his contact with his father-in-law there (variously called Reuel or Jethro), who may have been important in forming his religious ideas. According to the Bible, God revealed himself to Moses in the burning bush and gave him the new holy name, Yahweh. Pharaoh was threatened by the plagues, which may be based on natural causes which still exist in Egypt. The actual escape was preceded by a cultic rite which was the ancestor of the celebration of Passover. In their flight, the Israelites crossed the Reed Sea (*not* the Red Sea). The details of the "forty years" wandering in the wilderness are somewhat obscure including the site of the mountain (Horeb or Sinai) where the commandments were given. What was of paramount importance was the belief of the people that they and their god, Yahweh, had concluded a covenant together. This covenant was the beginning of the Hebrew nation.

Conquest and Settlement of Canaan (13th-11th centuries B.C.)

There is probably no period of Israel's history more disputed by scholars than the centuries of the Conquest. It is clear that the "Promised Land" Canaan, was inhabited by a mixed population. The Biblical accounts mention Hittites, Amorites, Perizzites, and Jebusites, as well as Canaanites. Later, the most formidable enemies were the Philistines, a sea people of Greek origin. According to one Biblical tradition, the twelve tribes invaded Canaan *en masse;* but closer scrutiny shows that there were many Israelites in Canaan who never went to Egypt, though they may from time to time have fought with their kin, the Joseph tribes who had been through the Egyptian and Exodus experience.

It is usual to contrast the account in Joshua of a long but successful struggle led by Joshua in which the whole of Canaan was eventually overcome, with the older account in Judges 1, which pictures a piecemeal series of efforts by different tribes. This older account has been usually regarded as more

accurate, but again closer scrutiny suggests that this is an oversimplification. There are indications in the book of Joshua that many areas were not subjugated (see for example Joshua 13). Even in the time of Saul, the Israelites held only the hills and parts of Trans-Jordan. They could not expect to defeat the Canaanites with their war chariots on the plains. On the other hand, archaeological evidence shows that several hill cities, Lachish, Hazor, Bethel, Debir, Eglon, underwent violent destruction in the thirteenth century. This would seem to support the picture in Joshua of a quick, decisive conquest. (See "Archaeology and the Bible" for the negative evidence at Jericho and Ai.) After this initial attack the conquest was more gradual and was assisted by treaties and intermarriages. In time the Israelites were able to settle in Canaanite territory.

According to Joshua 24, Joshua called a great assembly at Shechem where the covenant made with Yahweh at Sinai was reaffirmed. Shechem was never attacked by Joshua, and scholars have supposed that it was in control of Israelites who had never been to Egypt; possibly an alliance of six tribes who at that time chose to serve Yahweh and associate themselves with their kinsmen who had already covenanted with Yahweh at Sinai. (See B. W. Anderson, *Understanding the Old Testament*, pp. 92-94.)

Period of the Judges (12th-11th centuries)

Early in this period the political power of Egypt and Mesopotamia was weakened, but parts of Canaan were endangered by invasions by a number of smaller powers, such as Edom, Moab, Sihon, and Og. The most dangerous of these enemies were the Philistines, because they were well organized and especially because they had iron implements and weapons of war. They settled in Gaza, Ashkelon, Ashdod, Ekron, and Gath along the southwest coast of Palestine and acted in concert when there was a common danger. Israel in this period is thought to have been organized loosely into a tribal federation focused around a central shrine perhaps Shiloh, which was the center of their religious and political loyalties. Some historians think they are analogous to, even related to, the "amphictyonies" (leagues of tribes, united for mutual protection) of Greece and Italy.

The "judges" of this book — we do not know for sure if they were so called in their own time — were local leaders who often acted against these enemies. In the book of Judges, their "rule" is made to appear successive, but it is much more likely that they overlapped. They usually attacked external enemies, such as the Moabites, the Midianites, or the Ammonites. The exception was the campaign by Deborah and Barak (see Judges 4-5), who overcame a Canaanite alliance under Sisera in about 1152. The Philistines, whose possession of the secret of iron smelting gave them a hold over the Israelites (see I Sam 13:19-22) made frightening inroads into the country, and about the middle of the eleventh century they defeated the Israelites at Shiloh and captured the Ark of the Covenant. Their success made a united monarchy imperative.

The United Monarchy (1020-931/30 B.C.)

The need for a strong central military authority found its answer in the rise of Saul the Benjaminite. He was both a warrior and a charismatic leader, that is, he was (like some of the judges) divinely inspired and spoke ecstatically. He was also subject to fits of melancholy and jealousy. He was anointed by Samuel to fight the Philistines in the name of Yahweh. His first success, however, was against the Ammonites at Jabesh-gilead.

For some years he defended the central hills from the Philistines, but he and several of his sons fell in the disastrous battle of Gilboa, and the Philistines once more occupied the hill country. However, Saul had succeeded in uniting the Israelite tribes under one king.

David (1009/8-970/69), one of Saul's warriors, who had aroused the king's jealousy, had retreated to the southern desert. He and his personal band of followers served the Philistine king of Gath for a time. He gained strength in Judah, where he was proclaimed king c. 1009/8. Like Saul, he was regarded as a charismatic leader. He was anointed king of Israel in 1002/1.

David had great gifts both as a military leader and as an organizer. His first significant military feat was the capture of Jerusalem. With great foresight he made this town, independent of both northern and southern factions, his capital, and brought the Ark of the Covenant there. The city thus became both a political center and a symbol of religious unity, an indication that he meant to rule in the spirit of the covenant. He also established his authority over all of Canaan and confined the Philistines to their coastal towns, subject to his overlordship. Finally, he established buffer states around his country by defeating the Edomites, the Moabites, the Ammonites, and the Aramaeans, all of whom had to accept a measure of his authority.

David's administration was well-organized, and perhaps modeled on that of Egypt. Wright (pp. 70-71) notes that the titles and functions of the "recorder" (who organized palace ceremonies and was a liaison between king, officers and people) and the "scribe," who combined the offices of private secretary and secretary of state, were very like those in Egypt. In spite of his success, the last part of David's reign was marred by the revolts of his son Absalom and of some of the Benjaminites, and by a tendency to display autocratic qualities more appropriate to an oriental despot. However, he should be remembered for his very real military and political achievements, his zeal for justice, and his loyalty to Yahweh.

Solomon (970/69-931/30), the son of David and Bathsheba, often described as "born to the purple," displayed from the first an arrogance and love of luxury which were inappropriate to a king anointed in the name of Yahweh. He seems also to have been insensitive to the problems facing him, selfish, vain, pretentious, and unscrupulous. His reputation for wisdom seems to have been based on the episode of the disputed baby (I Kings, 3) and a certain turn for epigrammatic wit. Many wise sayings were later attributed to him.

In spite of the fact that he had a larger army than David's, we have no evidence that he ever fought a battle. He was notable for his commercial ventures and had a fleet of ships based at Eziongeber, which traded with Ethiopia and the Arabian Yemen, bringing back precious metals, ivory, and baboons (I Kings, 9:26; 10:22). He had a passion for building and imported both expensive materials and trained workmen from Phoenicia to build his richly ornamented temple. He soon used up the resources left him by David and had to raise money by taxes and by ceding some land to Hiram, King of Tyre. These practices, his use of forced labor, and his marriages to foreign princesses, who brought their pagan cults with them, made him unpopular in his last years.

The Divided Kingdom: Israel to the Fall of Samaria (931/30-723/22)

Dissatisfaction with Solomon's policies led to a revolt after his death. His son, Rehoboam, refused to make the reforms demanded by the northern tribes, and they broke away under the leadership of Jeroboam, who made Shechem his capital. The division between Israel and Judah continued until the fall of Samaria in 723/22, though religiously and culturally the two nations continued to have much in common. In 926/25, both underwent a common disaster when Shishak of Egypt despoiled Jerusalem and destroyed cities in both Israel and Judah. In the south, the Davidic line continued to rule, but in the north one dynasty was frequently ousted by another. (For a full list of the kings, see the date chart.)

Omri was an important and able ruler in the north. He made his capital at Samaria, formed an alliance with the Phoenicians, and revived Israel's control over Moab. His son, Ahab, married the Phoenician princess Jezebel, whose introduction of Baalism into her husband's country so outraged Elijah, the first of many prophets who protested against the worship of pagan gods and against social injustice. Ahab overcame Syria, but joined with her against Assyria, whose strength was beginning to revive in this period. Together with some other small nations, they fought against the Assyrians under Shalmaneser III at the battle of Qarqar (Karkar) in 853 B.C. Shalmaneser claimed a victory, but it is likely that he suffered heavy losses. Three years later Ahab died in battle in an attempt to win back part of Trans-Jordan. Jezebel and many of their sons were massacred by Jehu (841 B.C.), who was supported by Elisha and others who wished to bring the worship of Baal to an end. Under Jeroboam II, Jehu's grandson, Israel became more prosperous than at any time since Solomon's reign. However, from the middle of the ninth century, changes had been taking place in the distribution of land. Large landowners were forcing out peasant landholders, and the gulf between rich and poor widened. This weakened the state, which, with other eastern Mediterranean nations, fell victim to the Assyrians under Tiglath-Pileser. The plight of the poor began to arouse the sympathy of the prophets. Israel's disunity was increased by a series of short, unsettled reigns, some kings being murdered by their successors. Assyria was still strong and Shalmanazer V laid siege to Samaria which fell in 723/22 B.C., possibly to his successor, Sargon II. Many of the people of Israel (Sargon claimed 27,290) were sent into exile.

Judah to the Fall of Jerusalem (931/30-586)

In Judah the line of David continued to rule. Jezebel had a sort of parallel in Athaliah, her daughter, who married Jehoram. When their son was killed, Athaliah killed the other claimants to the throne, and seized power herself. When her grandson, who had been hidden by a priest, was proclaimed king, she in turn was murdered. While Jeroboam was king in Israel, the great Uzziah ruled in Judah. His son, Ahaz, was forced to pay tribute to Assyria. He was succeeded by Hezekiah (in whose reign Isaiah preached), who with other small rulers warred against Assyria. The ruler of Assyria, Sennacherib, responded by marching across Judah, capturing many cities, and laying seige to Jerusalem. Some kind of disease (perhaps bubonic plague) afflicted the Assyrian army and Sennacherib spared Jerusalem, made Hezekiah pay tribute, but kept him on the throne. Assyria remained powerful until about 630, when it was threatened by Scythians, Medes, and Babylonians.

It was in this period, in the reign of the great king Josiah (641/40-609), that Jeremiah and Zephaniah preached. Both viewed the disturbed political conditions of the time as an indication that the Day of the Lord (a day of doom) was at hand. Another prophet, Nahum, prophesied the fall of Nineveh, which actually took place in 612, when the city was overcome by the Medes and the Babylonians.

The most significant event of Josiah's reign was the discovery of the old lawbook in the temple (623/22; almost certainly part of Deuteronomy, probably chapters 12-28), which became the basis of the Deuteronomic Reforms. Local altars were abolished, pagan cults eradicated, and sacrifical worship centered in the temple at Jerusalem.

Pharaoh Necho of Egypt took the side of the Assyrians (KJV is wrong in saying he opposed them, II Kings 23:29) in the battle of Megiddo (609 B.C.). Josiah fought against him and died in the battle, much mourned by his people. He was probably the *greatest and most democratic king since David*. His successor was deposed after three months, and Jehoiakim was put on the throne by Necho as an Egyptian vassal. He was ostentatious and arrogant like Solomon, and like him a great builder. About this time (c. 607) Habakkuk began his prophetic career.

At the battle of Carchemish (605 B.C.) the Egyptian forces were all but annihilated by the Babylonians. Jehoiakim accepted Babylonian rule, but when he intrigued with the Egyptians, Nebuchadrezzar (the preferred spelling for Nebuchadnezzar), the king of Babylon, attacked Jerusalem. Jehoiakim was probably killed; at any rate his body was thrown outside the city, and his young son Jehoiachin was carried away captive to Babylon, together with many of the most prominent and able people of Judah (597 B.C.). Jehoiachin's uncle Zedekiah, a well-intentioned but weak man, was put on the throne as a Babylonian puppet. (It was during his rule that Ezekiel was called to prophesy.) Under Egyptian influence Zedekiah revolted against Babylon, and Nebuchadrezzar besieged Jerusalem for a year and a half. In 586 the city was utterly destroyed, the temple was burned, and all but the humblest peasants were carried away captive to Babylon. Zedekiah was forced to watch the execution of his sons, then was blinded and led away in chains.

The Exile (586 B.C. and after) and The Return (538 B.C. and after)

After 586, Judah was completely devastated. The walls and public buildings of Jerusalem, including the temple, were destroyed, other towns were leveled, and the more educated and skilled people were transported to Babylon. A Judaean noble, Gedaliah, was made governor, but he was murdered. After his death, many of the remaining inhabitants fled to Egypt, taking the prophet Jeremiah with them.

The exiles in Babylon were allowed to settle down in their own communities and to work perhaps on public projects. They were never entirely absorbed into the general population for they kept up their familiar observances, such as the Sabbath and the rite of circumcision. They began to worship in synagogues. Records (for example from Nippur, near Babylon) show that many Jewish names were retained. The prophets Ezekiel and Second Isaiah encouraged the people to believe that the exile was part of Yahweh's plan; they had sinned, but through suffering they would be renewed and purified, and become fit servants of the Lord. Second Isaiah foretold the return of Yahweh to Jerusalem, where "all flesh should see it together." Meanwhile, scholars began to compile collections of law, history, and prophecy.

Cyrus, king of Persia, conquered Babylon in 539 B.C. Unlike the Babylonians and Assyrians, he did not believe in forcing people to live outside their homelands and in 538 B.C. proclaimed freedom for the captive peoples including the Jews. Many of them remained in Babylon but a small group returned under Sheshbazzar and began to rebuild the temple. Sixteen years later under Zerubbabel, a relative of Jehoiachin, a larger group returned and, with the help of the prophets Haggai and Zechariah, continued the restoration. In 445 B.C. Nehemiah was appointed governor of a small area around Jerusalem and given permission to rebuild the walls of that city. He forbade "foreign" marriages (thus coming into conflict with the Samaritans) and supported the observance of the Sabbath and temple worship. Ezra, who came to Jerusalem c. 397, completed Nehemiah's work by promulgating "the law" and getting the people to accept it. This "law," probably the Pentateuch (the first five books of the Bible) in some form, helped to give a sense of unity to the struggling community. Ezra was a purist in religion and insisted that Jews who had married foreign wives should divorce them. (The book of Ruth is thought by some scholars to be a literary answer to this fiat.) Priests were very important in Ezra's regime and the High Priest was the main authority in the state.

Besides the Jews in Babylon, there were Jews in Egypt and in other parts of the Near East. This disturbed period really inaugurated the Jewish "diaspora," the scattering of the Jewish people to all parts of the world.

Hellenistic Rule and Maccabean Revolt (334 B.C.-143 B.C.)

Alexander the Great began his conquest of Persia in 334, marched through Syria and Palestine in 332, and overcame Egypt in 331. There he founded Alexandria, later to be an important center for Hellenistic Judaism. He died in 323 and was succeeded in Palestine first by the Ptolemies and later by the Seleucids, both of whom permitted a reasonable degree of independence and self-government. Hellenistic influences, however, remained important, for excavators at Samaria uncovered Hellenistic fortifications, dated slightly later than Alexander's time. In the city of Alexandria, where Alexander had settled Jewish merchants, there was the nucleus of an important Jewish community which became Greek-speaking. For its use the Jewish scriptures were translated (c. 280-250) into a Greek version known as the Septuagint (see "The Canon of the Old Testament"). Job, Ecclesiastes, and other examples of Wisdom Literature may have owed much to the free, questioning spirit of Hellenism.

In Jerusalem, two parties gradually emerged, a conservative group, who wished to preserve the religion of Yahweh as it had come down to them, and a more liberal group who were hospitable to Greek thought and art. This struggle is reflected in the book of Daniel. The Seleucid ruler, Antiochus IV (175-163 B.C.), wished to impose Hellenistic culture on all his realms and to use the power of the pro-Greek party to do so in Palestine. After a series of intrigues, murders, and quarrels, Antiochus exerted his power openly. The Jerusalem temple was desecrated and a shrine to Zeus set up in it. It was forbidden, on pain of death, to obey the Mosaic law, to keep the Jewish holidays, to observe the Sabbath, or to practice the rite of circumcision.

Antiochus' policy sparked off what is known as the Maccabean revolt, initiated by one Mattathias and his three sons, Judas, Jonathan, and Simon. Judas, called Maccabeus ("the Hammerer"), had the support of the conservative party and much of the rural population. He defeated Antiochus' forces, retook Jerusalem, and rededicated the temple. (This is celebrated in the feast of Hanukkah.) Under Antiochus' successor, the Mosaic law was restored. So far, Judas had achieved his religious objectives; but now he and his brothers wished to attain complete independence. As the Seleucids were distracted by internal feuds and wars elsewhere, Judas was able to win several important victories and to add Gilead and Galilee to his realm. After Judas died in battle in 160 B.C., his brother Jonathan took command of the revolt, and taking advantage of a power struggle between rival claimants to the Seleucid throne, managed to become High Priest and provincial governor under the Seleucids. Not all his people were in favor of this combination of functions, and it may have been at this time that the Qumran community was formed (see "Archaeology and the Bible," under "Dead Sea Scrolls"). Jonathan was murdered in 143 B.C. With his rule the Maccabean regime had really begun.

Judean Independence and Conquest by Rome (142 B.C. - 63 A.D.)

The last brother, Simon, expanded his territories with the aid of his sons and obtained from Demetrius II, the Seleucid ruler, recognition as High Priest and as the ruler of Judea. After he was murdered in 134 B.C., his son John Hyrcanus succeeded him. In spite of initial difficulties, he subdued most of Palestine and forced many of his new subjects to accept the Jewish religion and to become circumcised.

It was during his rule that the Sadducees and the Pharisees emerged as distinct parties. The

Sadducees, an upper-class faction, supported the Maccabeans in their bid for independence as well as in their religious policies. The Pharisees, on the other hand, thought Judas should have ceased his efforts after he had restored the temple worship. They had considerable popular support and were already characterized by that attentiveness to religious minutiae for which they are so well known in the New Testament. John at first supported them, but later turned against them, and is thought by some students of the Qumran writings to be the "wicked Priest" who persecuted the "Teacher of Righteousness." (See "Archaeology of the Bible," under "Dead Sea Scrolls." p 46.)

With John's death (104 B.C.) the great days of the Maccabeans ended, for his successors were personally ambitious, jealous, and quarrelsome. There was a decline in the idealism and moral standards, not only of the family but of the nation. After Aristobulus'

short reign (104-103), his brother Alexander Janneus married his widow, causing some scandal, as he was also the High Priest. He was disliked by his own people, particularly the Pharisees, and because of his cruelties is another candidate for the position of the "Wicked Priest" of the Qumran writings. On his death (76 B.C.), his widow Salome Alexandra became queen and her son Hyrcanus High Priest. The Pharisees were very powerful during her reign (76-67 B.C.), while the Sadducees supported Hyrcanus' brother, Aristobulus. When Salome Alexandra died, she left the throne to Hyrcanus, but Aristobolus, backed by the Sadducees, tried to take it by force. Bitter fighting ensued and at length both parties looked to Rome for support. A third popular party wanted neither brother. Pompey captured Jerusalem and took the temple, but set up Hyrcanus as High Priest. From this time on, Judea was regarded as part of the Roman province of Syria and Roman rule dominated her history.

THE COMPOSITION OF THE OLD TESTAMENT

This is an extremely complex and controversial topic, and only the broad lines of development can be indicated here. The composition of the Pentateuch and other special problems will be dealt with later at appropriate points. The reader would do well to bear in mind that *the books of the Old Testament were not written in the order in which they stand and that almost all are composites of materials from different periods*. We do not know the author of any one book in its present form, though we may know the author of part of it. The parts of the various books may be difficult to date. And there is certainly much disagreement among schol-

ars about both dating and authorship.

Once these warnings are clear, some positive points may be made.

We know, for example, that Hebrew literature must be seen in the context of the literature of the whole Near East. For example, early storytellers of Israel borrowed from the Babylonian flood story and other myths of origins, and Biblical psalms sometimes owed much to Canaanite and other Near Eastern models.

We know, too, that, as in all national literatures, a long period of *oral composition* preceded the widespread writing down of literature. Stories would be told of the beginnings of the world, of heroic deeds, of strange events, and of the mysterious origin of a sacred shrine. These would be passed on by word of mouth and it is known that folk memories are very retentive. Songs or fragments of songs, sometimes associated with exciting events, would be sung and remembered, wise sayings treasured, and wise judgments embodied in a primitive law code. Eventually, as more people became literate, some of this, material would be written down. In this way some very old material has found its way into our Bible. Some documents, however, have been lost; we hear, for example, of "The Book of the Wars of Yahweh" and "The Book of Jashar," which have not survived. Scholars have speculated that other now lost works have contributed in important ways to our present scriptures. For example, it is thought that there were *literary as well as oral sources for the four documents, called J, E, D, and P, which make up our present Pentateuch* (the first five books of the Bible).

Ancient Poetry. Poetry usually precedes prose in oral literature, and some very old poems or parts of poems can be found scattered throughout the Pentateuch. The English scholar H. H. Rowley in *The Growth of the Old Testament*, distinguishes tribal songs, curses and blessings, oracles, and national songs. Some examples (of which he cites a great many) are the Song of Lamech (Gen. 4:23-24), the Blessing and the Curse of Noah (Gen. 9:25-27), the Blessing of Rebekah (Gen. 24:60), the Oracle of Amalek (Num. 24:20), and the Song of Miriam (Ex. 15:21). This last song is perhaps contemporary with the crossing of the Reed Sea, and all are very ancient. The war song of Deborah in Judges 5 may have been written soon after the killing of Sisera which it describes. Joshua's Address to the Sun and

Moon (Josh. 10:12-13) is also of ancient date. Some scholars would place the *decalogues* and *an early code of law* in this period, the early version of the Ten Commandments (Ex. 20) in the thirteenth century, and the later decalogue (Ex. 34) as well as the Book of the Covenant (sometimes called the Canaanite Code, Ex. 20:23-19) in the twelfth or eleventh centuries.[1]

Some splendid *literature* comes *from the age of David and Solomon,* partly an expression of the newfound pride and confidence of the people. Besides David's beautiful Lament over Saul and Jonathan (II Sam. 11-27) and his Lament over Abner (II Sam. 3:33), we have a lively account of David called the Court History (II Sam. 9:20; I Kings 1-2), contemporary or nearly so with the events it describes. Some stories of the "judges" (local leaders) in their original forms may also have been set down at this time; perhaps also some wise sayings attributed to Solomon.

National Epics. But the most ambitious product of the period of the United Monarchy was the *national epic of Israel* by the writer or writers whom we call J or the *Yahwist.* Composed about 950, it forms the earliest strand in the Pentateuch. Inspired perhaps by national pride in the accomplishment of Israel, the saga tells of the creation of the world, the first sin and its punishment, the flood, the promise to Abraham, the Joseph story, the Exodus from Egypt, and the subsequent history of the chosen people down to the Conquest of Canaan and perhaps further. (This point is disputed.) The J-narrative, a work of genius, will be considered in more detail when we take up

---

1 See N.K. Gottwald, **A Light to the Nations,** pp. 18-19. I have generally followed his datings in my account of the literature.

the composition of the Pentateuch. As indicated above, J probably derived from both oral and literary sources.

The wonder-working prophets Elijah and Elisha flourished in the ninth century and some scholars think the accounts of their doings (I Kings 17:1-19, 20, II Kings 1:1-8, II Kings 2:1-8:29) were written down not long after their activities ceased.

Another national epic, designated E, was composed in the northern Kingdom about the middle of the eighth century. It begins with the story of Abraham and later follows some of the same ground as J, but is more fragmentary, perhaps because parts were lost or cut out. At some point, perhaps c. 700 B.C., the two epics were blended together or "conflated" to form what is called the document JE.

In the eighth century, too, the great prophets began to appear on the scene, *Amos* and *Hosea* in mid-century, *Isaiah* about 740 B.C., and *Micah* (chapters 1-3) just before the fall of Samaria. Their oracles protested the religious and social abuses of their time. Their original oracles were probably very short, spontaneous utterances though some compositions may have been longer. These oracles many have been memorized for a time and eventually written down, whether by the prophets themselves or by their disciples is not known. There are also autobiographical narratives (e.g., in Amos 7, Hosea 3, Isaiah 6), and third-person accounts of incidents associated with the prophets in question. These narratives were very likely written down fairly soon after the events they describe. It must be remembered that all the prophetic books were subsequently revised and much later had material added. (See below, under the prophets, for a fuller account of the composition of these books.)

D-Code. Some scholars think the nucleus of the *D-Code* (usually identified as Deut. 12-28) was assembled in the eighth century, while others would place it at some time in the seventh. It is generally agreed by scholars that this is the "book of the law" found by Hilkiah the priest during repairs to the temple in 622 B.C. and used as the basis of King Josiah's reform. As we have it, it is sandwiched between two speeches by Moses and forms the third document (D) of the Pentateuch, so far designated by the letters JED. It called for the centralization of worship and sacrifice in Jerusalem, the destruction of local shrines and cult objects (such as sacred images and pillars), and an end to divination and sacred prostitution. There were also rules concerning war, divorce, diet, the treatment of slaves, and other matters of law.

The discovery of the D-code and the reforms of Josiah evidently stimulated a great deal of activity among the *Deuteronomists*, as the scholars associated with D are called. They began to compile and edit a large body of material composed at various dates from the time of the United Kingdom on. These sources are far too numerous and their origins and dating too disputed for them to be listed here, but from them the Deuteronomists compiled *Joshua*, *Judges*, *Samuel*, and *Kings*, bringing the history of Israel down to their own time. As editorial methods in the various books differ somewhat, it is probable that a series of groups worked on the project, which was certainly completed by the middle of the sixth century, perhaps earlier. The purpose of their work was religious, and they edited and rewrote their sources so as to bring out their own beliefs in worship at the central shrine in Jerusalem, in divine retribution (God's reward for obedience and punishment for evil) and in the credibility of God's promises to his people. Leaders and events were judged according to the religious and ethical principles of the editors.

New Prophets. While the Deuteronomists were at work, new prophets appeared. *Zephaniah* seems to have been active in Josiah's day, probably when the Scythians were a source of danger, c. 630 B.C. *Nahum* foretold the fall of Nineveh in 612 B.C., and near the end of the seventh century, but before 587 B.C., *Habakkuk's* oracles represented the Chaldeans as the instruments of God's chastisement. Meanwhile a greater prophet had appeared upon the scene. *Jeremiah* was called to prophesy in 628/27 B.C. and his ministry extended into the period of the Exile. He was preoccupied with fellowship with God, independent of temple ritual or rites such as circumcision. The book that bears his name contains both autobiographical and biographical material, probably contemporary or nearly so. We know, too, that he did dictate some of his oracles to his disciple Baruch, who read them in the temple. (Naturally, there are additions to the original material in his book, as in the other prophetic books). The book of *Lamentations* is traditionally ascribed to Jeremiah and was placed after it in the Greek version of the scriptures; but both style and ideas are very unlike his. The oracles are laments for the fall of Jerusalem, and some of them may be close to that event and thus contemporary with Jeremiah.

Prophets of the Exile. *Ezekiel's* oracles must next be considered. Ezekiel has long been thought of as the prophet of the Exile, carried away to Babylon with the captives of 597 B.C.; but some recent scholars think that part of his ministry was spent in Palestine. By all accounts he was the most eccentric of the prophets and his concern with the temple and the rights of the priests is unusual in prophetic literature. There is little agreement as to which of the oracles in his book are genuine. The little book of *Obadiah* was also probably written in the exilic period.

To a later period of the Exile belong the glorious poems of *"Second Isaiah."* (His real name is unknown, but he is so called because his works appear on the same scrolls as those of the eighth-century prophet, Isaiah.) He proclaimed that God would forgive his chastened people and would restore them to their homeland, where all flesh should see the glory of the Lord and the redeemed should rejoice in his presence.

After the return to Jerusalem, two more prophets emerged, *Haggai* and *Zachariah*, c. 530 B.C. Both are concerned with the restoration of the neglected temple and both are hostile to the Samaritans, who from now on are considered outsiders by the Jews. Later still, perhaps c. 560-50 B.C., before Nehemiah was appointed governor of Israel in 445 B.C., the prophet *Malachi* pointed out various abuses which should be corrected and voiced his objections to mixed marriages (Note: *Micah* chapters 4-7 is placed by Gottwald and others in this period; *Joel* is also postexilic.)

P Materials. We must now return briefly to the *composition of the Pentateuch*, in which J, E, and D had already been combined. The next step was the addition of a body of *priestly material*, emanating from a group of priests some time after the Babylonian exile. While it may have contained ancient traditions, it was composed during the fifth century. The priestly writers were interested in temple rituals, the ordering of the priesthood, the sacred holidays, the rite of circumcision, and worship at the Jerusalem shrine. With these additions (designated by P), the Pentateuch was complete by c. 410 B.C., more than 500 years after the Yahwist composed the J-epic. The Pentateuch or part of it was perhaps the "Law" read to the people by Ezra in Jerusalem in 397.

Later than P and influenced by the Priestly group are all the books of *Chronicles, Ezra, and Nehemiah*. In the opinion of many scholars, they are all by the same author, referred to as the Chronicler. He uses most of the Old Testament from Genesis to Kings for his sources, plus a number of other documents, but rewrites the history of Israel from a priestly viewpoint, idealizing it considerably. He emphasizes David as the founder of the temple and of its rites and priesthood, and omits the scandal of David and Bathsheba and other unedifying events. He is concerned with the religious community as inheritors of ancient Israel, the legitimacy of the temple rites, the authority of the priesthood and its responsibilities. He shows a special interest in temple music and in genealogies. His books are very valuable for the light they throw on the preoccupations of the post-exilic community in Judah. The Chronicler's works are dated variously from 380-300 B.C.

A number of books still have to be added to complete our Old Testament, but most of them are of uncertain date. Both *Ruth* and *Jonah* are often interpreted as reflections of liberal opposition to the various and exclusive policies of Ezra and Nehemiah, who objected to mixed marriages. The author of Ruth seems to show that an "outsider" who marries a Jew can become a good and loyal member of the family and of the Jewish faith. However, other interpretations are possible, since the book does not have a polemical ring about it. Jonah is also opposed to narrow nationalism and favors tolerance, but neither book can with certainty be associated with the time of Ezra and Nehemiah, although both are certainly post-exilic.

The Wisdom Literature, comprising *Proverbs, Job*, and *Ecclesiastes*, is also variously dated from the fifth century on, though the book of Proverbs may contain wise sayings which go back to the time of Solomon. *Ecclesiastes* is almost certainly the latest of the three, dating perhaps from the third century. The *Song of Songs* is sometimes associated with the Wisdom Literature, but is really a collection of love-songs, perhaps composed early in the fourth century. The book of *Psalms*, like Proverbs, a collection from many periods, was completed by 100 B.C., perhaps earlier.

It seems likely that *Esther* and *Daniel* are the latest books in the Old Testament. Esther, a fictional account of the triumph of the Jews of Persia over their enemies, is a fiercely nationalistic book which has been associated with the Maccabean struggle, or, more probably, with a later celebration of the Maccabean victories. The book of Daniel describes the "abomination of desolation," the desecration of the temple by Antiochus Epiphanes in 167 B.C., and was intended to give hope to the people during the struggle which followed. It was composed before the death of Antiochus in 164 B.C.

We can see from this account that the books of the Old Testament contain materials from well over a thousand years of history.

LITERARY FORMS IN THE OLD TESTAMENT

The Old Testament is a library, not only of many books, but of many different literary forms.[1] Many of these forms are common to other literature of the Near East from which Israel for centuries borrowed and adapted poems, stories, and laws. It is difficult to set up exact categories, because the genres are often mixed and exact criteria are not agreed on by scholars; however, the types mentioned in this section can all be found in the Bible. The reader is merely warned that he will often find passages that are difficult to categorize, since they may contain elements of two or more forms. For example, the story of Samson, given a genuine historical context, the struggle with the Philistines, nevertheless includes folk tales and riddles which are much older, and, some scholars think, vestiges of a sun-myth. The reader should also remember the changes that must have taken place when songs or stories were circulated orally, and indeed when they were copied and recopied over the centuries.

Hebrew Poetry

While early Hebrew poetry made use of rhythm, and, on rare occasions, rhyme, e.g., the Song of Lamech (Gen. 4:23-24), its basic technique is a balancing of lines called *parallelism*, common in other Near Eastern poetry. The most usual forms of parallelism are 1) *synonymous parallelism*, in which the second line repeats the thought of the first line in different words; 2) *antithetical parallelism*, in which the second line throws light on the first by means of contrast. Both can be illustrated from Psalm 1:

Synonymous parallelism:

But his delight is in the law of the Lord
And in his law doth he meditate day and night.

Antithetical parallelism:

For the Lord knoweth the way of the righteous;
But the way of the ungodly shall perish.

Synonymous parallelism can have a third line, as in the first verse of this same psalm. 3) In a third type, *synthetic parallelism*, the second line is not only parallel, but supplements the statement in the first line, for example:

And he shall be like a tree
by the river's waters,
That bringeth forth his fruit
in his season.

These two-member and three-member units can be combined into strophes or stanzas. Parallelism is found in all types of early songs, in the prophets, and in Wisdom Literature.

All sorts of occasions gave rise to poetry and song, sometimes accompanied by dancing. The variety of the songs is indicated in the list which follows, beginning with those associated with war.

Victory Songs celebrate triumphs over Israel's enemies. Probably the earliest we have is the Song of

---

[1] The study of Biblical and other Near Eastern forms is called "form criticism" and was pioneered by the German scholar Hermann Gunkel.

Miriam, perhaps composed after the escape from the Egyptians at the Sea of Reeds (Ex. 15:21):

Sing ye to the Lord, for he hath triumphed gloriously;
The horse and the rider hath he thrown into the sea.

A later writer enlarged the poem and it became attached to the more important leader, Moses. Famous also is the Song of Deborah (Judg. 5) and the women's triumph song at David's victory over the Philistines:

Saul hath slain his thousands
And David his ten thousands.

Both are probably contemporary with the events they describe.

Taunt Songs, illustrated in the satirical picture of the Amorites (Num. 21:27-30), who have been conquered by Israel and cannot now be expected to defeat the Moabites. It begins with the ironic

Come into Heshbon,
Let the city of Sihon be built
and prepared,

which implies that the Amorites no longer have the strength to do this.

Incantations were also employed in war. Perhaps the most famous is Joshua's appeal for a long day to win the battle of Gibeon:

Sun, stand thou still upon Gibeon;
And thou, Moon, in the valley of Ajalon.

Work Songs in Egypt and Canaan were associated with the harvest or the gathering of grapes. The Bible does not preserve these, perhaps because they were so closely associated with pagan religions, but the Song of the Well (Num. 21:17-18) expresses rejoicing at the digging of a new well in the desert, and the complaint of workers to

Yahweh (Num. 4:4) has been called a "strike song."

Blessings and Curses were treated very seriously, as we can see from the story of how Jacob outwitted Esau and deprived him of his father's blessing. Esau "cried with a great and exceeding bitter cry ... 'Bless me, even me also, O my father'." The point was that the blessing mistakenly given to Jacob could not be revoked. The same was true of curses.

Both are employed in the story of Noah, when his sons Ham and Shem find him "uncovered" (RSV, Gen. 9:25-6):

Cursed be Canaan;
A servant of servants shall
he be unto his brothers
Blessed by the Lord my God
be Shem.
And let Canaan be his slave.

Some scholars think this passage and the blessings of Jacob and Joseph were composed, at least in their present form, after David had contained the Canaanites. Their association with the great patriarchs helped to preserve them when many other poems were lost.

Dirges or Laments were appropriate in a house of mourning and could be sung by the relatives and friends of the dead, or by professional mourners, always women. The most famous, David's personal expression of grief at the death of Saul and Jonathan, begins

The beauty of Israel is slain
upon the high places.
How are the mighty fallen!
Tell it not in Gath
Publish it not in the streets
of Askelon ...

an excellent example of synonymous parallelism. There were also "collective" dirges for whole tribes or cities. Amos made good use of this tradition when he composed the dirge for Israel (RSV, Amos 5:2):

Fallen, no more to rise,
Is the virgin Israel;
Forsaken on her land,
With none to raise her up.

Oracles in verse were one form in which the prophets conveyed their message. Perhaps originating in response to inquiries addressed to the prophet, or to God through him, these oracles often begin, "Thus saith the Lord" and express a judgment on an individual or on whole nations, as Amos does in his opening poem. First he warns the foreign nations, then Israel. All the stanzas are the same in structure and announce the "transgressions" of each particular nation and the punishment which is to follow. The sudden attack in the country in which Amos is preaching has a fine shock effect. The attack on Israel and the announcement of the punishments which are to follow became standard in Isaiah and the other great prophets, though there are occasional favorable promises in Jeremiah and Ezekiel, e.g., the latter's promise of "hearts of flesh" instead of "hearts of stone." The great change comes in Second Isaiah, whose oracles promise deliverance and a new order. "Comfort ye, comfort ye, my people, saith your God," he begins, and continues,

Prepare ye the way of the Lord,
Make straight in the desert a
highway for our God,

for

The glory of the Lord shall
be revealed,
And all flesh shall see it together.
(Isa. 40:1, 3, 5.)

Love Songs. A large collection of these appears in the Song of Solomon, though it is disputed whether this is just a collection of love-songs or a little drama. It contains many delightful verses, such as (in Ch. 2)

Stay me with flagons
[really "raisins"]
Comfort me with apples
For I am sick of love.
[i.e., from love].

and

My beloved is like a roe or a
young heart...
He looketh forth at the windows
Showing himself through the
lattice.

Psalms are perhaps the most familiar poems in the whole of the O.T. They are also the most difficult to categorize, since they are sometimes grouped according to subject matter (e.g., "royal" and "wisdom" psalms), and sometimes according to form (laments, oracles, etc.) "Purity of type is the exception rather than the rule" (Gottwald p. 24). These problems will be dealt with when we come to the book of Psalms.

Poetic Prose

Myths are invented stories, often explaining the origins of man, the world, the feats of gods and heroes, curious natural phenomena, and puzzling customs and facts of existence. In Near Eastern mythology, as in Greek mythology, many of the stories portray the relationship of the gods, their marriages, their jealousies, and their partialities for certain members of the human race. Typically, mythology is polytheistic. When Israelite writers borrowed myths from Canaanite or Babylonian sources, they transformed them to fit the religion of Yahweh. However, we shall see when we study them that many vestiges of polytheism remain. Most of the material in Gen. 1-11 is mythological.

Miracle stories and other folk tales have also been borrowed from neighboring literatures. Moses has a magic rod like miracle workers of Egyptian stories. Elijah's magic mantle, the jar of oil which is miraculously never empty, and the metamorphosis of Lot's wife into a pillar of salt all have parallels in Near Eastern literature, as do the tales of enmity between brothers, Cain and Abel and Jacob and Esau. There are several parallels to the tale of Solomon's judgment over the live baby, which are said to go back to an Indian original. Balaam's ass is like the talking animals of many nations. The element of supernatural power dominates the miracle story, while the folk tale may have many motifs, for example, the efforts of a strong man, such as Samson, or the rise to power of a peasant, such as Saul or David.

Sanctuary legends usually explain why certain sacred trees, altars, or shrines are held sacred, usually because an angel or deity appeared there or because a famous ancestor was associated with it. Thus Peniel was remembered because Jacob wrestled with the angel there, Shechem because he erected an altar there.

Cult legends supply justifications for cult practices, such as circumcision (performed by Abraham, Gen. 17) or the presence of the serpent image in the temple (Num. 21:4-9).

Parables, short simple stories illustrating a moral or religious lesson, are far more common in the N.T., as they were one of Jesus' most effective teaching devices. The best parable in the O.T., and the closest to the N.T. form, is Nathan's tale of the rich man who stole his neighbor's one ewe-lamb to make a meal for a guest. It showed David how wrong he was in taking Bathsheba and destroying Uriah. Isaiah's account of Israel as Yahweh's vineyard is another simple parable which reminds the people that God will be disappointed in their "wild grapes." Some writers interpret the "sign" of the prophets as acted-out parables, for example Hosea's taking a harlotrous wife to remind his hearers that they are being unfaithful to Yahweh.

Short stories are difficult to differentiate from folk tales and other narratives, except that they are usually somewhat longer and more elaborately constructed. The story of Joseph, while it is linked to the account of his ancestors, does differ from these in its length and its unified construction. *Like every story in the Bible, it has its message, the providence of God.* Much later the story of Ruth inculcates respect for a foreign girl whose loyalty shows that she can be a worthy member of the community. The book of Jonah probably ridicules the fanaticism of some prophets and certainly the absurdity of provincialism. The story of Esther defends religious freedom and gives a traditional origin for the feast of Purim. The fact that some scholars classify Jonah as a satire and Esther as a historical romance shows how tenuous many of these classifications are.

Fables, brief narratives about animals or plants which illustrate some moral truth, are relatively rare in the O.T. Perhaps the best example is Jotham's tale about the trees trying to choose a king and finding that only the useless bramble is willing to take the position.

History

Legends, unlike myths, may have some distant roots in history, but like myths are often poetic and imaginative. They are often difficult to disentangle from history, for legendary elements may be incorporated into a historical narrative as (according to some historians) the slaying of Goliath has been incorporated into the account of David.

Annals, year-by-year records of important events, were kept perhaps by Saul and certainly by David and later kings. The authors of Samuel and Kings refer to such records, now lost, the Chronicles of the Kings of Israel and the Chronicles of the Kings of Judah. The high priests at Jerusalem may have kept records of their own, describing, for example, Solomon's temple and Josiah's reformation.

History. The materials of history proper include stories about local leaders (called "judges" in our Bible), about Samuel, and about Elijah and Elisha. The magnificent "Court History of David" (II Sam. 9-20 and I Kings 1-2), written by someone who witnessed, perhaps took part in the events he describes, antedates the so-called "father of history," Thucydides, by over 500 years. The "J" and "E" histories and the work of the Deuteronomic school of historians will be described later.

Law

Israel's laws, like other forms, are related to the laws of the surrounding countries, yet reflect the unique insight of Yahwism.

Early short forms include "apodictic" sayings, brief commands, such as, "Thou shalt not uncover the nakedness of thy mother's sister." (See Lev. 18 for many examples.) The Ten Commandments were originally such brief, pithy commands, and some remained so, e.g., "Thou shalt not kill." Ex. 22:17 probably read originally, "Thou shalt not covet thy neigh-

bor's house," the other items being added later.

Another short form is the "conditional" form: "If thou buy a Hebrew slave, six years shall he serve and in the seventh he shall go out free for nothing." Both these forms may have circulated orally, but gradually written collections were made, short collections such as the Decalogue, and longer ones, of which the most important are the Covenant Code, the Deuteronomic Code and the Holiness Code.

The Book of the Covenant, Ex. 20:23-19 is the earliest of these and contains both the apodictic and conditional forms. It is well planned and covers (a) laws concerning persons, e.g., problems of slavery, murder, assault; (b) laws concerning property, such as animals, fields, vineyards, money; (c) social laws, which deal with sojourners and debtors; and (d) religious laws, which concern images, sacrifices, and cult.

The Deuteronomic Code, Deut. 12-26, contains some of the same provisions, but adds more dealing with centralization of worship, the rights of Levitical priests, the administration of justice (e.g., the establishment of cities of refuge), the rules for conducting a holy war, and many other topics. Like the Covenant Code, it is a compilation perhaps of the seventh century. Many historians think that it is the scroll of laws found in the temple in 623/2 and made the basis for Josiah's reform.

The Holiness Code, Lev. 17-26, as its name suggests, is concerned less with moral law than with the purity of the cult as expressed in special feasts, Sabbath years, the sacrificial slaughters of animals, and other practices which distinguish the religion of Yahweh from other cults and make its people and priests holy. However, the Holiness

Code also includes strict laws about sex, the treatment of the poor and the stranger, usury, and false testimony. The code contains the law adopted by Jesus, "Thou shalt love thy neighbor as thyself." Here, however, "neighbor" meant "fellow Jew."

The Priestly Code, so called, is not really a formal code at all, but miscellaneous rules in the P portion of the Pentateuch, where cultic laws are often related. These and great historical events, for example, the laws about the Passover and the first-born are associated with the Exodus.

Wisdom Literature is often said to include the wise sayings collected in Proverbs, the somewhat cynical and pessimistic reflections in Ecclesiastes, and the questionings

in the book of Job, in the Apocrypha, the Wisdom of Solomon and Ecclesiasticus. As these books reflect the "Wisdom" outlook in different ways, they will be treated separately as the different works are discussed. Job and Ecclesiastes, as we shall see, really cast doubt on the assumptions of other wisdom writers.

Apocalyptic works offer a prophecy or picture of a future, usually through dreams or visions, as the book of Revelation pictures the summoning of the redeemed to heaven, the New Jerusalem. The single apocalyptic book in the O.T. is Daniel, a mixed form containing court tales and dream-visions vaguely related to Babylonian and Persian history. It was probably written during the Hellenistic period.

THE CANON OF THE OLD TESTAMENT

The Greek word *canon* comes from a Semitic word for "reed." As reeds were used for measuring, the word came to mean a "measuring rod," and thus eventually signified "that which regulates, rules, or serves as a norm or pattern" (Arthur Jeffery, "The Canon of the Old Testament," *Interpreter's Bible*, Vol I, p. 34). Ultimately the word came to mean a body of literature which had a special authority.

The Hebrew Canon is divided into these parts:

I. *The Law,* that is the Pentateuch (meaning five scrolls).

II. *The Prophets,* including the Former Prophets, Joshua, Judges, I and II Samuel and I and II Kings, which are mainly historical, but which do contain stories of Elijah,

Elisha, and Samuel; and the Book of the Twelve (Hosea to Malachi).

III. *The Writings,* a very miscellaneous collection, including the "poetic books," Psalms, Proverbs, and Job (although poetry is certainly not confined to these books), the Song of Songs, Ruth, Lamentations, Ecclesiastes, Esther, Daniel, Ezra, Nehemiah, and the Chronicles.

Roughly speaking, these bodies of literature were canonized in this order, first the Law, then the Prophets, then the Writings. When the D-Code was discovered by the priest Hilkiah and adopted by King Josiah in 622 B.C., this event, says Gottwald, "marked the first time in Hebrew History that a particular book became authoritative"

(p. 30). The whole Law was recognized as authoritative by 400-350 B.C. A signal event was the reading of the Pentateuch, or part of it, to the people of Jerusalem by Ezra in 397 B.C., though it should be emphasized that Ezra and his hearers were actually recognizing a body of writings which were already regarded as authoritative by their usage in the religious service.

The books of the Prophets gradually came to be reverenced on a level with the Law, perhaps by 200 B.C. There is evidence of this in the book of Ecclesiasticus by Jesus Ben Sira. To this book Ben Sira's grandson added a prologue when he translated the book into Greek c. 130 B.C. In his prologue he confirms the impression given by Ecclesiasticus itself that "the Law and the Prophets" are equally sacred. The phrase indeed became a standard one, used for instance by Jesus (Matt. 22:40).

The third group of sacred books, which Ben Sira referred to as "the other books of our fathers," was a more mixed collection. Books such as the Psalms had the sanction of usage in the synagogues, but certain works met with pertinent objections. Gottwald (p. 32) well summarizes the difficulties presented by the Song of Songs, Ecclesiastes, and Esther: "To some the love poetry of the first seemed profane and vulgar, the skepticism of the second shocking and irreverent, and the lack of reference to God in the third disconcerting"; however "all three were rescued for the Canon. The Song of Songs and Ecclesiastes were accepted as the work of Solomon, Esther was approved because it had become a symbol of Jewish survival in the face of overwhelming odds."

Closing of the Canon. The two events which led to the final closing of the Jewish Canon were the fall of Jerusalem in 70 A.D. and the rise of Christianity. The fall of Jerusalem and the destruction of the Temple deprived the Jews of the center of their religious life, gave rise to fears that the faith would be diluted or destroyed, and made it vital that the authentic scriptures should be carefully guarded. The rise of Christianity, with its claims to its own interpretation of the Old Testament and its vast body of apocalyptic and Messianic literature, generally unacceptable to the Jews, was another danger.

The institution which dealt with this crisis was the academy at Jamnia in Palestine, where many of the best minds of Judaism had congregated. There at the so-called Council of Jamnia, c. 90-100 A.D., some books accepted by Hellenistic Jews or by Christians were excluded and the Hebrew Canon established more or less in permanent form. There was still some conflict over the books of Esther and Ecclesiastes, even as late as the fourth century. It should be emphasized that the works retained in the Canon had long been recognized as sacred and vital in the religious life of the community. The Council of Jamnia merely confirmed what had long been accepted.

The uncertainty as to what books should be included in the Canon is reflected in the Septuagint,[1] the Greek version translated in Alexandria in the third century B.C. for the use of Greek-speaking (Hellenistic) Jews. It included fourteen books not found in the Hebrew Canon, among them Judith, Tobit, Susanna, and Ecclesiasticus. These constitute the Apocrypha (from the Greek word meaning "hidden" or "obscure"). The Septuagint was substantially the Bible of the early Christians, and quota-

---

[1] Means "The Seventy"; according to tradition seventy-two scholars made the translation.

tions in the New Testament are generally from it. There remained some uncertainty, however, as to how much of it was to be accepted as canonical. St. Jerome, the fourth century scholar who translated the Latin Vulgate, "was inclined to follow the Palestinian tradition and to relegate the extra writings found in the Septuagint to a secondary place. But his contemporary, Augustine ... insisted that the catalog of Old Testament books should also include books found in the Septuagint" (Anderson, p. 558). This uncertainty persisted. The Roman Catholic Church accepted certain of the Apocryphal writings at the Council of Trent (1545 and after). Protestant practice was often to print the Apocryphal books between the Old and New Testaments, and this was done in the King James Version of 1611. *In modern times the Apocrypha is frequently omitted from Protestant Bibles.* This is a pity, as *the books are interesting in themselves and inspired many works of art and literature, particularly in the Renaissance.* Brief summaries of the Apocryphal books will be found at the end of this book.

A Note on the Vulgate

As Roman rule spread and Latin became more important as a common language, the Old Testament began to be translated into that tongue, but these efforts were scattered and unsatisfactory. St. Augustine is scathing about the "barbarisms" of the Old Latin versions, as they came to be called. In 382 Pope Damasus commissioned Saint Jerome, the greatest Biblical scholar of his day, to make a more reliable translation of both the Old and New Testaments. The original intention of the project was to revise and correct the Old Latin texts, but in 386 Jerome moved to Bethlehem, where he used the original Hebrew versions as well as the Greek Hexapla (which compared Greek versions in six columns). He also obtained the help of outstanding Jewish scholars. The whole Bible was completed in 405 and is a masterpiece in its own right. However, the Vulgate, as it was called (meaning it was in the common or Vulgar tongue) met with immediate criticism from worshipers more familiar with the Old Latin versions. Its text suffered various vicissitudes in the Middle Ages and it was only pronounced authentic and free from doctrinal error by the Council of Trent in 1546.

The Masoretic Text

The Hebrew text has been transmitted from ancient times to the present with remarkable care and fidelity. From the time of the Exile, the scriptures were carefully copied by theologically trained scribes, who eventually tried to establish a standard text. In the second century, after the Canon was established, the responsibility for preserving the text became the task of the Masorete scholars, so called from the "Masorah," the collections of critical and explanatory notes which they added to the text. From the study of the Dead Sea Scrolls (see under "Archaeology"), many scholars have recently concluded that an early version of the Masoretic Text, called "Proto-Masoretic," was in use at Qumran along with other versions, including one similar in some respects to the Septuagint. The Masoretes copied the text with great care and gradually added "vowel points," dots and dashes which helped to indicate the pronunciation, as originally only consonants were used. This "pointing" had been begun even before the Christian era, but was continued and systematized by the Masoretes. Their work was complete by the tenth century, from where our earliest complete Masoretic text dates.

ENGLISH TRANSLATIONS OF THE BIBLE

Old English Translations

Translations into Old English (Anglo-Saxon), the language of *Beowulf*, were the exception rather than the rule. People who read at all generally used the Latin Vulgate. Indeed, some churchmen opposed the whole principle of vernacular translation. Caedmon's poems on the Creation and other Biblical topics were verse paraphrases rather than true translations. King Alfred translated, or had translated, parts of the Bible. One of the most beautiful books of this period is the illuminated *Lindisfarne Gospels* in which some scholar (Alfred?) has written an interlinear translation in the Northumbrian dialect between the lines of the Latin text.

Middle English and John Wycliffe

John Wycliffe was the leading figure in bringing out a Bible in Middle English, the language of Chaucer. An Oxford theologian and reformer, he wished to use the Bible to attack the abuses in the church, notably the wealth of the higher clergy and the encroachments of papal power. He hoped an English translation would bridge the gap between the church authorities and the common people. He and his colleagues translated from the Vulgate, their N.T. appearing in 1380 and the O.T. in 1382. Their first effort was stiff and literal, but a revision, perhaps by John Purvey, Wycliffe's curate, is smoother. The prologue to this version is very interesting, for it shows that the translator consulted all the Latin texts he could get

hold of "to make a Latin Bible somewhat true" — i.e., he was trying to establish a reliable Latin text and saw that what he had done was not perfect. In spite of a strict law against the reading of the Bible in English — readers caught would "forfeit land, cattle, life and goods for their heirs forever" — Wycliffe's Bible evidently circulated quite widely, for about 170 manuscripts have survived. Copies were owned by Henry VI, Henry VII, Edward VI, and Elizabeth I.

The Reformation Era

Better texts make for better translations. Two important texts were issued by reformers within the Catholic church, Erasmus' Greek text of the N.T. in 1516, and Cardinal Ximenes' *Polyglot*, so-called because it printed the Bible in the original languages (1522). Naturally, the invention of printing in the fifteenth century facilitated the reproduction and circulation of new texts and versions. Gutenberg had already printed the whole Vulgate in 1453-6.

"If God spares my life, ere many years I will cause a boy that driveth the plough shall know more of the Scriptures than thou dost." So vowed William Tyndale to a conservative clergyman. A student of both Oxford and Cambridge (where perhaps he studied under Erasmus), Tyndale was skilled in many languages, including Greek and Hebrew, and determined to get a reliable translation into the hands of common people. Using Erasmus' Greek text and comparing it with the Vulgate, he worked urgently, possibly consulting with Luther, whose great German translation had appeared in 1522. As it was not safe to print Bibles in England, Tyndale took his N.T. to Cologne, but before the work was finished the printers carelessly betrayed him. He had to escape up the Rhine to Worms, taking the sheets with him. Here the first edition was completed and gradually smuggled into England. Tyndale next translated the Pentateuch and Jonah, meanwhile revising his N.T., which appeared in several versions. While he was working from Joshua on (it is uncertain how far he got), he was seized by the Roman Catholic authorities, and strangled and burned as a heretic in 1536. But his work survived and is of primary importance both because of his excellence as a scholar and his skill as a writer. The vigor, grace, and directness of his style set the standard for the King James Version and to some extent survive in it. For example, Saint Paul's hymn to love (I Cor. 13) survives almost intact in the KJV, and I John and Ephesians are almost all in Tyndale's words.

The English authorities of his day, however, disliked the "Lutheran" flavor of his N.T., for instance the substitution of "elder" for "priest" and "congregation" for "church." Copies were bought up and burned by the bishops. Henry VIII, too, was unsympathetic — hence Tyndale's traditional last words; "Lord, open the king of England's eyes!"

It is ironic, then, to find an English Bible using some of Tyndale's work appearing in England some months before his death, dedicated to Henry VIII, defender of the faith. Cranmer, the Archbishop of Canterbury, had persuaded King Henry that popular feeling demanded an English Bible. The version used was compiled by Miles Coverdale, who, like Tyndale, had many contacts on the continent. He apparently did not know much Hebrew or Greek, so he used the trans-

lations of Luther and Zwingli, the Vulgate and another Latin text in making his version, incorporating what Tyndale had already done in the O.T. In the N.T. he restored many of the more churchly words which Tyndale had removed, so his work was uncontroversial and found wide acceptance. Printed in Zürich, Switzerland, in 1535, it was the first complete printed Bible in English. Another English Bible appeared in 1537, containing all of Tyndale's O.T. translation. It was completed by the martyr's friend, John Rogers. Rogers naturally suppressed his own name and used the pseudonym Matthew, so his version is called the *Matthew Bible.* It found favor with Cranmer and Cromwell and circulated freely, though some of its marginal comments were controversial.

Cranmer and Cromwell now wished to issue a large Bible which could be available in parish churches. Coverdale, whose tact and favor at court made him acceptable, was put in charge of the project. *The Great Bible,* as it was called, was so large that it had to be printed abroad in Paris, where, unfortunately, the printer and the sheets fell into the hands of the Inquisition. Coverdale escaped and by great good luck retrieved his sheets — the official who was supposed to destroy them sold them for scrap and they were sent on to him! Eventually a large press was shipped to England and the Great Bible appeared in 1539. Coverdale had revised the Matthew Bible, i.e., the work of Tyndale and Rogers, with some assistance from a new Latin translation.

The Geneva Bible. The next important English translation was made while Queen Mary was trying to restore Catholicism in England. Many of the leading Protestants took refuge in Geneva during her reign, among them Coverdale, John Knox (the leading Calvinist of Scotland), and William Whittingham, an able scholar who was already working on a N.T. translation. This group produced the most important and influential Bible of the century. Dedicated to Queen Elizabeth in 1560, it was a landmark in several ways. It was printed in Roman, not Gothic type, which made it much easier to read. For the first time in an English translation, the verses were numbered, making it much easier to refer to. The very full notes, with their strongly Calvinistic flavor, helped to promote the rise of Puritanism. Small in size, it became a household Bible and went through about 140 editions. It influenced writers from Shakespeare to Bunyan, was taken to America by the Pilgrims, and was, in an a-bridged version, issued to Cromwell's troops.

However, its Calvinistic flavor did not entirely commend it to Queen Elizabeth, who was endeavoring to build a *via media,* a church which would include all but the most extreme of her subjects. The Archbishop of Canterbury, Parker, agreed with her and planned a revision of the Great Bible by scholars whom he appointed. Nine of these were bishops, so this official translation was called *Bishops Bible.* Uncontroversial, even in literary quality (as each translator worked on his own), this work was used in churches for about forty years, but the Geneva Bible remained the Bible of the people.

The Douai Bible. Meanwhile the Roman Catholics were producing a vernacular Bible of their own. Like the Geneva Bible, it was initiated by English exiles, this time at Douai, in Flanders, where an English college had been founded to train priests. There Gregory Martin, another Oxford scholar, and his colleagues began a literal, accurate translation of the Vulgate, making use, however, of Cover-

dale's version and of the Great Bible and the Bishops' Bible. Their N.T. appeared in 1582 and the O.T. in 1609-10 and is called the *Douai-Rheims,* as the college was at one time in that French city. The most important revision of the Douai-Rheims was by Richard Challoner, the N.T. in 1738 and the O.T. in 1749-52. The Douai translation was sufficiently well known in England to influence the King James Version.

The King James Version. James I, who succeeded Elizabeth in 1603, knew the Geneva Bible well and had himself worked on the Psalms and the book of Revelations. At the Hampton Court Conference in 1604, he encouraged a proposal to produce a new translation "by the best learned in both universities; after them to be reviewed by the bishops and the chief learned of the church." By that same year fifty-four men, Church of England ecclesiastics, Puritans, and laymen, had been chosen for their scholarly ability and organized into six groups, two in London, two at Oxford, and two at Cambridge. Each group was given a number of books to work on. Guiding principles were agreed on, for example, the old ecclesiastical terms were to be used, the previous translations were to be consulted (the translations which most exactly fitted the ancient texts being selected), and all marginal notes except for different readings and cross-references were to be cut out. As they were translated, each book was to be sent to the other group to be rechecked. Thus each man could have a say in the entire work. The whole was carefully gone over by a committee of revisers.

The KJV appeared in 1611, according to the title page "newly translated out of the original tongue," but, as we have indicated, it was really a careful revision using all important previous versions, though the available Hebrew and Greek texts were consulted. The work of Tyndale was still the single most important influence on the style, which had even then a slightly archaic flavor. The translation was praised by its nineteenth-century revisers for "its simplicity, its dignity, its power . . . the music of its cadences, and the felicities of its rhythm." It has had an enormous influence on English literature and remained the Bible both for the Church of England and the nonconformists for nearly three hundred years. (The Geneva Bible competed with it for about fifty years, but gradually went out of use.) The KJV was published in the American colonies from 1752 onward.

Modern Versions

In the nineteenth and twentieth centuries, the discoveries of new texts, and the advances made in our knowledge of Hebrew and Greek, and in Biblical studies generally, have given rise to a large number of new translations, Protestant, Catholic, and Jewish. This account will concentrate on the most recent. Neither of the "official" Protestant versions of the late nineteenth century, the *British Revised Version* and the *American Revised Version*, was satisfactory, and both are outmoded. Still useful is *The Complete Bible: An American Translation* (1939; N.T. 1922, O.T. 1927) by J. M. P. Smith, Edgar Goodspeed, and their colleagues. As its title suggests, it is distinctively American and somewhat colloquial. In England and Scotland *James Moffatt's* was a popular translation which employed different types to show different documentary sources (N.T., 1913; O.T., 1924). Just after World War II, J. B. Phillips' *Letters to Young Churches*, an attempt to present the epistles in language that modern readers would understand,

found a wide public. Phillips finally completed the N.T. and parts of the O.T. A recent American venture is the *Anchor Bible*, an interfaith and international project. The volumes are by different scholars of repute, each responsible for his own translation and study aids. Genesis, Psalms, and John are particularly good.

There has also been much activity in Roman Catholic circles. *The Westminster Version of the Sacred Scriptures*, still incomplete, is being translated from the original languages. The translation by Msgr. Ronald Knox is from the Vulgate, but has the advantage of being a one-man translation by a master of English prose (N.T. 1945, O.T. 1950). The *Confraternity Version*, under the auspices of the Confraternity of Christian Doctrine, was started as a revision of the Douai-Challoner translation, using the Vulgate, but it was decided to translate the O.T. from the Hebrew. The *Jerusalem Bible* (1960) is a translation by English Catholics from the original languages, using the text on which the French *Bible de Jerusalem* is based. The notes from this French version have been translated into English, thus providing Catholic readers with a modern annotated edition. *The New American Bible*, issued in 1952 and the complete translation in 1970, is the work of the Catholic Biblical Association of America. It is a scholarly work from the Hebrew and Greek and is increasingly known and used outside Catholic circles.

Jews have traditionally been favorable to vernacular translations. A version by Rabbi Leeser (1853) was widely used here and in England. Under the auspices of the Jewish Publication Society, *The Holy Scriptures According to the Masoretic Text*, the work of a committee of scholars, was issued in 1917 and reissued in 1955. Its aims were "to combine the spirit of Jewish tradition with the results of modern scholarship." The *New Jewish Version*, under the editorship of Harry M. Orlinski, is in preparation.

Two important "official" Protestant translations remain to be discussed, one American, the other English.

The Revised Standard Version. The *Revised Standard Version* (N.T. 1946, O.T. 1952), was undertaken under the auspices of the International Council of Religious Education, which represented most Protestant churches in the U.S. and Canada. Their aim was to preserve "those qualities which have given the King James Version a supreme place in English literature" and to "embody the best results of modern scholarship as to the meaning of the Scriptures." The translators, who included Goodspeed and Moffatt, had to take into account new discoveries in archaeology, philology, and historical criticism. Nearly five hundred words in the KJV had changed in meaning since 1611. Thus "cunning" had to be changed to "skillful," "forwardness" to "readiness" and "Libertines" to "Freedmen." In some cases a new word was used when a Hebrew concept was better understood. The most striking example of this is the substitution of "steadfast love" for the KJV "mercy" to convey Yahweh's absolute loyalty, founded on love. The term is used only of the deity. (*An Introduction to the Revised Standard Version*, by members of the revision committee, explains and records some of these changes.) Some of the changes offended conservatives. For example "A virgin shall conceive," in Isa. 7:14, traditionally interpreted as a prophecy of the birth of Christ, was altered, quite correctly, to "A young woman shall conceive." One angry minister burned this page in front of his church. Other changes brought proposals to send copies of the KJV to Iron Curtain countries by balloon!

In spite of these protests, the RSV sold over twelve million copies in its first ten years, is widely used both in England and America, and has become the basic text for recent commentaries both Catholic and Protestant, concordances, historical studies, and even liturgical materials. An excellent student's text based on it is the *Oxford Annotated Bible*, edited by Herbert G. May and Bruce M. Metzger. As a result of Vatican II, which commended translations "made in collaboration with our separated brethen," an RSV Catholic N.T. was sanctioned in Scotland in 1964 and in 1966 *The Oxford Annotated Bible with the Aprocrypha* was given the *imprimatur* by Cardinal Cushing. In 1968 the Vatican confirmed the RSV Catholic Edition as one of the three English translations which could be read at Mass. It has thus become a truly ecumenical Bible.

The New English Bible. The British counterpart of the RSV, in that it was initiated by the leading Protestant churches in England and Scotland, is the *New English Bible*. (N.T. 1961, O.T. 1970). However, as the title indicates, it was not to be a revision but a fresh translation into modern, idiomatic English. Three panels of scholars, for the N.T., were chosen. Like the American translators, they took great pains to find exact English equivalents, whenever possible, for Hebrew and Greek words. For example, the Hebrew word "lilith" was translated "nightjar" not "nighthag" as in the KJV to convey the idea that it was not an evil witch but a kind of desert creature. Similarly, in Matt. 13:24 KJV "tares" has been changed to "darnel," which the N.T. committee felt was closest to the Greek word. When each panel had completed its translation, the typescripts, with marginal alternative translations were passed on to a fourth panel of writers and clergy, who made suggestions for improving the literary quality of the work. The aim of all the collaborators was to achieve a simple, graceful style, and "to secure the tone and level of language appropriate to the different kinds of writing."

It is too soon to tell if the NEB, will be as influential as the RSV, though it has been praised by reviewers for its "fresh, living language" and its "superb reflection of the meaning of the original." Like the RSV committee which, it will be recalled, wished to preserve the qualities which had made the KJV a great piece of literature, the NEB collaborators had literary aspirations. However, it is in just this area — literary achievement — that both have been criticized, and by literary men. For example, in a review of the RSV in 1953 (*New Yorker*, Nov. 15), Dwight MacDonald, while accepting many necessary changes for the sake of accuracy, complained of many changes which merely restated perfectly clear KJV passages in flat modern English, lacking in poetic intensity. In the Sermon on the Mount, for example, "the exalted has become flat, the pungent bland, the rhythms crippled, phrases dear for centuries to English-speaking people have disappeared or are maimed." Of the NEB, T. S. Eliot (In *The Sunday Telegraph*, Dec. 16, 1962) voiced similar criticisms. He notes the change from "Neither cast ye your pearls before swine" to "Do not feed your pearls to swine," which changes a perfectly comprehensible figure to an absurd one. Pigs do not *appreciate* pearls, but even "the youngest and most illiterate of us know[s], that they cannot be *nourished* on pearls." Eliot regards the translation as "a symptom of the decay of the English language in the middle of the twentieth century."

Despite these critics and many who agree with them, we must of course have new translations to embody the results of modern scholarship, and these do not necessarily constitute bad writing. For example, David's lament for Saul and Jonathan in the RSV is far clearer than in the KJV and has a force and rhythm of its own. Even Eliot admits that the modern translations of the Epistles help us "to get to grips with the mind of St. Paul" and serve to emphasize the complexity and difficulty of his ideas.

In "The Noblest Monument of English Prose," John Livingstone Lowes writes of the KJV with enthusiasm.

Its phraseology has become part and parcel of our common tongue....Its rhythms and cadences, its turns of speech, its familiar imagery, its very words are woven into the texture of our literature....The English of the Bible...is characterized not merely by a homely vigor and pithiness of phrase but also a singular nobility of diction and by a rhythmic quality which is, I think, unrivalled in its beauty.

Time will show whether any of these modern translations can displace their great competitor.

TEXTS THROUGH THE CENTURIES

The following texts show some of the changes in translation from the *Lindisfarne Gospels* to the *New English Bible*.

Psalm 23:1-3a

Wycliffe:
(1380)
He nurschide me on the watir of refreischyng; he conuertide my soule.

Coverdale:
(1535)

> and ledeth me to a fresh water.
> He quickeneth my soule,

Geneva:
(1560)

> and leadeth me by the stil waters.
> He restoreth my soule.

Douai-Rheims:
(1582)

> Vpon the water of refection he
> hath brought me vp, he hath
> conuerted my soule.

KJV:
(1611)

> He leadeth mee beside the still
> waters. He restoreth my soule:

RSV:
(1952)

> He leads me beside still waters;
> he restores my soul.

NEB:
(1970)

> and leads me beside the waters
> of peace; he renews life within
> me.

Proverbs 15:17

Wycliffe:
(1380)

> Betere is to be clepid to wrtis
> with charitie, than to a fat calf
> with hate.

Coverdale:
(1535)

> Better is a meace of potage with
> loue, then a fat oxe with euell
> will.

Geneva:
(1560)

> Better is a dinner of grene her-
> bes where loue is, than a stalled
> oxe and hatred therewith.

KJV:
(1611)

> Better is a dinner of herbes
> where loue is, then a stalled oxe
> and hatred therewith.

American Transl:
(1931)

> Better a dish of herbs, where
> love is. Than a fatted ox, and
> hatred with it.

RSV:
(1952)

> Better is a dinner of herbs where
> love is than a fatted ox and
> hatred with it.

NEB:
(1970)

> Better a dish of vegetables if
> love go with it than a fat ox
> eaten in hatred.

The Lord's Prayer: Matthew 6:9-13

Lindisfarne
Gospel (Anglo-Saxon):

> Fader uren thu in Heofnas, Sie
> gehalgud Nama thin; To Cymeth
> ric thin; Sie fillo thin.

Luther:
(1522)

> Unser vater ynn dem hymel. Deyn
> name sey heylig. Deyn reych
> kome. Deyn wille geschehe.

Wycliffe:
(1380)

> Oure fadir that art in heuenes,
> halwid be thi name; thi kyng-
> dom cumme to, be thi wille don.

Tyndale:
(1525-6)

> O oure father, which art in heven
> halewed be thy name. Let thy
> kyngdom come. Thy wyll be ful-
> filled.

KJV
(1611)

> Our father which art in heauen,
> hallowed be thy name. Thy king.
> dome come, Thy will be done.

RSV
(1946)

> Our Father, who art in heaven, hal-
> lowed be thy name. Thy king-
> dom come, thy will be done.

Luke 2:14

Wycliffe:
(1380)

> Glorie be in the higheste thingis
> to God: and in erthe pees be to
> men of good wille.

Tyndale:
(1525-6)
Glory to God an hye, and peace on the erth: and vnto men reioysynge.

Geneva:
(1560)
Glorie be to God in the high heauens, and peace in earth, and towards men good wil.

Douai-Rheims:
(1582)
Glorie in the highest to God: and in earth peace to men of good will.

KJV:
(1611)
Glory to God in the highest, and on earth peace, good will towards men.

RSV:
(1952)
Glory to God in the highest, and on earth peace among men with whom he is pleased!

NEB:
(1961)
Glory to God in heaven and on earth! Peace to the men he favors!

ARCHAEOLOGY AND THE BIBLE [1]

Introduction

Meaning and Importance of Archaeology. Archaeology is the study of the remains of past civilizations and includes both excavation and the study of texts. It is a relatively new tool for exploring the Bible. The Palestine Exploration Fund, founded in London in 1965, defined its goals as "the accurate and systematic investigation of the archaeology, the topography, the geology the manners and customs of the Holy Land, for biblical illustration." Since that time there has been remarkable progress in accomplishing these aims. Biblical sites have been identified and many of them excavated, inscriptions deciphered, documents or fragments translated, and fragments of weapons, kitchen utensils, tools and ornaments located and photographed. In addition, an accurate chronology for events in the Bible, carefully related to the chronologies of Egypt and the lands east of Palestine, has been worked out and is being continually refined.

These achievements have been the joint work of men from universities and other organizations both in America and in Europe. The most important organization in America is the American School of Oriental Research, which has a center in Jerusalem. It has taken part in excavations at Jericho, Bethel, Gibeah, and many other sites, and issues a valuable quarterly, *The Biblical Archaeologist*, which describes recent discoveries in terms an intelligent layman can understand. Other important bodies are the British School of Archaeology, the Pontifical Institute, the German Oriental Society, the French Institute of Archaeology, and the Dominican School in Jerusalem. Distinguished archaeologists have come from all Biblical faiths. Some notable examples include Judith Marquet-Krause, Nelson Glueck, Yigael Yadin, Father Vincent, Father de Vaux, Dorothy Garrod, W. F. Albright, and G. Ernest

1 Though I have consulted many works, I found G. Ernest Wright's **Biblical Archaeology** the clearest and most intelligible account for the layman. I have read this book with delight and profit, both in the large illustrated edition and in the abridged paperback. Page references here are to the latter, unless otherwise indicated.

Wright. Biblical archaeology is truly a great international and interfaith project.

Early Discoveries and Development of Techniques.

Dramatic archaeological discoveries during the nineteenth century were important in advancing techniques and in illuminating the nearly forgotten civilizations of Egypt and Mesopotamia. The Rosetta Stone, found by scholars who accompanied Napoleon on his Egyptian campaign, was important because it contained inscriptions in three languages: hieroglyphics (the old picture writing), the usual cursive Egyptian hand, and Greek. Through the Greek, the French linguist Champollion was able to decipher the other inscriptions (by 1822), thus providing the key to thousands of Egyptian inscriptions and manuscripts, many of which throw light on Egypt's dealings with Israel. The Behistun Rock in Persia likewise carried inscriptions in three languages, Old Persian, Elamite, and Babylonian, celebrating Darius the Great's victories over his enemies. In the 1840's a curious British officer, Major Rawlinson, copied and compared the first and third inscriptions, and through his efforts and those of others, the ancient language Akkadian was recovered. This "cuneiform" language (so called because the letters were wedge-shaped) had been used by the Assyrians and Babylonians, and now their literatures could be read. In the same period (the 1840's), the civilization of the Assyrian kings, who had troubled Israel in the days of Isaiah and Jeremiah, was gradually revealed to Europe by the work of French and English archaeologists. The greatest of these, Sir Austen Henry Layard, discovered the magnificent *library of King Asshurbanapal*, containing historical records, religious epics, hymns, prayers, lists of plants, animals, and minerals, letters and addresses of rulers and officials and dozens of other types of records. Among them were myths analogous to those found in Genesis, such as the stories of the Creation and the Flood. We can now see how the Israelites borrowed and modified these myths.

One of the most romantic events in the history of archaeology was Heinrich Schliemann's excavation of Hissarlik, the site of Homer's Troy, in 1870. Schliemann, once a grocer's apprentice, had adored Homer since he was a boy and had vowed that he would find the city where the epic events had taken place. He was not experienced enough to distinguish Homer's Troy from the other layers which made up the historic mound. However, others who came after him were able to do so, and the principle was established of excavating layer after layer of such a mound or "tell" to find remains of older and older settlements. Since Schliemann's day, hundreds of tells have been excavated in Palestine and elsewhere which have shed light on the Bible.

The great problem for the early archaeologists was the dating of the layers or "strata" of the tells. The solution to this problem was the work of the great British "dean of diggers," William Flinders Petrie, who was employed by the Palestine Exploration Fund. A man of boundless energy, he worked fourteen hours a day, lived thriftily on tins of sardines, and continued his studies until he died at eighty-nine during the Second World War. In 1890, he began to excavate Tell el-Hesi, a mound in Southern Palestine. Here he worked out his pioneer system of dating strata by the broken pottery which he found in every layer, since pottery vessels are cheap, used for all sorts of purposes, and easily broken. Petrie soon noticed that different styles and shapes could be associated with different periods. Since his day the techniques of dating pottery have been enormously refined and are very reliable.

Other excavating techniques have been evolved. Since it is often impractical to remove layers of the tells, sometimes shafts are sunk to see what can be deduced from the different layers and to decide whether further exploration is worthwhile. Similar in principle is the trench method, used by a pioneer of Palestinian archaeology, R. A. S. Macalister, before and after the First World War. With native help, he dug ditches forty feet wide at Gezer, where he found dwellings, burial sites, inscriptions, and an obelisk. Sometimes a site is partly cleared when either of these two methods indicates that the results may be worth the expense, or when the importance of the site invites exploration, as at Jerusalem. The total clearance method, however, is often impractical because of its great expense. It was attempted at Megiddo in the 1920's and 1930's by the Oriental Institute of Chicago, largely financed by Rockefeller money. The Institute bought the site and planned to excavate it completely layer by layer. The work, although impressive, was never completed, and many archaeologists now feel that total clearance has the great disadvantage that future archaeologists, possibly with better techniques, can never explore the site.

Of course, whatever the method of excavation, the finds on each layer are carefully cleaned, labeled, and photographed, and their exact location is recorded on a grid, so that other archaeologists can get a picture of what was found and where.

Since about 1950 a new method of dating which supplements dating by pottery has been evolved. It was first developed by Dr. Willard Libby of the University of Chicago and is called radiocarbon dating. All organic matter contains a constant proportion of carbon 14, which has a half-life of about 5,500 years. It disintegrates at a constant rate. Thus if a small portion of wood, for instance, or material, or charcoal is burned, its age can be calculated for many thousands of years with an error of only 5-10%. This method has been used to check the dates of, for example, the earliest settlement at Jericho, a mortuary boat of King Sesostris of Egypt, and cloth from the Qumran caves. (See "New Radiocarbon Method for Dating the Past," *Biblical Archaeologist*, I, pp. 330-342; cited hereafter as *BA*.)

Archaeology and the Old Testament

The Age of the Patriarchs. A variety of finds throws light on the book of Genesis. As mentioned above, Layard found in Asshurbanapal's library in Nineveh tablets recording myths similar to those in Genesis. The most striking of these is the Gilgamish Epic which has several likenesses to the Biblical story of the Flood. There are also analogies to the stories of Creation and the Garden of Eden, and it seems likely that the story of the Tower of Babel was inspired by the great ziggurat of Babylon, reaching in ever-narrowing steps toward heaven, with a temple to Marduk at its summit. These stories were probably brought by the patriarchs to Canaan, and gradually refined in accordance with the religion of Yahweh until they were written down, perhaps in David's reign. Most (though not all) of the polytheistic elements of the originals were removed.

Speaking of the Flood, there have been archaeological attempts to find evidence of a catastrophic flood such as is described in the Bible and in widely divergent literatures. So far these efforts have not succeeded. Sir Leonard Woolley did indeed claim to have found such proof in alluvial deposits of the city of Ur, but it is clear from his own account that the flood which left the deposits did not even cover the whole city of Ur. Later excavations at Kish and Nineveh have been similarly negative. It is important to make this point, since Woolley's claims have been widely disseminated and accepted.

We are on safer ground when we turn to the historical period of the patriarchs. The Mari Tablets of the 18th century B.C., found by French excavators, contain places and personal names such as Haran, Abram, and Jacob, and refer with some frequency to the "Habiru," a mixed group of outsiders who might be invaders, mercenaries, captives, or slaves. There seems to be a connection here with the word "Hebrew," although the word originally referred to a group of low-cast outsiders, not to a religious or racial group.

The Nuzi Tablets, fifteenth century archives of a town near Nineveh, contain laws of the Hurrians (called "Horites" in the O.T.) which throw light on practices mentioned in Genesis. They show, for example, how a childless couple like Abraham and Sarah could adopt an heir, who in return for looking after them, could expect their property (Gen. 15). We find also that a childless woman could give her handmaiden to her husband as Sarah gave Hagar to Abraham, that one son could sell his inheritance for a foolish price, in this case a fine grove for three sheep, just as Esau sold his for a "mess of pottage," and that a blessing once given could not be revoked, as in the case of Isaac's mistaken blessing of Esau. One tablet shows that the possession of the "teraphim" (family gods) was a sign of the ownership of the family property. This is why Laban was so upset (Gen. 30-31) when Rachael hid the teraphim.

The Code of Hammurabi, inscribed on a tall stone shaft, was compiled in the patriarchal period by the great king of Babylon from the laws of previous rulers. Many of its rulings are similar to those in Hebrew secular law, probably because both drew on common traditions. To turn to Egyptian sources, several Egyptian documents and pictures attest to the frequency of famines and of the admission of foreigners to Egypt, both of which we read about in the Joseph story. Perhaps the most striking is the tomb at Beni-hasan, which shows Asiatics in brightly colored garments walking toward linen-clad Egyptian scribes who seem to be directing them to an official.

Moses and the Exodus. The store-cities Pithom and Raamses, mentioned in Ex. 1, have been identified. It is likely that the Israelites worked on the temple built by Rameses II in the latter city. A stele of his times, erected c. 1320-1300, celebrates the 400th anniversary of the city, which must accordingly have been founded by the Hyksos early in the eighteenth century. There is a fine granite statue of Rameses II.

The Conquest of Canaan. The Tell el-Amarna Letters, found in Egypt in 1887, were written in the fourteenth century by local kings of Palestine and Syria to their Egyptian overlords. They complain that the "Habiru" have captured some fortifications and are a future danger. It is tempting, but uncertain, to identify these "Habiru" with the Israelite invaders of Canaan, but it seems more likely that they were internal trouble makers. The letters do show the jealousy, suspicion, rivalry among the various rulers, and this disunity may have been a factor in the conquest, as far as it went.

The archaeological evidence for the destruction of the hill cities has already been mentioned in the historical account. It has fixed the conquest firmly in the thirteenth century. The great puzzles for the archaeologist have been the sites of Jericho and Ai. Everyone knows how the Israelites marched seven times around Jericho, with seven priests blowing seven trumpets and blowing "til the walls come tumbling down." Unfortunately three excavations have turned up only negative evidence. The last one, a joint effort of Americans and British under Miss Kathleen Kenyon, showed that the walls were destroyed some time in the third millennium B.C. "In fact, thanks to the process of erosion," concludes Wright, p. 48, "virtually nothing remains of the last period of occupation between 1500 and 1200 B.C. Thus Jericho provides no evidence either for the manner or for the precise date of its fall to the Israelites." The case of Ai is similarly puzzling. It was destroyed in the third millennium and not inhabited again until about 100 B.C. The probability is that it was confused with nearby Bethel, which *was* destroyed during the Conquest.

The Stele of Merneptah (the son of Rameses II) celebrates that pharaoh's conquest of Canaan:

Israel is laid waste, his seed is not.
Hurru [Canaan] is become a widow for Egypt.

Merneptah was somewhat overconfident. However, the inscription is interesting as it contains the first reference to Israel outside the Bible.

The Period of the Judges. It is in this period that the Philistines begin to appear as a threat to the Israelite tribes. "The Peoples of the Sea," as they were sometimes called, came from Crete or Greece, or perhaps Sicily, and began to move into the Near East. A group of them attacked Egypt, as is re-corded on the wall in Rameses III's temple at Medinet Habu in Upper Egypt. Rameses claims to have defeated them, but, according to one reasonable hypothesis, used them as mercenaries in Canaan, giving them Gaza, Ashkelon, and Ashdod as bases. The picture at Medinet Habu shows that the invaders were accompanied by women and children in carts, so they clearly meant to settle and perhaps to conquer the whole land, which did eventually derive from them its name, Palestine. They seem to have burned the Canaanite Ashkelon, as a layer of ashes indicates, then built their own city on top of the ruins, and probably followed the same procedure in Gaza and Ashdod and later in Gath and Ekron. At any rate they eventually occupied and ruled all five cities.

Both their pottery and their tombs differed from those in the Canaanite settlements. The designs on their pottery included spirals, interlocking semicircles, and decorative birds, imitated from the pottery of the Greek world from which the Philistines had come. The tombs were also different. Instead of roughly rounded tombs, those of the Philistines were trapezoid in shape, with shelves around the sides to receive the bodies. Among the finds in the tombs were bronze bowls, an iron dagger with a bronze hilt, and an iron knife. These finds symbolize the fact that the Bronze Age was giving way to the Iron Age.

The possession of the secret of iron smelting (which had also been known to the Hittites but was never revealed by them) explains why the Israelites were at such a disadvantage in competing with the Philistines, both in farming and in war. As late as the early years of Saul, we hear that every Israelite had to go "down to the Philistines to sharpen his plowshare, his mattock, his axe, or his sickle" (I Sam. 13:19-22). Originals of the "pim" used in payment (RSV verse 21) have been found; they are little weights marked with this name and show the high prices charged for the sharpening process.

Excavations have shown how wealthy many of the Canaanite cities were, yet how vulnerable to destruction. For example, the splendid twelfth-century palace of the king of Megiddo yielded beautiful carved ivories and objects of gold and alabaster, yet the town was destroyed in the last quarter of the twelfth century, perhaps by the Philistines. It was rebuilt and an excellent water-supply system constructed, so skillfully engineered that it was in use until about 600 B.C. However, the system is an indication that the city still feared a siege in which a water supply would be essential. Beth-shan, another wealthy Canaanite fortress city, was also destroyed and rebuilt, probably by the Philistines.

The Israelite hill towns, such as Shiloh, Gibeah, and Bethel, were very simply and roughly built compared with the great Canaanite cities. It is interesting that this was the case while the tribes were moving toward unity and nationhood. All three towns mentioned were destroyed in this period, Bethel no less than four times. When Shiloh and other cities fell to the Philistines, Israel seemed at the bottom of her fortunes.

The United Monarchy. What is thought to be Saul's palace-fortress at Gibeah has been excavated. It was strongly built and surrounded by a double wall. The unornamented pottery, spinning wheels, working pots, rubbing stones (to make flour), and a whetstone are like those found in other Israelite homes, and indicate the simplicity of his life — a great contrast with what we know of Solomon. The palace was destroyed before he died.

Jerusalem, the "city of David," has unfortunately not yielded much in the way of evidence for the reigns of David and Solomon. The system of tunnels and shafts which supply the city with water has been explored, but its date is uncertain. However, the "water shaft" through which Joab entered to attack Jerusalem from within while David besieged it from without (II Sam. 5:8) has been identified. The establishment of Jerusalem added greatly to David's power and he began to make trade contacts with other nations, including the Phoenicians, who, as both archaeology and literary evidence show, exerted an important artistic influence on Israel during his reign and particularly during Solomon's. It is generally agreed that Solomon's famous temple was Phoenician in style. This is clear both from the description of it in I Kg. 6 and from finds in the area. The temple itself is inaccessible beneath modern Jerusalem. We do know that it was quite small, more like a royal chapel than a Roman temple or a medieval cathedral. Its thick walls suggest that is could also be used as a fortress.

Recent excavations at Megiddo by Yigael Yadin (of the Hebrew University of Jerusalem) and others have somewhat changed our ideas of Solomon's building activities there. Yadin attributes the famous stables, long thought to be Solomon's, to a later date, but describes his "metropolis with stately buildings of official and ceremonial character. This city is surrounded by a casement wall with a gigantic gate of six chambers and two towers, and has a secret passage... leading to the water spring" (*BA*, Sept. 1970, p. 95).

The Divided Kingdom. Some of the most striking discoveries belong to this period concerning victories over Israel. For example, the revival of Egyptian ambitions and Pharaoh Shishak's invasion of Palestine are confirmed both by archaeological evidence of destruction of a number of towns and by Shishak's own record, a list of the towns conquered and a picture of the pharaoh defeating his enemies while the god Amon looks on. The list and picture are in the great temple of Karnak, near Luxor.

The ninth-century Moabite Stone, found in Dibon in Trans-Jordan, commemorates King Mesha's successful revolt against Israel, earlier dominated by Omri. "Israel hath perished forever," he exclaims. The Black Obelisk of Shalmaneser III depicts King Jehu of Israel kneeling before the Assyrian king, while thirteen Israelites bring tribute. Tiglath-Pileser, who took much of Israel's territory about 733, recorded his triumphs in a number of handsome stone bas-reliefs. One shows the citizens of Ashtaroth being deported and another Tiglath-Pileser himself in his royal chariot.

Among the most interesting domestic finds of this period are objects discovered at Samaria and Megiddo which show that the prophets' attacks on luxury and vanity were justified. Brooches, rings, beads and other ornaments, a limestone palette for mixing cosmetics, all testify to women's vanity as the fine masonry and strong fortifications at Samaria indicate the wealth of Omri and Ahab. The ivory inlay in the furniture and the fragments of ivory plaques, also from Samaria, show that Amos was not exaggerating when he denounced the "houses of ivory" (Amos 3:15). As he prophesied, they perished — when Sargon II destroyed the city in 723/22 B.C.

Judah to the Fall of Jerusalem. Ivory figures again in Sennacherib's account of his attack on Hezekiah, whom he shut up in Jerusalem "like a bird in a cage." Among the luxury items which He-

zekiah was forced to send him were couches and chairs inlaid with ivory. Also mentioned were precious stones, gold and silver, elephant hides, and ebony and boxwood. Sennacherib's capture of Lachish is celebrated in an elaborate relief in the walls of his palace at Nineveh. It shows both the siege itself and the submission of the captives, elders of the city.

Another striking monument of this period is the Siloam tunnel, cut through 1,777 feet of rock to bring water within the walls of the city. In 1880 some boys found the Siloam Inscription which tells how the workmen, working uncertainly toward each other, "heard the voice of one calling unto another," "while there were yet three cubits to be bored through." The inscription has been moved to the Istanbul Museum, but one can still wade through the tunnel.

The fall of the Assyrian empire to a coalition of the Medes and the Babylonians, in particular the fall of Nineveh (612), foretold by the prophet Nahum, is recorded in the clay tablets of the Babylonian Chronicle. As Pharaoh Necho was going to the aid of the Assyrians, Josiah attempted to bar his way at Megiddo, but was defeated and killed. The excavations at Megiddo show the destruction of that level of the city, which never really recovered from this blow. More tablets of the Babylonian Chronicle continued the story, telling how Nebuchadrezzar defeated Necho at Carchemish in 605 and besieged Jerusalem in 598/597.

The most important documents for the last years of Judah are the Lachish Letters written in Hebrew on ostraca (broken pieces of pottery). Several of them are from a commander of a fortified post to the governor of Lachish, saying on one occasion, "For the signals of Lachish are we waiting, for we do not see [the signals of] Azekah." According to Jer. 34:7,

Lachish and Azekah were the last surviving fortified cities. The letter seems to indicate that Lachish is now alone. Shortly thereafter, Lachish was itself destroyed; in fact, the letters were found in its ashes.

The Exile and After. According to contempory authorities the low ebb of civilization in Palestine, which lasts for the next three centuries, makes it very difficult for archaeology to recover any evidence. Town life suffered a severe setback, and few artifacts or buildings can be attributed to this period. Many sites were not occupied at all and in others the people left behind, the poorest in the nation, seem to have lived in such shelter as they could find. The most interesting archaeological finds for the early part of this period come from Babylon and Egypt.

It will be recalled that the young King Jehoiachin (or Joiachin) was carried away captive to Babylon, while his uncle Zedekiah was made governor of Jerusalem. Two finds throw light on his status (see Albright, "King Joiachin in Exile," BA, I). Three jar-handles found in Palestine stamped "Belonging to Eliakim, steward of Yaukin" (i.e., Jehoiachin), suggest that the young king's property was being held for him, even though he was in Babylon. Certainly many of his countrymen would regard him as the rightful ruler and it was in fact his grandson Zerubbabel who began rebuilding the temple about 520 B.C. with the encouragement of Haggai and Zechariah. (Also, St. Matthew traces the ancestry of the Messiah through him, rather than through Zedekiah.) The other source consists of a number of cuneiform tablets found in Babylon. These were administrative documents, some of which listed deliveries of rations in oil and grain to people listed by name and profession or nationality. Among them are Yau-

kin (i.e., Jehoiachin) king of Judah and five of his sons. Wright (p. 123) suggests that "Yaukin" was "being held as a hostage for the good behavior of the Judaeans."

Considerable light has been shed on a colony of Jews in Egypt by the *Elephantine Papyri*, fifth-century letters in Aramaic from the Island of Elephantine in the Upper Nile. Many of the settlers were Jewish mercenaries guarding Egypt's southern boundary from the Persians. They observed the Passover and had a temple to Yahu (Yahweh). They seem to have been somewhat unorthodox, as they apparently intermarried with the Egyptians and made offerings to foreign deities, Ishumbethel and Anathbethel. (Wright suggests, however, p. 135, that these deities may have personified "certain qualities or aspects of Yahweh.") The temple was certainly unlawful according to Josiah's reform, which forbade animal sacrifice except at the Jerusalem temple, and it is of interest that when it was destroyed during some disturbances, the priests promise that if they are allowed to rebuild it, they will *not* offer animal sacrifes, only incense, meal and presumably a drink offering. Wright theorizes (p. 134) that this was a concession offered "in order not to rouse opposition from Jerusalem or from the commissioner of Jewish affairs in the chancery" of the Persian governor.

The Dead Sea Scrolls. Of a special nature, since it throws light on the New Testament as well as the Old Testament and since it has so enormously increased our knowledge of the Old Testament texts, is the discovery of the Dead Sea Scrolls. The scrolls are the most spectacular discovery of our century and certainly rank with the greatest archaeological finds of all time.

In the spring of 1947 a bedouin boy, looking for a lost animal near the Dead Sea, casually tossed a stone at the cliff. The crashing sound it made, although it scared him at first, made him curious. When he and his friends investigated, they found in a small cave, safely stored in jars, eleven ancient scrolls. Eventually these scrolls came into the hands of scholars at the Hebrew University and the American Schools of Oriental Research. Early in 1948, Dr. Millar Burrows, then the head of the Schools, was able to announce to the press that the scrolls from Cave I, as it came to be called, included a complete text of Isaiah, other portions of the same book, and a commentary on Habakkuk. Since then, observes Wright dryly, "scholars and bedouin have been vying with one another in the search for still more manuscripts, with indefatigable bedouin having by far the greatest success." (Wright, p. 217). In the next two decades, eleven caves of the Qumran area[1] were explored yielding manuscripts and tens of thousands of fragments. In Cave 4, for instance, were found almost a hundred Biblical manuscripts and in Cave II substantial parts of Leviticus and Psalms. More material was found in caves to the north of Qumran area and in Herod's fortress at Masada, to the west of the Dead Sea, where their owners had apparently hidden them before a last stand against the Romans.

The scrolls and fragments are the remains of the library of the Essenes, an ascetic Jewish community, known to classical historians, which was formed sometime in the second century B.C. and continued to exist throughout the life of Jesus, and until their center was destroyed by the Romans about 68 A.D. This center, Kirbet Qumran, excavated 1951-56, consisted of a monastery-like group of buildings including a dining hall, also used as an assembly room, a library, kitchen, pantry, storerooms, and washing facilities. In the scriptorium or writing room the excava-

tors found the long table used by the scribes and even the inkwells they used.

The Qumran library included several kinds of religious literature: psalms, hymns, and other liturgical literature, apocalyptic writings, and works which tell us about the beliefs and practices of the community, such as the Manual of Discipline, the Damascus Document, and the Temple Scroll. The picture of the Essenes which emerges from this literature is of great interest in itself and for its possible influence on the New Testament, but for the Old Testament the chief interest lies in the Biblical texts, about one fourth of the whole. The prophetic books are particularly well represented but there are samples from every canonical book except Esther.

What is the importance of these manuscripts? The full answer to this question is extremely complex and as yet incomplete, as the study of the scrolls is still going on. Their value will be appreciated, however, when it is realized how very late in date are the Hebrew texts which were available before the Dead Sea discovery. The earliest complete Masoretic Text comes from the tenth century A.D., besides which we have some sixth-century fragments and a Samaritan Pentateuch from the seventh century. Only a single sheet comes from an early date, the Nash Papyrus containing the Ten Commandments and a verse of Deuteronomy, c. 100 B.C. The Dead Sea Scrolls are thus of immense importance for textual scholars, for they take us back a thousand years nearer to the originals. In the case of the book of Daniel, the fragments may be only about a century later than the composition of the book. Frag-

1 Named after the Wadi Qumran; a wadi is a usually dry watercourse, which has a stream running in it only during the rainy season.

ments of Jeremiah and Samuel may be as old as 200 B.C.

The most surprising result of the study of the texts so far is the extent to which they confirm the accuracy of the Masoretic Text. Many scholars believe that a "Proto-Masoretic" text was already in existence in the Qumran community, though it is not supposed that it was the most highly regarded or the closest to the originals. Sometimes other Dead Sea Scrolls give better readings. For example, in working on Isaiah the RSV translators used thirteen readings in the scrolls which made better sense than the MT.

The reliability of the Septuagint, of which we have two fourth-century manuscripts, has also been confirmed by many passages which are very close to the Septuagint. "This proves," concludes Wright (p. 219), "that the Greek tradition does indeed rest on a real Hebrew text tradition which was actually known and used in Palestine during and before the time of Christ." The two books of Samuel provide an excellent instance of this. The MT of these books has long been regarded as incomplete and in parts garbled, while the Septuagint seems clear and more sensible. Fortunately, among the Qumran scrolls were portions of 46 of the 54 chapters. The texts of these scrolls were very close to the Septuagint, thus vindicating its general accuracy.[1]

It may be some time before there is a find as exciting as the Dead Sea Scrolls, but the work of archaeology goes on, as there are still many pottery inscriptions to be read, manuscripts to be studied, and sites to be explored. Perhaps some readers of this little guide may in the future take part in the hunt for evidence to illuminate our Old Testament studies.

---

[1] An excellent color slide-and-tape program on the Dead Sea Scrolls is available. Inquiry should be addressed to Dr. John C. Trevor, Department of Religion, Baldwin-Wallace College, Berea, Ohio 44017.

SUMMARIES AND ANALYSES OF OLD TESTAMENT BOOKS

INTRODUCTION TO THE PENTATEUCH

The word Pentateuch comes from the Greek for "five scrolls." The Hebrew name for the five books is the "Torah," meaning "the law" or simply "teaching." The books comprise stories, songs, riddles, laws, etc., written over a long period, perhaps 500 years. The process by which the Pentateuch was put together has been reconstructed by scholars, at least as to its general lines, though there is disagreement over details and some fundamentalist scholars of all faiths reject the hypothesis.

The main sources of the Pentateuch, according to modern scholars, are indicated by the letters J, E, D, and P.

The letter J stands for the Yahwistic writer, who calls God Yahweh (in German Jahweh). He wrote in the southern kingdom Judah, probably in the tenth century B.C. Some historians think he was inspired by the brilliant victories of David and the nationalistic spirit which they nurtured. His work is marked by a naive anthropomorphism which records God as making man, planning a garden for him, and walking in the garden in the cool of the evening. Angels are not often mentioned in his stories. J is interested in the beginnings of things and takes his story back to the week of creation. Many of the stories of the early days of mankind in Genesis 1-11 are his work and his account of the patriarchs is epic in scope. His style is simple but very effective, vivid, informal, and dramatic. He is a great storyteller who makes brilliant use of dialogue and narrative.

E stands for the Elohist, so called because he calls God Elohim until the burning bush episode (Ex. 3), when the divine name, Yahweh, is revealed. His work is variously dated c. 850 - c. 750 and reflects interest in personages of the northern kingdoms, such as Rachel, Joseph, and Ephraim, and in northern shrines such as Bethel and Shechem. His anthropomorphism is less marked than J's. He has a fondness for angels representing God and for dreams which convey God's messages. His epic lacks the universal scope of J and begins with the first of the patriarchs, Abraham. He is somewhat less dramatic than J, but makes good use of pathos, as in the touching story of the sacrifice of Isaac and in various scenes of blessings and farewells. He emphasizes miracles, especially the miracles of Moses.

Both J and E describe the patriarchs as worshiping by sacred wells and trees and offering sacrifices without an official priesthood. It is not always possible to distinguish the J and E narratives and, for uncertain passages, the symbol JE is used, commonly, for example, for the Book of the Covenant: Ex. 20-33.

D stands for the Deuteronomic writings, the core of which is the Deuteronomic Code (Deut. 12-26) around which the book of Deuteronomy is built. The chief interest of D is in the purity of Israel's religion and the need to root out all pagan (i.e., Canaanite) rites and symbols. Sacrifices were to be offered only at the temple. The ethical laws of Deuteronomy show considerable sensitivity to human needs and concern for the poor and the enslaved. The D writers have influenced the other books of the Pentateuch little, if at all, but their characteristic conviction that piety will be rewarded with prosperity and sin punished by disaster recurs in the historical books which follow. Some would date the nucleus of D as early as the middle of the eighth century. The D code is certainly no later than c. 640, but the whole of D was probably revised after the Exile.

P, which stands for the Priestly writings, preserves many ancient traditions, probably oral as well as written. It uses three names for God, Elohim, in the early period, El Shaddai, after the covenant with Abraham, and Yahweh, after God reveals himself in the burning bush. The P writer (or writers) is interested in the regulations for sacrifice and in the priesthood. He has an exalted idea of God, conceives of the covenant with Moses as the great turning point in history, and thinks of the covenant community as the worshiping community. He is particularly concerned with the origins of religious observances such as the Sabbath and the Passover. The Holiness Code in Lev. 17-21 exhorts Israel to be holy, even as God is holy. This block of teaching is notable for its ethical fervor and contains the law made famous by Jesus as the second great commandment, "Thou shalt love thy neighbor as thyself." Though P absorbed many earlier traditions, it is late in composition and, in fact, some scholars think it was written as a supplement to J, E, and D after they were finally combined.

At some time after the fall of Samaria (723/2), J and E were combined, with J predominating. At some time in the late seventh or the sixth century, the D document, under the guise of discourses by Moses, was inserted in the account of the wanderings in the desert, just before Moses' death. The addition of P, however it was carried out, was made in the late fifth century.

The theory that the Pentateuch is composed of these four docu-ments is sometimes called the Graf-Wellhausen hypothesis after the two German scholars who finally put the documents in the correct order, with J first and P last. Earlier scholars had sorted out the four sources, but for a long time it was believed that P was the first source. For a fuller account of the sources and arguments for dating them in this order, see Rowley, *The Growth of the Old Testament*, Ch. 2.

Genesis

Introduction. "Genesis," the name given to the book in its Greek trans-lation, means "beginning" and is taken from the first word of the Hebrew text. Genesis falls natural-ly into two main parts. Chs. 1-11 deal with the creation of man and his early troubles. Many of the stories in these chapters are "etio-logical," dealing with origins or causes, such as how were people created? Why do they sin? Why do they speak so many languages? Why are certain places regarded as holy? Chs. 12-25 tell the stories of the patriarchs. Their exact his-torical value is variously judged, but some of the narratives, such as the sacrifice of Isaac, the rival-ry of Jacob and Esau, and the tales of Joseph, are masterpieces of story-telling, polished by repetition and full of human interest.

J, E, and P (see previous sec-tion) are combined, resulting some-times in two or even three accounts of the same events. These different strands will be indicated where it seems important. Scholars are not in agreement about the assignment of every verse, but a recent and reliable breakdown may be found in *The Interpreter's One-Volume Commentary*, p. 2.

P Account of Creation 1-2:4a. "In the beginning God created the heaven and the earth." God's crea-tion is accomplished in six days, three for the creation of the world and three to fill it with vegetation, living creatures, and man. As the Jewish day started with sundown, the day began in the evening. The refrain "the evening and the morn-ing were the first day" gives a liturgical quality to the passage. Creation is out of darkness and chaos by divine fiat: "And God said, let there be light and there was light." (Note: all quotations, unless otherwise stated, are from the King James Version.) These commands anticipate a *major theme* in the Bible, that God is creator and Lord of all. On the second day, he makes the "firmament," thought of as a translucent dome. The "waters which are above the earth" fall through openings as rain. Then, on the third day, the land appears, floating like a disc on the seas, together with trees, plants, and other growing things. Next are created the heavenly bo-dies, sun, moon, and stars. On the fifth day appear the living crea-tures of the deep, and on the sixth day the animals, from cattle to creeping things. Last of all comes the crown of creation, man, through whom God's purposes are to be carried out. "Male and female created he them," "in his own image" to "rule the earth" and to "be fruitful and multiply." God's creation, according to this P version, is marked by order and abundance and God is satisfied with his work, for "behold, it was very good!" On the seventh day, in keeping with the Jewish Sabbath, he rests and blesses the day. (The word "Sabbath" is connected with "rest.") It is characteristic of P to emphasize the divine origin of this special day, when man, too, should rest and keep the day holy.

P's account is solemn, impressive, majestic. It should be thought of as poetic rather than scientific. Attempts to turn the days into geological periods or to show that the order is illogical (e.g., light appearing before the sun is created) ignore the artistic intentions of the original authors, who were putting into narrative the religious and theological assumptions of their time.

J Account of Creation 2:4b-25. In this more primitive story, the account is much simpler and the order is different from P's. First come the heavens and the earth, as yet without vegetation, then a mist which waters the earth. God forms man out of the earth, as an artist might make a figure of clay, and breathes life into him. Thus man becomes "a living soul." For him, God plants the garden of Eden (means "delight"), full of beautiful trees and flowers.

Notice the "anthropomorphic" or man-like conception of God here. A brief note describes the four rivers of Eden, certainly the Tigris and Euphrates, less certainly the Ganges *(or the Indus?)* and the Nile. Man is warned not to eat of the tree of knowledge of good and evil. In this account, the emphasis is not so much on a supreme creator working by divine fiat, but on a loving God who makes man with his own hands and who puts him to live in the beautiful garden. He even realizes that man will be lonely. The beasts and birds who are brought to Adam to name are not enough company for him, so God gives him a "help meet" for him (KJV; RSV "a helper" fit for him). God sends Adam *(the name just means "man")* to sleep, takes one of his ribs, and creates woman. Adam expresses his joy, saying, "This is bone of my bone and flesh of my flesh." This emphasizes their closeness, as the comment "they were not ashamed" emphasizes that in their nakedness, they felt unselfconscious and innocent.

Temptation and Fall 3. Meanwhile, we must not forget that among the trees in the garden was "the tree of the knowledge of good and evil," probably symbolizing knowledge gained by experience. The serpent who now enters the story is the clever, mischievous talking animal familiar in folk stories, not "evil" or the devil as in later Christian thinking. He plays his part by hinting that God has not told Eve the truth about the tree. It will, in fact, confer wisdom, and she will be like a god. She will not die. Eve's rationalization of her disobedience is a masterpiece of psychological truth. She tells herself that the fruit is good and attractive and that it will make her wise. She eats it and offers it to Adam. Immediately, their innocence is lost. They are embarrassed by their nakedness. God, who is walking in the garden, confronts them and conducts a short inquisition. *(Such an appearance of God before man is called a theophany.)* Adam blames Eve, Eve blames the serpent. God announces their punishments: the serpent is to crawl on its belly, women are to suffer greatly in childbirth, and men will toil painfully in a ground full of thorns and thistles. However, God does clothe them in skin garments. This is sometimes interpreted as a mark of grace. But they are dismissed from Eden as cherubim (winged celestial beings of the second order in the angelic hierarchy) bar their return. Their exclusion from Eden represents their estrangement from God because of their disobedience.

Notice in this story, too, the thoroughly anthropomorphic concept of God (who, for instance, walks in the garden and makes clothes), the vivid, economical narrative, the use of dialogue, and the perceptive portrait of two human beings falling into sin through arrogance and weakness.

Cain and Abel; the Rise of Other Peoples 4, 5, 6:1-4.

Cain and Abel, the sons of Adam and Eve, quarrel because Abel's offering of "the firstlings of his flock" is accepted, while Cain's "fruit of the ground" is not. In anger and envy, Cain kills Abel and tries to deceive God by asking "Am I my brother's keeper?" God's reply, "The voice of thy brother's blood crieth unto me from the ground," assumes that the blood is sacred and cries out for vengeance. This sentence is echoed in many literary passages, for example, in Shakespeare *Richard II*, when Bolingbroke claims that the Duke of Gloucester's blood, "like sacrificing Abel's, cries, / Even from the tongueless caverns of the earth, / To me for justice and rough chastisement."

The mark of God set on Cain is not, as is often supposed, the brand of a murderer, but a sign to protect him from blood revenge. Even so his sin, like that of his parents, estranges him from God, and he is condemned to be a wanderer.

In 4:17, Cain is represented not as a fugitive, but as a married man and a city builder. Perhaps J got this part of the narrative from another source. He names the city after his son, Enoch, possibly the same man who is said in 5:27 to have "walked with God." (n. b. This is from P.)

The existence of other people is assumed. The beginnings of civilization are hinted at: the sons of Lamech, one is the father of those who dwell in tents and have cattle, another is the author of lyre and the pipe, and a third, Tubal-Cain, makes tools and weapons of bronze and iron. "The Song of Lamech" 4:23-24, is a fragment of an ancient revenge song. Note the parallelism in both verses.

The J-genealogy in Ch. 4 may be contrasted with the P-genealogy in Ch. 5 which does not refer to the fall and attempts by attributing incredible ages to some of the patriarchs to cover the ten generations from Adam to Noah. The oldest of all is Methuselah, 969 years old, hence the expression "as old as Methuselah."

A curious little fragment about the giants or Nephilim is apparently included by J here in accordance with his idea that sin was spreading even to the heavenly beings, for the "sons of God" marry women, perhaps very large women, and produce a race of supermen. There are other stories in Near Eastern mythology of heroes of huge size; and also the Greek hero, Hercules. The passage is much disputed.

Noah and the Flood 6:5-10:32.

It is of great interest that many peoples have in their traditions tales of ancient, catastrophic floods. A Babylonian account has come down to us from a variety of sources; from it the Hebrew account was derived and very possibly the Greek and Roman stories, too. But flood stories occur also in the mythologies of cultures quite widely dispersed. Persians, Indians, Melanesians, American Indians and Eskimos, and Australian aborigines all have their flood stories. The Bible account is closest to the flood story in the Gilgamesh epic of Babylonia, for both stories involve the intervention of a god or gods, the warning given to a favored human being, the refuge ship, trial flights made by birds to find land, the landing on a mountain, and the final sacrifice to the god or gods.

Discrepancies in the Flood Stories.

The account as we have it in these chapters is somewhat confusing, as *it is made up of two different traditions, blocks of P being interwoven with blocks of J*, with consequent repetitions and discrepancies. The basic story is so well known that instead of retelling it, it seems best to point out some of these repetitions and to indicate differences between J and P. God's anger at man's sins, his warning that the flood is coming, the entry into the ark, the coming of the flood, and the destruction of all life on earth, the end of the flood, and the promise that there will never be another, are all repeated in both versions. The contradictions, however, are also very striking. J has one pair of unclean animals, seven pairs of clean, while P has one pair of every species. In J the flood is caused by rain, in P by "all the fountains of the great deep" (RSV). The chronology also is different. In J the flood lasts 40 days and 40 nights, so that together with the days for the rising and falling of the waters, there is a total of 61 days. In P the time is much longer, a year and ten days. In J, first a raven and then a dove are sent out, the dove returning on her second trip with an olive leaf. In P, Noah waits for the divine command before he and his family leave the ark. In J, as in the Gilgamesh epic, the hero offers a sacrifice after his safe landing; in P he does not, because acording to P's view, sacrifice was not commanded by God until later (see Lev. 1).

The promise that there will never be a flood again is also stated differently in the two accounts. J ends his account with the beautiful sentence, "While the earth remains, seed time and harvest, cold and heat, summer and winter shall not cease." P has God declare that he will set the rainbow in the clouds as a sign of a covenant that there will be no more floods. This promise anticipates the other covenants with the patriarchs.

The rest of the chapter tells how Noah, the first tiller of the soil (note the contradiction here with the similar identification of Cain), plants a vineyard, becomes drunk and is covered up tactfully by his sons. Ch. 10, the "Table of Nations" gives a long account of the descendants of Noah.

Tower of Babel 11:1-9.

This story is from J (note the contradiction with P, 10:5), and was originally etiological. It explains the multiplicity of languages among men — as puzzling to ancient man as to a modern ignorant workman. It is set in Shinar in the Tigris-Euphrates plain; the author had in mind the characteristic Babylonian ziggurat, a series of platforms forming a stepped pyramid whose summit reached toward heaven. According to a folk etymology, "Babel" — which in Akkadian meant "gate of God" — is here punned with the Hebrew word for "confuse." Whoever put the story in its final form gave it a theological meaning. God is angry at the builders for their presumption (one is reminded of the story of Prometheus and of the Greek concept of hubris, arrogating to oneself something that properly belongs to the Gods). He suggests to the heavenly court that they go down and confuse the languages of the builders, so that they won't understand each other. Thus the men are scattered over the face of the whole earth.

Abraham, Lot, and Isaac 11:10-20:18. The story of Abraham begins patriarchal history, and an ancestry for him going back to Noah and showing his descendants down to Jacob and Esau has been supplied by P at the end of the previous chapter, thus linking the myths of human origin with the history of Israel. Abraham's career has been dated variously in the first 300 years of the second millennium, certainly not later than the seventeenth century. As indicated in the introductory articles on history and archaeology, many details of the patriarchal period are supported by archaeological findings. There are certainly historical as well as legendary elements in the narratives which follow. However, the documents J, E, and P are combined, as in the flood story, so we shall find narratives repeated ("doublets") and contradictions, particularly in Abraham's character.

In Ch. 12 he is depicted as the man of faith (cf. N.T., Heb. 11:8) who without question obeys God's command to leave his country and family. He is promised that he will receive a new land, that his descendants will be a great nation, and that through him shall all the families of the earth be blessed. His call marks a new stage in the history of mankind, in that through Abraham (as later through Moses) Israel is called by God to become a new nation with special privileges and responsibilities. *The delays before the promise begins to be fulfilled through the birth of a legitimate heir provide dramatic tension in the narrative.*

Abraham and his nephew travel by way of Haran, passing through Shechem near which, at the sacred oak of Mamre, God appears and repeats the promise that this land is for Abraham's descendants. Because of a famine, Abraham goes down to Egypt. Here the curious story is told of how Abraham protects himself by having Sarah pretend she is his sister. (According to 20:12, she *was* his half-sister; according to Hurrian law, a wife *could* become legally her husband's "sister" to ensure her legal standing.) The Pharaoh deals well with Abraham and admires Sarah's beauty, but is punished by plagues because he took her into his house (harem?). He recognizes that he has been deceived and sends them both away. In this story, Abraham appears deceitful and cowardly. *The motif of a wife pretending to be a sister is repeated twice in Genesis.*

Because of their many possessions, Abraham and Lot decide to separate. Abraham generously lets his nephew choose first. Providentially, he chooses the Jordan valley (becoming the ancestor of the Moabites and the Ammonites), while Abraham dwells in the promised land of Canaan and is once more told that his descendants will be numberless as "the dust of the earth."

Ch. 14 is from another source and depicts Abraham in another role — a powerful chieftain with troops under his command. None of the kings he defeats can be satisfactorily identified. The theme of Abraham's longing for an heir is picked up in Ch. 15. In a vision he is told by God that his descendants will be as numberless as the stars. A heifer, a goat, a ram, a dove, and a pigeon are sacrificed, all the animals, except the birds, perhaps because they were so small, being cut in half. At nightfall, Abraham is in a trance and sees a smoking pot and a flaming torch pass between the carcasses. This was evidently a covenant ritual, but its exact meaning is disputed. A very optimistic promise as to the extent of the future land of Israel is made (vss. 18-19). However, "river of Egypt," i.e., the Nile, may be a mistake for brook of Egypt, a wadi near Gaza.

Sarah, in despair because she and Abraham have no son, gives her maid, Hagar, to Abraham as a second wife. Hagar conceives a child. *(Such a practice is paralleled in the Nuzi laws, according to which the child would be legally Sarah's.)* Hagar is, not surprisingly, contemptuous of her mistress, who treats her badly, so that she flees toward her own homeland. (Her name may be a pun on the word "flee.") God tells her to return, for her child, though a "wild man" (i.e., a Bedouin) will also be the father of numerous progeny. The child is born and Abraham names him Ishmael. This account is from J, with some passages, perhaps 16:15 and most of Ch. 17 being from P, who emphasizes infant circumcision. There is a variant account from E in Ch. 21.

Sodom and Gomorrah. Now Abraham and Sarah are visited by three "angels," one of whom is God, in the guise of men. In accordance with the eastern traditions of hospitality, Abraham hastens to prepare the best meal he can for his guests, meal cakes and a tender calf. These details, and Sarah's exclusion from the meal, are typical of desert life. The visitors predict that Sarah will have a son. Listening at the tent door, Sarah laughs *(notice the motif of laughter in this story)*, but is reminded that nothing is too hard for God to do. Abraham goes with his visitors and learns that they are concerned with the wickedness of Sodom. He pleads for the city on behalf of its righteous men, but the men of Sodom betray their depravity by demanding, "Bring them (the visitors) out to us that we may know them." *(Sodomy was widespread in the ancient East.)* Lot, who is their host, in what seems to the modern reader an excess of hospitality, offers his virgin daughters instead. The "men," i.e., angels, advise him to escape with his family and both Sodom and Gomorrah are destroy-

ed, together with other cities, Zoar being excepted. The "fire and brimstone" used to be thought a memory of volcanic action, but it is now thought more likely that the cities disappeared as a result of an earthquake. The story of Lot's wife, turned to salt for her disobedience, is clearly etiological, suggested by a pillar shaped like a woman. Lot's daughters are disturbed that their line may die out, so they make their father drunk and each in turn lies with him. Their sons are Moab and Ben-Ammi, the ancestors of the Moabites and the Ammonites. *(The folk etymologies, according to which Moab is supposed to mean "by one father" and Ben-Ammi "son of the parent," are false.)* The Abraham-Abimelech story (Ch. 20) is a variant, probably from E, of the Pharaoh story in that there is a pretense that Sarah is Abraham's sister. Sarah is protected and Abraham is at fault, more so than Abimelech; E seems to be struggling with the problem of the guilt of his ancestors.

Abraham and Isaac 21:1-25:18. At last *(notice how long the reader has had to wait in suspense!)* the long-expected heir, Isaac, is born. J, E, and P are all used, P contributing the point that the child is circumcised on the eighth day, a late practice. The neighbors laugh *at*, or according to a pleasanter interpretation, laugh *with* Sarah. But when the child grows old enough to play with his half-brother, Sarah is very jealous and makes her husband cast out "this bondwoman." The story of Hagar in the desert as told by E (Ch. 21) is much more touching than the J parallel in Ch. 16. Abraham is compassionate, giving her bread and water. Even so, the water is soon gone and Hagar in desperation puts her son under a shrub saying, "Let me not see the death of the child." God pities her and promises that her child, too, will live and become the father of a great nation. Hagar sees a well and gives the boy water. "And God was with the lad; and he grew, and dwelt in the wilderness and became an archer." He is the ancestor of the Ishmaelites. From E also is the moving account of Abraham's faithful obedience when he is told "take now thy son, thine only to make a burnt offering of Isaac, whom thou lovest," emphasizing the magnitude of the sacrifice. The story would, indeed, be unbearable if the reader did not understand from the opening verse that the order is a "test" (RSV; the KJV "tempt" is now misleading) of Abraham's faith. They go up to the mountain and gather firewood, but just as Abraham is raising his knife, an angel of God stops him and he is able to substitute a ram providentially caught in a thicket. Of course the Hebrews knew and even preached human sacrifice (Ahaz sacrificed his son, Jephtha his daughter), but *it is reasonable to suppose that E told this story to show that animal sacrifice could be substituted.* Ch. 23 (P) describes the buying of some property in Machpelah and Sarah's burial there. It becomes a family tomb where Isaac, Rebekah, Jacob, and Leah are all buried.

Abraham is now very old, and in a final act of faith he sends his servant back to his homeland (the Haran area) to find a wife for Isaac. The servant swears with his hand "under the thigh" of his master to fulfill his task faithfully; i.e., he swears by the reproductive organs, the source of life. Abraham acts in full belief that God will choose the right wife for his son; he has faith in God's "steadfast love" (the RSV rendering of the Hebrew, which expresses the love and loyalty of God toward those with whom he is in covenant). The charming scene where Rebekah gives the servant a drink and waters his camel follows. *(Unfortunately, archaeologists tell us there is no evidence of domesticated camels until the twelfth century.)* The servant presents his gifts, a nose-ring and bracelets. The arrangements are made with the bride's brother Laban (her father is evidently dead), more gifts are presented, and she is brought back to Isaac. As the servant addressed him as "my master," we may assume that Abraham has meanwhile died. This is later stated by P, 25:7. The last verse of Ch. 24 should probably read "Isaac was comforted after his father's death."

Jacob and Esau 25:20-35. The series of struggles between the brothers probably reflects the early hostility between Israel and Edom. The struggle actually within the womb of Rebekah presages a struggle between the two tribes. *There is word-play in the account of the birth of the twins.* Esau is "red," a play on the word Edom, and "hairy," a play on the word Seir where the Edomites lived. Jacob clutches his brother's heel, by a folk etymology related to the word "supplant." Jacob is to become a supplanter of his brother. Esau, the "cunning hunter" and Jacob, the herdsman, typify two ways of life. The characters of the two appear when Esau gives up his birth right, perhaps a double share of his inheritance, for the "red pottage," which is merely a stew of lentils. He appears greedy and careless of his heritage, while Jacob is quick, opportunistic and selfish. Subsequent events show that he does not get much personal benefit from his trickery, for he has to leave his homeland and returns in fear. *(Ch. 26, from P, tells a story of Isaac in Gerar passing off Rebekah as his wife. It resembles the Abraham-Pharaoh and Abraham-Abimelech stories described above and is an intrusion into the Jacob-Esau narrative.)*

Jacob's next trick is to cheat Esau out of his father's deathbed blessing. His mother, whose favorite he is, really plans the deceit, preparing the savory food, taking Esau's clothes and making gloves for Jacob so that he will appear suitably hairy. She also assumes the responsibility: "Upon me be thy curse, my son." Isaac is deceived and Jacob receives the blessing, which promises him "the fatness of the earth" and power over the nations, including his brother. Jacob's descendants probably enjoyed the story, admiring the shrewd opportunism of their ancestor and laughing at the slow-witted, boorish brother, whose garments still smell of the outdoors. Esau comes in from the hunt too late, to find that the blessing, which was considered irrevocable, has been given to Jacob. His despairing cry, "Bless me, even me also, O my father" produces only the promise that he must live by his sword and serve his brother though he will eventually force himself from his yoke (Edom did eventually gain independence from Israel). He plans to kill Jacob, but Rebekah hears of this and sends her favorite to Laban for protection, while Esau is out of favor because he marries Canaanite women.

So far we have a folk tale with no religious theme, but en route to Haran Jacob sleeps at Bethel with his head on a great stone and dreams of the famous "ladder" *(perhaps more correctly a ramp or stairway, reaching to heaven like a ziggurat)*, with God's angels ascending and descending. God repeats the promise to him. On awakening he exclaims, "How awesome is this place" (RSV; the KJV "dreadful" has lost its force) and sets up the great stone as a sacred memorial of his experience. The story gives credence to Bethel's reputation as a sacred place.

Another pastoral scene in Haran follows, but this time the wooer acts on his own behalf. The common well covered with a stone, so heavy that only several men could lift it, reflects a contemporary precaution against its use by the casual passerby. Presumably Jacob dismisses the shepherds because he wants to be alone with Rachel, and his removal of the stone by himself shows his great strength, already indicated in the setting up of the pillar at Bethel. He weeps as he kisses Rachel, preferring her to her older sister Leah, whose eyes lack luster, and promises to serve seven years (presumably instead of the bride-price) for Rachel. In Laban, however, he has met his match and the "overreacher" is fooled. Leah, heavily veiled, is given him instead of Rachel, for whom he is obliged to serve another seven years.

Origin of the Tribes. The account of Jacob's children gives folk history of the origin of the twelve tribes and throws light on a polygamous marriage. God pities the neglected Leah and gives her four sons. In envy and despair, the childless Rachel gives Jacob her maid, Bilhah, who produces two sons, whom Rachel names, thus assuring her right to the maid's offspring. Leah's maid in turn bears Jacob two sons, whom Leah names. For a few mandrakes (thought to stimulate conception) Leah wins the right to sleep with Jacob and she bears two more sons and a daughter, Dinah, after which God listens to Rachel's appeals and she bears a son of her own, Joseph.

Now follows a contest between the scheming Jacob and his wily uncle. In an apparently modest claim, Jacob, as a reward for further services, asks for the "speckled and spotted" sheep, goats (RSV; the KJV "cattle" is incorrect) and the black lambs, which Laban then removes from Jacob by three days' journey. Meanwhile Jacob places wooden rods peeled in streaks before the rest of the animals as they drink. In consequence they bring forth the abnormally colored animals which Jacob can claim. *The episode shows a belief in sympathetic magic.* Laban's sons are jealous of Jacob's wealth. While Laban is busy with the sheep-shearing, Jacob takes his household and flees. Rachel steals and takes with her the teraphim (household gods like the Lares and Penates of the Romans), which, if an analogy with one of the Nuzi documents is correct, insured the rights to the family property. Eventually Laban overtakes them. Rachel hides the teraphim by sitting on them, excusing herself for not getting up by explaining that she is in her menstrual period. Jacob and Laban make a covenant (two accounts are combined here) and part.

Jacob's Fear of Esau. Now Jacob has to face his injured brother, Esau. His preparations (again, two accounts are combined), which include sending messengers with gifts and dividing his people and flocks into two companies, show his fear of reprisal and perhaps not a little guilt. In his prayer to the God of his fathers, he admits, "I am not worthy of all the steadfast love ... which thou hast shown to thy servants" (RSV). That night occurs the mysterious wrestling with some kind of supernatural being, *perhaps in an early form a river demon,* but later interpreted as being God himself, whom Jacob with his great strength about overcomes until his thigh is sprained. In its context the story seems to give an explanation of the name Peniel (Penuel), "the face of God," Jacob's new name, Israel, and the custom of not eating the sciatic muscle. But since Jacob refuses to let go until he has been blessed, the story has from early times been interpreted as God's persistence against man's stubbornness, as in Wesley's beautiful hymn, "Come O Thou Traveller Unknown." Certainly we are to understand that from now on Jacob, or

Israel, is in a new relationship with God. He and Esau at last meet. Jacob and his family are very courteous, bowing and offering presents. Unexpectedly, Esau falls on his brother's neck and kisses him. His forgiveness is not explained, but it seems to be sincere.

Ch. 34 contains two somewhat contradictory accounts of the rape of Dinah which do not fit in the time-scheme of Jacob's story as we have it. It has been suggested that it comes from a later date. Jacob makes a pilgrimage to Bethel (perhaps there was a tradition of such a pilgrimage) and, as a preliminary, calls on his family to put away all objects connected with foreign religions, perhaps such as crescent earrings connected with moon worship, and to purify themselves by ritual washing. In an insert from P, Jacob is told, somewhat unnecessarily, to be fruitful and multiply. Rachel gives birth to her second and last child, whom she names "son of my pain," an unlucky name which Jacob quickly changes to Benjamin, which means "son of the right hand" or "son of the South." Rachel dies. If Jacob grieved for her, the text does not say so, except to record that he set up a pillar in her memory. Isaac dies and is buried by his two sons. Ch. 31 is devoted to Edomite genealogies.

Joseph 37-50. The story of Joseph, *a literary masterpiece,* is more unified than any other patriarchal narrative, in spite of the fact that it is a harmonization of accounts from J and E, with occasional rather obvious contradictions. It is also longer and more elaborate, less interested in shrines, cult practices, and tribal history, than any of the previous patriarchal narratives. *These differences suggest that a story of separate origin has been inserted here to link the early narratives with the Exodus story.* It is given an Egyptian setting which is correct in many details, such as the prominence of magicians, the use of signet rings, the titles of the officials, the habit of shaving and the custom of embalming, to name only a few.

The problem of dating the story is more controversial. According to a recent chronology, Joseph may have held office under Akhenaton, the monotheistic Pharaoh of Egypt in the fourteenth century. Another recent hypothesis, presented by the French historian Vergote, relates the story to the 18th dynasty who ruled Egypt in the sixteenth century.

Joseph, represented here as much younger than his brothers, arouses their hostility by bringing an "evil report" to his father's concubines. His father's preferential treatment of him in giving him a luxurious long robe, different from the short working tunic, had already alienated them, and his account of his dreams, in which they all bow down to him, annoys his father as well as his brothers. Joseph is sent to see if all is well with his brothers, who comment, "Behold this dreamer cometh. Come now therefore and let us slay him." Reuben (probably from E) and Judah (probably from J) each tries to defend him, arguing that blood guilt cannot be concealed (cf. the comments on Gen. 4:10). According to one account, he is put in an empty pit or cistern, or, according to another account, sold to Ishmaelites. Following the pit story, Midianites take him from there and take him to Egypt. Reuben is distraught.

The brothers dip Joseph's robe in goat's blood. Jacob is convinced that his favorite has been eaten by wild beasts, and mourns in sackcloth and ashes. (Here the Joseph story is mysteriously interrupted by an account of Tamar and Judah.) Meanwhile an Egyptian captain of the guard, Potiphar, has bought Joseph from the Ishmael-

ites (in 37:36 he was sold by the Midianites). The Lord is with Joseph and he is made overseer in the house. Unluckily for him his good looks attract Potiphar's wife, who attempts to seduce him. He refuses because he respects the master who confided in him and because such a deed would be against morality and religion. In revenge, she one day grabs his garment and pretends to her husband that he tried to seduce her. *(This part of the Joseph story is much like the Egyptian Story of Two Brothers, where the wife of the elder tries to seduce the younger.)* Put into prison, Joseph becomes the supervisor of the other prisoners, including Pharaoh's chief butler and chief baker, whose dreams he correctly interprets, telling the butler that he will be restored to his position and the baker that he will be executed. His reputation as a dream interpreter reaches Pharaoh, from whose dreams of seven fat cows and seven thin ones, seven plump ears and seven spoiled ones, Joseph rightly forecasts seven good years, then a famine. He recommends that Pharaoh appoint a discreet man to oversee the storing of grain for the lean years. Pharaoh chooses Joseph himself to be this discreet man, his viceroy, giving him the authority of his signet ring, fine linen, a gold chair, horses and chariot, an Egyptian name, and a wife from a priestly family. The names chosen for his sons show that he has put aside the memory of his thirteen years' imprisonment and is grateful for his success.

Reunion of Joseph and his Brothers. When the famine comes, Joseph sells the grain which has been stored up. Among those who come to buy are his brothers, whom Joseph at first treats harshly, accusing them of being spies, imprisoning them for three days, and insisting that they bring their youngest brother, Benjamin, who has been left behind. Reuben tells his brothers they are being punished for their treatment of Joseph. Understanding this, though his prisoners do not know it, Joseph keeps the next brother, Simeon, and has the brothers' money put back in their sacks. When they find it, they are dismayed. At first they cannot persuade Jacob to let Benjamin go as Joseph requested. But when they need more grain, Judah finally persuades the old man to entrust the boy to him. Jacob sends the choicest products of Israel to placate the Egyptian viceroy, as well as doubling the money for the grain. The steward tells them that they are to dine with the viceroy at noon. Joseph is almost overcome with emotion when he sees his young brother and hears news of his father. However, he masters his emotions and entertains his guests, who are seated separately from the Egyptians, according to Egyptian custom. Once again the money is put back in the bags of grain, and Joseph's silver cup in Benjamin's sack. When the money and cup are found, the brothers are distraught and return to the city, where Judah makes a dignified appeal for compassion on Jacob's love for the child of his old age. He would die if the child is not returned to him. Judah offers himself and his brothers as hostages if Benjamin is returned safely. Joseph can no longer restrain his feelings, and, sending out the onlookers, reveals his identity to his brothers. They are dismayed, but he comforts them by assuring them that they have acted in accordance with Divine Providence. "Now therefore be not grieved nor angry with yourselves, that ye sold me hither: for God did send me before you ... to preserve you a posterity in the earth and to save your lives by a great deliverance." They embrace each other and Joseph sends them back with many provisions to bring their father back to Egypt. God assures Jacob that all will be well and at last he and Joseph are reunited. Pharaoh is pleased by these events, and employs Joseph's family as shepherds in the land of Goshen. After seventeen years Jacob dies, after blessing first Joseph's sons and his own sons, the latter in an elaborate poem. Jacob is embalmed and buried in the cave of Machpelah, where Abraham, Isaac, Rebekah, and Leah are already buried. Joseph's brothers are anxious, thinking he may choose this moment for his revenge, but he repeats that he forgives them and that everything took place under God's providence. Joseph lives to see his great-grandchildren and promises, "God will surely visit you and bring you out of this land."

Exodus

Introduction. The name of the book is from the Septuagint (LXX). "Exodus" means "going out" or "road out." It does not do full justice to the contents, which also includes accounts of the wanderings in the wilderness and the Sinai covenant, together with moral laws and directions for cultic practices. Like Genesis, Exodus is a composite mainly of J, E, and P, with only short passages from D; but the whole has been worked over during a period of perhaps 500 years. In Israel's history, the Exodus, the deliverance from bondage, is crucial, and the covenant at Sinai the beginning of a theocratic community.

The dating of the events is controversial. For a long time it was widely held that it was Ramses II who began to oppress the Hebrews and that they escaped under Merneptah. However, exploration of sites conquered, according to the book of Joshua, by the invading Israelites, show that they were actually destroyed during Merneptah's reign. This would push back Moses' return to Egypt to early in Ramses' reign, perhaps about 1290-1280. In that case his adoption by a royal princess and his upbringing in the court would be under Seti I and the Exodus about mid-century. This would make Seti I "the king who knew not Joseph" (i.e., the Israelites) and Ramses II the Pharaoh of the Exodus. The store-cities Pithom and Raamses, mentioned in Ch. 1, were built at this time, and the capital moved to Avaris, in the Nile delta. Building projects were carried on by forced labor, as described in Genesis. If the Israelites did increase in large numbers, the authorities may well have been nervous about a large body of foreigners near their borders.

Oppression and Early Life of Moses 1-2. The Pharaoh of Exodus 1 is indeed represented as being concerned about the number of the descendants of Jacob, and telling his people to "deal shrewdly" (RSV) with them. His measures include not only forced labor on the building projects, but hard labor in the fields and the killing of the male babies. This last measure, however, is circumvented by the wit of the midwives who tell Pharaoh that the Hebrew women give birth to their babies before they can get there. (*Notice that the total of two midwives for the whole community indicates that the large numbers given later [12:37] are exaggerated.*) A general order is given that all male babies must be thrown into the Nile. Moses, the baby son of a Levite family is in danger, but like many other ancient heroes, he is saved by a miraculous piece of luck. His basket of reeds is seen by the daughter of Pharaoh, she adopts him, and he is brought up in the Egyptian court. (*A very similar story is told of Sargon, the Akkadian conqueror c. 2300 B.C.*) He is even given an Egyptian name (*the folk etymology of vs. 10 is false*), probably meaning "son" as in "thutmose," which means "son of Thut." Even so, Moses feels identified with his own people, kills an Egyptian who is beating a Hebrew, and is forced to flee. He takes refuge (*a "sojourner" is a protected alien*) among the Midianites and marries one of the daughters of a priest called Reuel (sometimes Jethro). Some historians thinks Moses' religious ideas were at least in part formed by his father-in-law.

Call of Moses 3-4. While he is watching the sheep, Moses, like some of the canonical prophets, experiences a theophany in which he receives a spectacular call. At the "mountain of God" (*called both Horeb and Sinai and commonly but not certainly identified with Jebel Musa*) an angel of God calls to him from a burning bush, which in spite of the fire (*often a symbol of God*) is not consumed, telling him to take off his shoes because the place is holy. Moses is fearful, knowing that the actual presence of the Deity may destroy him, but God tells him that he has seen the affliction of his people in Egypt, that he means to rescue them and lead them to "a land flowing with milk and honey": an ideal description of Palestine as it appeared to nomads. The honey may be wild honey or a syrup from the juice of grapes. Moses is to be their leader. He raises four objections to such a responsibility: 1) that he is of no importance, 2) that he does not know this god's name (*note the implication that there are* *other gods),* 3) that he will not be believed, and 4) that he is a poor speaker. God overrules all his objections — he promises to be with him and to give a sign (not identified) announcing his name "I am who I am" (the Hebrew letters YHWH, hence Yahweh), endows him with magical powers, and indicates that his brother Aaron can speak for him. God even knows that Pharaoh will be obstinate, and gives Moses a rod with which he will do miracles before Pharaoh on behalf of his people. He calls Israel his first-born son, and for whom if necessary he will slay the first-born of the Egyptians. With Jethro's permission, Moses travels with his family toward Egypt. On the way, Aaron, sent by God, meets him and Moses tells him of God's promise. They gather the elders and do signs so that the people believe. *(Contained in this narrative, 4:24-26, is a probably ancient fragment which tells how Moses' wife, Zipporah, circumcises her son with a flint and touches Moses' "feet" — really his genitals — evidently a substitute circumcision. The use of flint suggests the antiquity of the story; the directions given to Abraham about circumcision are from P and are naturally much later.)*

Contest between Pharaoh and Yahweh 5-12:33. This is made as dramatic as possible. The conflict is intense and the drama heightened by repetitions such as "Let my people go" and "Pharaoh hardened his heart." Pretending that they want to hold a feast in the wilderness, Moses and Aaron ask that the people may go into the wilderness, perhaps to the sacred mountain. Pharaoh contemptuously asks "Who is Yahweh?" and increases the burden of work by forcing the people to find their own straw to bind the bricks. Yet they must produce as many bricks as ever. The old JE narrative here is interrupted by a P account of

Moses' call and the victory of Aaron over Pharaoh's magicians— they all turn their rods to serpents, but Aaron's serpent eats up theirs. The JE narrative is resumed with the account of the plagues, although P has contributed two items here, the gnats and the boils. *The whole account is literary, stylized, and repetitious, yet there is enough variation to keep up the interest. The first nine plagues could all occur in Egypt and could all be explained by material causes, e.g., mud particles and tiny organisims would make the Nile look red, cattle diseases are certainly possible, locusts can still be a frightening threat to crops, thick darkness may describe the effect of the hot wind blowing dust in from the desert, and so on. But it is clear that to all three writers these are deliberate acts of God in his contest with Pharaoh.*

Each writer's approach is a little different. According to J, God acts directly, but in E's narrative Moses usually does something such as holding out his rod or hand. In P's gnats incident, God tells Moses to tell Aaron what to do and both brothers toss up the ashes which cause the boils. In the final form of the narrative, the number was certainly artificially rounded out to ten: 1) the pollution of the Nile, 2) the frogs, 3) the gnats, 4) the flies, 5) the diseased cattle, 6) boils, 7) the hail (this would be very unusual and frightening in Egypt), 8) the locusts, 9) the darkness, and 10) the killing of the first-born. Pharaoh alternately relents, and hardens his heart. His advisers eventually intervene and when the plague of darkness comes, Pharaoh is willing to let the people go, but wants the herds left behind. Moses insists that the herds must go, too, and Pharaoh threatens to have him killed if he comes before him again. Thus the conflict is intensified and the account gathers momentum until the time comes for the tenth and most terrible plague, which is prefaced by a warning from Moses and two accounts of the Passover, P in 12:1-20 and J in 12:21-27.

The J directions for the Passover are much simpler and given directly by Moses. Hyssop, a sweet-smelling herb, is dipped in lamb's blood and the doorposts touched with blood so that the Lord will "passover" the houses of the Israelites as he goes to destroy the Egyptians. The Passover is a memorial, for parents shall ever after tell their children how God delivered them. The directions in P are represented as being given by God and are more elaborate, involving the killing of an unblemished lamb, the anointing of the doorposts, and the eating of the lamb with unleavened bread and bitter herbs. As before, the day is to be kept as a memorial.

On the stroke of midnight, the tenth plague smites the first-born from Pharaoh's son to the sons of prisoners. Even the cattle are executed. There is a great cry in Egypt. Pharaoh is now thoroughly cowed: "Rise up and get you from my people ... also take your flocks and your herds ... and bless me also". His subjects, too, are unnerved, for they said "We be all dead men."

Escape 12:34-15:21. After taking jewelry and clothing from the Egyptians, the people of Israel set out from Raamses with their bowls of unleavened bread on their shoulders. The Lord goes before them as "a pillar of cloud" by day and "a pillar of fire" by night. *These are manifestations of the divine presence and do not need to be given naturalistic explanations.* The lengthy P expansions make the original J narrative difficult to follow and confuse the itinerary, but the water crossed was certainly not the Red Sea, but a "sea of reeds," perhaps Lake Timsah. Pharaoh gives chase, but the

Lord drives the sea back and the Israelites pass over dry land. The wheels of the Egyptian chariots stick, the waters return, and all Pharaoh's host is overwhelmed. Moses' sister, Miriam, leads the song of victory (15:21), later enlarged in the Song of Moses (15:1-18).

Wanderings in the Wilderness 15:22-18. Of course the itinerary cannot be determined with any certainty, especially since there are three or more candidates for Mt. Sinai. The "forty years" is also an indeterminate round number. The rather straggling narrative, in which J, E, and P are combined, is held together to a degree by a recurring pattern: there is some privation, the people "murmur" against Moses, who, advised by God, solves the problems in some more or less miraculous way. The bitter water of Marah is sweetened by a bough, the people's hunger is appeased by manna (perhaps a viscous substance from the tamarisk) and by quails, while more complaints about thirst lead to Moses' striking water out of the rock.

The Amalekites, long to be an irritant to the Israelites, are defeated. In this incident Joshua is first mentioned, here as a warrior who mows down the Amalekites. (Later he appears as a young servant of Moses.) There is an encounter with Moses' father-in-law, Jethro, which is interesting for its courteous interchanges, joint sacrifice, and sacred meal, also for Jethro's suggestion that Moses should choose able, trustworthy men to judge the people, reserving only the most important cases, perhaps those without a precedent, for himself.

Mount Sinai 19-40. The Lord announces that he is coming in a cloud, that Moses should consecrate the people and have them wash their garments, ready for the third day when he will appear, which he does, accompanied by a tremendous storm *(probably from E)* and perhaps volcanic action *(probably from J)*. The end of vs. 18 reads "all the *people* trembled" in some Hebrew versions and the Septuagint. God himself issues the *Ten Commandments* (20:1-17, sometimes called the Decalogue, Greek for "ten words"), probably the work of P in their present form, but in the short forms (as in vss. 3 and 13-15) much more primitive, conceivably from Moses' time. *Whatever its date, the commandments present ethical standards of a remarkably high order.* The observation that the people are fearful and tremble in the presence of God is a return to the E narrative, but immediately we have another late and very important insertion, the *Covenant Code* (20:22-23:33), a compilation of laws made over a long period, some perhaps going back to the early days of the settlement of Canaan, since no king is mentioned. Many of the laws reflect a settled rather than a nomadic life. They include directions for worship, laws about slavery, the punishments for capital crime and for various injuries (including the injury of a pregnant woman), a list of compensations for property losses, and miscellaneous laws regarding sorcery, moneylending, the treatment of aliens, etc. The people accept the covenant and according to E it is ratified in a ceremony including a sacred meal, peace offerings, and the reading of the whole book by Moses. Blood is thrown on the altar and the worshipers to symbolize the new relationship between God and his people.

God invites Moses to go up to the mountain (here he is accompanied by Joshua as a servant) to receive the tablets. *E evidentally intended to go straight on to the golden calf story, but P interrupts with a new description of the theophany.* God appears like a devouring fire on the mountain and gives extremely elaborate instructions for the building of the sanctuary, its furnishings (ark, lampstand, altar, etc.) together with directions for the consecration of priests, and other details (25:1-31:18). All these laws and customs of a much later date are given authority by being associated with the covenant at Sinai.

The JE narrative is picked up again in Ch. 32. While Moses is on the mountain ("forty days" is again a round number meaning "quite a long time"), the people fall into sin with scandalous celerity. With Aaron's connivance, they use their rings to make a golden calf, resembling the Baalite bull, a cult symbol of fertility. They worship it, thereby breaking the prohibition against worshiping idols in the Decalogue. E constructed a very neat narrative in which Moses and Joshua first hear the revelry and then discover the calf (vss. 17-19), but the editor has spoiled the surprise by prefacing it with a J extract in which God tells Moses all about it. Moses is very angry, breaks the tablets, and burns the calf. Aaron calls on the sons of Levi to kill a number of the people, and finally intercedes with the Lord for the sinners *(the J version of this is in vss. 7-10)*, but the people are punished by a plague. Nevertheless, a new start seems to be made in the J narrative in Ch. 27. The promise is repeated and the "tent of meeting" (RSV; KJV "tabernacle") described. It is a small, portable shrine, pitched outside the camp, used as a meeting point and perhaps the source of oracles. God is represented as speaking to Moses face to face "as a man speaks to his friend" (RSV). The simplicity of the tent should be contrasted with the elaborate details given about the sanctuary. Joshua here, not Aaron, takes care of the tent. New tablets are made to replace the broken ones, evidently a symbol of the renewal of the covenant. God promises his "steadfast love" (RSV), though justice on the sinners is also stressed; *perhaps D has interposed or reshaped this passage.* Ch. 34:10-28 seems to be another version of the covenant, in this context a renewal; *but the whole chapter is difficult and critical opinion varies, some historians emphasizing its relationship to Hittite treaties between vassal and suzerain.* The curious passage describing how Moses' face shines and has to be covered with a "veil" is probably a recollection of a cultic mask of shining metal.

The last chapters of Exodus describe the construction of the sanctuary more or less according to the instructions in Chs. 25-31.

Leviticus

Introduction. The English title comes from the LXX via the Vulgate and refers to the duties of the priests in the sanctuary. Sometimes called "The Priest's Manual," Leviticus, however, does not only concern ritual, but also personal holiness. The Code, *chronologically the third of the four great codes in the Pentateuch,* contained in Chs. 17-26, calls upon Israel to be holy, because God is holy, and this holiness is defined in ethical as well as ritual terms. The Holiness Code is only the most important of several strata in Leviticus, but the whole collection has been reworked from the P viewpoint, assimilating much of the material. Of course the assumption, throughout, is that God gave these directions to Moses on Sinai. *In modern times, much light has been thrown on the vocabulary and content of the book by the Mari, Nuzi, Ras Shamra tablets.* While a collection of ancient laws is not light reading, Leviticus should certainly be sampled for its religious, ethical, and sociological interest.

The first four divisions of the book deal with sacrifices, the consecration of priests, the laws governing cleanness and uncleanness and the Day of Atonement. After the Holiness Code there is a short appendix on the commutation of vows and titles.

Laws Relating to Sacrifices 1-7. God's call beginning "If any man of you bring an offering to the Lord" emphasizes the voluntary nature of sacrifices. Ideally, they represent true contrition.

The Burnt Offering involved the burning of the whole animal at the great altar and symbolized the offering of the worshiper's self. Blood (vs. 5) was especially sacred to God.

The Cereal Offering (Cain's was the first we heard of) was an expression of thankfulness or perhaps was expected to gain some favor.

The Peace Offering is more difficult to define. It has been related to the words "sound" and "safe" and has been defined as expressing peaceful, friendly relations with God, with whom the worshiper joyfully shared a meal. It was often a festive occasion to which many people were invited. Some see in it a type or anticipation of the Eucharist. It can also be connected with the word "requite," which suggests some form of expiation.

The Sin Offering could also expiate sins, but was used as well to cleanse in cases which we would not consider matters of sin, as after childbirth and after recovery from leprosy. It could be used in the consecrating of a priest or in making a Nazarite vow.

The Guilt Offering seems to have been in reparation for damage and could be commuted into a money payment.

This is inevitably a simple listing. The actual breakdown in Leviticus is more complex and describes the ritual accompaniments to the sacrifices. *It is of interest that the poor did not need to bring an expensive animal, but could offer two doves or pigeons, one for a sin offering and the other for a burnt offering.*

Consecration of Priests 8-10. This section picks up the Sinai narrative after the building of the sanctuary (Ex. 35-40). According to God's directions, Moses anoints and initiates Aaron as the first High Priest (there is some repetition from Ex. 29) and his sons as ordinary priests.

Laws Governing Cleanness and Uncleanness 11-15. The distinction between cleanness and uncleanness is not limited to the Hebrews, but is very ancient and widespread. Uncleanness in the Levitical context meant ritual uncleanness, and in such a state people could not approach God. However, uncleanness was partly determined by hygienic considerations, as the many references to washing, in some cases under running water, attest; also the long list of skin diseases which were lumped together under the heading "leprosy," some of which required separation from the community. *Of course, washing also had a symbolic meaning.* In deciding which foods were unclean, there were certainly other considerations, including the repulsiveness of certain animals or their association with heathen rites.

Clean animals chew and have cloven hoofs, thus cows, oxen, sheep, goats, and certain deer are clean. The badger was included because it appeared to chew cud. The hare and particularly swine were excluded. Of aquatic creatures, only those with scales and fins were accepted. None are named, probably because the author did not know much about them. Birds of prey, such as the vulture, the kite, and the owl were unclean. "Swarming things," all insects which do not leap like the grasshopper, were unclean, perhaps because of associations with pagan worship. Of course, unclean animals could be touched, e.g., the camel, and dead carcasses, even of unclean animals, rendered those who touched them unclean only until evening. After all, someone had to haul them away!

Other sources of uncleanness were childbirth, various skin diseases, and genital discharges. Provisions are made for purification from these conditions. There is no hint that sex in itself was considered unclean, but reproduction was a mystery regarded with awe, so purification was considered necessary, lasting forty days for a male child and twice that for a baby girl. In the care of skin diseases, the priest has to decide how serious they are, and since they are often regarded as punishments for sin, sacrifice as well as washing and sometime shaving may be prescribed. A very ancient ceremony, *not really understood,* is described in Ch. 14. A real leper in the modern sense may appear like a mourner with loose hair and torn garments and cry "unclean, unclean." He should live outside the community. "Leprosy" of garments or buildings was probably some kind of fungus. If washing the garment does not remove it, it must be burnt. Similarly, if removing the "leprous" part of a house does not succeed, the house must be torn down and the materials taken to an unclean place. Genital discharges, whether due to venereal disease or whether they are normal discharges, such as menstruation, all render persons unclean, and again there is a great deal of emphasis on washing of the body and clothes as well as on sacrifice.

Day of Atonement 16. There are many very ancient elements in this composite account of the most sacred of Jewish holy days, Yom Kippur. The high priest (here Aaron) makes atonement for the whole people in the sanctuary. Of most interest is the choosing of two goats, one to be sacrificed for a sin offering, the other "to be sent away into the wilderness to Azazel." This name occurs only here in the Old Testament — perhaps a desert demon is intended. The meaning of the ceremony is clear. The priest, in laying his hands on the goat, lays the peoples' sins on the animal as well. He becomes an "(e)scape goat."

Holiness Code 17-25. The Holiness Code (H), as indicated in the introduction, calls on Israel to be holy because God is holy. Ritual and ethical prescriptions are combined. It contains laws about sacrifice, laws about sex, laws about poverty, defilement, and directions for feasts, the Sabbath year and the Jubilee year. The student interested in the development of the Jewish calendar should look at Sandmel's *The Holy Scriptures*, Appendix II. Of most interest to the non-specialist is the prescription (19:18) "Thou shalt not avenge, nor bear any grudge against the children of thy peoples, but shalt love thy neighbor as thyself." The prescription is specifically extended in vs. 34 to include "the stranger who sojourns with you" (RSV). *Jesus took the last part of the verse and gave "neighbor" a definition for his contemporaries.*

The Holiness Code, like the Code of Hammurabi, closes with an exhortation beginning, "If ye walk in my statutes . . . then I will give you rain in due season and the land shall yield her increase." However, "terror, consumption, and fever" (RSV) will follow disobedience, and the seed will be sown in vain.

Numbers

Introduction. "In the wilderness," a phrase from the first sentence of the book, is its Hebrew title and is much more appropriate than the English title, which refers to the census described at the beginning of the narrative. *The literary sources are JE (impossible to disentangle) and at least two levels of P.* Behind the literary sources lies a multiplicity of traditions, and the book is, like Exodus, a mixture of narrative with laws and ritual rules, though much more disjointed than Exodus. The three main divisions include: 1) the last days at Sinai, 2) the period in the desert, and 3) the entry into Trans-Jordan.

Last Days at Sinai 1-10:10. This continues the P account of happenings at Mt. Sinai. God tells Moses to take a census. No reason is given, though both taxation and the need for military readiness have been suggested. The numbers of the Israelites are given three times in the Pentateuch, when the Israelites leave Egypt, at this point, and when they are about to enter Palestine (Num. 21). *The number of males given here, 603,550, would mean a total of about two million, obviously absurd. Such a multitude could certainly not have been supported on the oasis of Kadesh. The camp is four-sided, with three tribes encamped on each side. The*

Levites are set aside by the Lord for their priestly functions. Lepers (as we have seen, a vague term including sufferers from various skin diseases) and other unclean persons are not allowed in the camp. Also considered ritually impure were those who had committed adultery or touched dead bodies. Regulations for Nazarites are given. A Nazarite (the word means "dedicated to God") vows for a specific period not to drink intoxicants cut his hair, or touch a dead body. At the end of the period, the hair was dedicated to God. If the Nazarite accidentally broke his vow by touching a dead body, he had to shave and make new vows. *Nazarites are mentioned all through Israel's history and include Samson and John the Baptist.* The beautiful blessing which Aaron is told to pronounce is given at the end of Ch. 6. It is still often used. "The Lord bless thee and keep thee: The Lord make his face to shine upon thee and be gracious unto thee: The Lord lift up his countenance upon thee and give thee peace."

Supplementary rules for the Passover are given and it is celebrated in the wilderness of Sinai. A more detailed description is given of the fiery cloud which rests over the tabernacle. When it is "taken up" it is a signal for marching on. Silver trumpets summon the people or announce when to break camp.

Period in the Wilderness 10:11-19. According to P, this period lasted 38 years. The "wanderings" are impossible to follow, as the book is so haphazardly put together. A modern theory is that the oasis of Kadesh was the center of activity and that much time was spent there. The fiery cloud leads the march from Sinai, which if the theory about Kadesh is correct is Jebel Hebal, south of the wilderness of Shur. In vs. 26 the old JE

narrative reappears, picking up Ex. 34:28. Moses invites his father-in-law, now called Hobab, to accompany them. *He is now said to be a Kenite, though previously he was called a Midanite. The two tribes were, in fact, very closely allied. The number of references to them and to Moses' father-in-law seems to support Albright's "Kenite hypothesis," which postulates that many of Israel's religious ideas derived from these tribes.* The complexity and multiplicity of the traditions which lie behind one present text make it quite impossible to be sure of the actual events. There is a repetition of the peoples' murmuring about the monotony of manna. The discontented remember the cucumbers, melons, onions and garlic of Egypt, and once again they are satisfied with quails, *whose migrations are common in this area,* but which now are gathered in miraculous numbers. However, God is displeased at the people and many suffer from a plague. One wonders if some greedy clamorers overate; of course, the narrative sees the epidemic as an act of God. A curious episode also suggesting rebellion against Moses' authority, relates how Miriam and Aaron challenge their brother's unique communication with God and imply that he is arrogant. He is really "very meek," i.e., humble, and God angrily punishes Miriam with leprosy.

Chs. 13 and 14, a composite of JE and P, tell how scouts are sent to report on the land of promise. According to P, representatives of the twelve tribes get as far as Dan, in the north of Canaan. In the JE account (13:17-20, 22-24) they are given very specific instructions to investigate the number of the inhabitants and the fertility of the land, and to find out whether the cities are camps or strongholds. They get as far as Hebron and bring back grapes, pomegranates, and figs, but say the cities are fortified and that enemies include not only the Amalekites, traditional harassers of the Israelites, but also the Nephilim, (the giants of Gen. 4). Only Caleb thinks they can overcome the land, though according to a P passage which follows, Joshua supports him. *Some historians think there was an unsuccessful attempt to enter Canaan at this point.* The purpose of the whole narrative, in both JE and P, is to explain the delay in entering into the promised land. The people are being punished for their lack of faith. Moses is included in this punishment which seems a little hard, only Caleb (JE) and Joshua (P) being excepted. The narrators look forward to Joshua's assumption of the leadership after Moses' death. A miscellaneous collection of ritual laws and directions for priests and Levites is inserted here.

Entry into Trans-Jordan 20-35.
"Then came the children of Israel ... into the desert of Zin," apparently on their way to Trans-Jordan, having failed to enter Canaan from the south. P's account is so lacking in details about the "wanderings" that we may conclude they were minimal. Disconnected events along the way are recounted: Miriam dies, Moses is once more goaded into striking water from a rock, the Israelites are refused passage by their kinsmen the Edomites, Aaron dies, and his son Eleazar succeeds him. After a struggle at Hormal (near Beersheba), perhaps an isolated account of another attempt to enter Canaan from the south, the people go "by way of the Red Sea," the caravan routes to the north and of the Gulf of Aquaba. The deaths due to poisonous snakes are interpreted as a divine punishment for rebellion. Moses is told to make a bronze serpent. Those who are bitten may look upon it and live. *Such a serpent was worshiped later (II Kgs. 18:4) and is used symbolically in*

the Gospel of John where it represents the crucifixion of Christ. The list of encampments on the way (in Ch. 21) is partial. There are three songs in this chapter, the most interesting of which is the Song of the Well, vss. 17-18. It was probably included to indicate another miraculous provision of water. The Amorites try to oppose the march and are dispossessed. Og, king of Bashan, seems to be another Amorite.

The story of Balaam and Balak (Chs. 22-24) is one of the most famous and ancient in Numbers. It is a combination of J and E with some contradictions. Frightened at the Israelites' success, Balak, king of Moab, sends to Pethor, near the Euphrates, 400 miles away, for a diviner to put a curse on the Israelites. In a series of incidents which build up surprise, it is established that even Balaam, a foreign diviner, not a member of the religion of Yahweh, must obey his will. At first he rejects Balak's mission altogether, because God tells him not to go. Next he is allowed to go on condition that he is obedient. He rides on an ass, which is opposed by an angel of the Lord and made to turn aside. When Balaam beats her, she protests in human speech with the angel and informs Balaam he would have been killed but for his mount's action. *Talking animals, such as the ass here and the snake in the Paradise story, are a common feature in folk tales.* The anxious Balak comes out to meet the diviner. He has prepared to sacrifice seven bulls and seven rams on seven altars. Balaam's four oracles are a great disappointment to him. In the first, he asks, "How can I curse whom God hath not cursed? ... Who can count the dust of Jacob?" Frantically, Balak leads him to another spot, where he can see the hateful Israelites, perhaps from a new angle, but Balaam still insists that God is with Israel, whom he brought out of Egypt and who will rise up like a lion. The disgusted Balak responds, "Neither curse them at all nor bless them at all." However, he takes the diviner to still another spot and assembles a new supply of rams, bulls, and altars. Now Balaam sees Israel encamped, tribe by tribe, and exclaims, "How goodly are thy tents, O Jacob," like long valleys, in the gardens behind a river, like aloes and cedars that the Lord has planted. This time Balak's "anger [is] kindled" and he dismisses Balaam, who, however, pronounces one more oracle, in which he foretells the coming of David and his victories over Moab and Edom. The king and diviner part.

Apostasy. At Peor, some of the Israelites are guilty of apostasy. They marry Moabite women, who tempt them to take part in idolatrous rites. *Intermarriage leading to apostasy is a recurring theme in the Old Testament.* Another census, again taken at an important point, just before Israel should enter Canaan, shows a decline in numbers from those given in Ch. 2. *The totals are still impossible for a migrant group.*

Joshua Appointed Leader to Succeed Moses. God tells Moses to go up into the hilly country of Abraham (Mt. Nebo, stated in Deut. to be the scene of Moses' death, is there). He will be gathered to his fathers and Joshua, "in whom is the spirit," will be appointed, though he will not have the great authority of Moses (28:20). Chs. 28-29, a supplement to P, gives regulations for public offerings on

various occasions, and Ch. 30 deals with the limitations on vows made by women. Only those on the widowed and the divorced are binding, daughters and wives being subject to fathers and husbands respectively. Ch. 31 (P) describes a holy war against the Midianites. This tribe, usually represented as friendly to Israel, is blamed for the apostasy at Peor, in contrast to the JE account. *The description of the assignment of lands in Canaan to the twelve tribes seems to have been rewritten by an editor, for J, E, and P cannot with any certainty be distinguished. It assumes that all twelve tribes were in Trans-Jordan, which was not the case.* Israel later adopted the history of the Exodus, the desert life and the stay in Trans-Jordan as her own. *The analogy has been made with America: citizens from many nations think of the Pilgrim story and the settlement of Virginia as part of their history.* After another attempt to list the encampments on the journey from Egypt, the boundaries of the Israel of the future are announced. They correspond roughly to David's empire. Special cities and pasture lands were to be allotted to the Levites, who did not have a right to a tribal inheritance. "Cities of refuge" were also set aside for those who killed accidentally; those who took refuge there need not be fearful of blood revenge from the next of kin. The last chapter (36) supplements the passage in 27 and is concerned with the inheritance of property by women. A women who inherits property must marry within the tribe to keep the tribal property intact.

Deuteronomy

Introduction. The name Deuteronomy goes back to the LXX where "a copy of this law" was rendered

as "this second law." However, the latter term is not really a misnomer, as Deuteronomy really presents a new statement of the covenant for its own day in the guise of Moses' farewell speeches. The second discourse, Chs. 12-20, contains the Deuteronomic Code.

Though it is *the last book of the Pentateuch*, Deuteronomy is also the first book of the D (Deuteronomic) history of Israel, which retraces some of the early history of Israel and continues in the subsequent books through Kings. It has a characteristic style, exhortatory, didactic and repetitious; it is the work of several hands and draws on much past work. It or part of it may be the "book of the Law" (II Kings 22-23) on which Josiah based his reforms in 622/3. It has in common with his reforms the centralization of worship, including the Passover, at Jerusalem, the destruction of sacred poles and pillars, and the proscription of magic, the worship of heavenly bodies, and cult sacrifice. In the words of the introduction to the book in the Ox. An. Bible, "although Deuteronomy rests upon ancient tradition, fundamentally it is a rediscovery and reinterpretation of Mosaic teaching in the light of later historical understanding."

Setting 1:1-2. This places Moses in the Arabah desert in Moab, in the fortieth year after leaving Mt. Sinai (here Horeb).

Moses' First Discourse 1:3-4:49. Moses summarizes the events since the people were told to leave the holy mountain and to take possession of the land. Officials were chosen to help him bear the burden of governing his unruly people. He recounts, with variations from Numbers, an attempt to enter Canaan and the march through Edom and Moab. The right of Edomites and Moabites to their own land is now recognized. Another point different from Numbers is that Moses now claims he

is punished on the peoples' account (vs. 37), not for his own rebellion, i.e., he endures a kind of vicarious suffering. The summary goes down to the defeat of Sihon and Og and the description of land described in Numbers. Moses tells how he begged God to let him cross over the Jordan, but was only allowed to go to Mt. Pisgah (Nebo) and look at the promised land. In Ch. 4 Moses issues an impassioned plea to the people to heed the laws, which should not be added to or removed. *(Note the focus on the written law.)* What other nation is so close to God or has been so spectacularly saved or has been given so many righteous laws? "Because he loved your fathers... therefore you should keep his statutes... that you may prolong your days in the land which the Lord your God gives you forever." If the laws are not obeyed, Israel may be scattered among other peoples.

Moses' Second Discourse 5-26. Moses emphasizes that God made the covenant "not with our fathers... but with us, who are all of us here alive this day" (RSV). This contradiction of the exclusion of the wilderness generation from the promised land must have been conscious and intended by the writers to underline the acceptance of the covenant by his contemporaries. The Ten Commandments are repeated, with slight variations, and the hearers are exhorted to obey them. The Shema ("hear"), "Hear, O Israel: The Lord our God is one Lord; and thou shalt love the Lord thy God with all thy heart and with all thy soul and with all thy might" (Deut. 6:4-5) is linked with a plea to teach the children the laws in the context of the home and everyday life. The holiness of God's chosen people is emphasized, his love for them, his many promises to the patriarchs, his care in bringing them out of Egypt. Love and obedience must be observed if Israel is to keep its inheritance.

The Deuteronomic Code is contained in Chs. 12-26:19. The Code contains about half the laws given in the Covenant Code, but it is thought that both codes draw on earlier collections. Sacred poles and pillars, heathen images and altars are to be destroyed. Worship is to be centralized to keep Israel from contact with pagan cults. Israelites who follow pagan rites are to be stoned. There are laws regulating tithes, the release of slaves and debtors, firstlings, annual feasts, and the establishment of a higher court to help weak judges. There are rules for the selection and ratifiying of a king and for his conduct. A king is permitted but not required. Criteria are set up to distinguish true prophets from false. A number of miscellaneous laws concern homicide, the stipulations for a holy war, the treatment of female prisoners, the punishment of rebellious sons (by stoning), the shelter of fugitive slaves, the payment of hired labor, and numerous other topics. The treatment of slaves, hired workers, and some animals, mother birds for example, is remarkably humane. The section and laws conclude with exhortations and bits of liturgy, including a very interesting credal summary beginning "A wandering Aramean was my father" (RSV) and summing up God's mighty acts in bringing the people out of Egypt and into the promised land (26: 5-10).

Renewal of the Covenant; Moses' Last Discourse and Death 27-50. The covenant is to be reaffirmed near Shechem on Mount Gerizim and Mount Ebal, where blessings and curses are to be offered, and repeated at every seventh Feast of the Booths at the central sanctuary. It was the curses which later alarmed King Josiah when he was shown the book of laws found in the temple. Chs. 29-30 describe another covenant made in the land of Moab, apparently one of the periodic renewals of the pact between Israel and God. Moses again sums up the Lord's favors and exhorts the people to avoid apostasy. Some critics think this is a very late passage, perhaps postexilic.

Finally, at God's behest, Moses commissions Joshua to be his successor, exhorting him, "Be strong and of good courage, for you shall bring the children of Israel into the land which I swore to give you." *The Song of Moses in Ch. 32:1-43 fits in broadly with the D point of view, but is thought to come from another source because it does not refer to the law or make Israel's prosperity depend on good behavior; rather, it is a manifestation of God's power.* Moses is told to ascend Mount Nebo, where he looks across to the promised land which he will never enter. He does and is mysteriously buried by God, so that no one knows the place of his burial.

Joshua

Introduction. If we judge by the overall impression it makes, the book of Joshua appears simple in structure. Chs. 1-12 show how the promise is fulfilled in the speedy conquest of Canaan, Chs. 13-22 describe the division of the land

among the twelve tribes, and the last two chapters tell how Joshua renews the covenant and bids his people farewell. *When the text is examined in detail, however, the book's complexity is revealed. It is a composite of many sources, some in poetry as well as in prose, all of which have been worked over by several editors.*

Scholars are not in agreement about this process, nor even about the continuity of the J and E traditions in this book. If they were used, their identity has been much obscured by rewriting. Some narratives record what were probably ancient oral traditions regarding Gilgal and Shechem, etiological stories explaining the origins of customs, and descriptions of early tribal boundaries. Lists of cities included seem to be later than the conquests and were added at a later date. The Deuteronomic editors, writing perhaps in the seventh century B.C., imposed their own ideas on this material. They thought of Yahweh as active in history as a defender of his people, rewarding the obedient with victory, but indifferent to non-Israelites. According to Martin Noth and his followers, the Deuteronomic school was responsible for all the books from Joshua through Kings, shaping the material to suit their ends and producing a continuous Deuteronomic history of events from the Conquest to the Captivity.

Preparations for the Conquest of Canaan 1-2. God appoints Joshua to succeed Moses and promises him the land stretching from the wilderness of the south and east as far as the Euphrates, and from the Lebanon mountains and the land of the Hittites (probably northern Syria) to the Mediterranean. Even David's empire, perhaps "prophesied" here, was not so extensive. The editor's emphasis is on Yahweh's generosity and care in personally commissioning Joshua to lead the attack. *The whole scene has a liturgical quality; the repeated exhortations to "be strong and of good courage" and to obey the law reflect the thinking of the Deuteronomic editor.* The people promise to obey Joshua.

The story of the spies is probably a very early one, though it has been altered by the editor to emphasize God's protection of the men. Joshua sends them to spy out the land, particularly Jericho. There they are protected, as often happens in folk tales, by one of the humblest inhabitants, the harlot Rahab, *who must be one of the earliest good-natured prostitutes in Western literature. (She is praised for her good deed in Heb. 11:31.)* She asks for protection in return, and a sign is arranged, a scarlet thread hanging from a window. The spies return to Joshua and report that the conquest will be an easy one, because the people are terrified.

Crossing the Jordan 3-4. The narrative is confused, perhaps as a result of combining two or more earlier narratives. It is meant to recall, of course, the crossing of the Red Sea by Moses, as again the waters are miraculously held back. *The whole passage has a liturgical flavor, describing, with several repetitions, how the people are purified, how the priest takes the lead, carrying the ark, how the procession passes over on dry land, and how twelve men, representing the twelve tribes, set up memorial stones. The whole account suggests a religious ceremony. Some scholars think the crossing was reenacted ritually in later times at Gilgal, in response to the anticipated question* (4:6) "What mean these stones?"

Circumcision and Passover 5. Since the men circumcised in the time of Moses have died, Joshua himself circumcised his men "with flint knives." The phrase may indicate that the writer knows the rite is very ancient (perhaps originating in the third millennium B.C.), or that flint knives were really used, which would be an example of conservatism in religious rites. In any case the ceremony implies dedication to Yahweh and a renewal of the covenant. It is followed by a celebration of the Passover. Obviously meant to recall the Passover in Egypt before the Exodus, it marks the last stage of the events which the Exodus initiated, the final entry into the promised land. The people eat the unleavened bread and parched grain; the next day manna, the wilderness food, ceases, for now the people can "eat of the fruit of the land of Canaan." In Exodus an angel passed by as the Passover was celebrated; similarly now a mysterious figure appears to Joshua. Joshua falls on his face, saying, "What saith my lord unto his servant?" and "the commander of the Lord's host" tells him, "Loose thy shoes from off thy foot; for the place whereon thou standest is holy." *Again we are meant to recall Moses at the burning bush, cf. Exodus 3:5, though here the Lord is represented as a military leader.*

The Siege of Jericho 6-7. *It may be disconcerting to readers of this dramatic and famous account of how "Joshua fit the battle of Jericho" to hear that archaeology, in this case, does not support the tradition. The latest excavation, under Kathleen Kenyon in 1952-7, showed that the ruins of Jericho were of a much earlier date than the conquest.* Perhaps these ruins were impressive and were associated by the tellers of the story with Joshua's conquest. In any case the original account or accounts have undergone great transformation, and now display the same liturgical quality that we noticed in the story of the crossing of the Jordan. It is a magnificent instance of Yahweh's mighty acts. "See, I have given into thy hand Jericho, and the king thereof, and the mighty men of valor." At the Lord's command, the people march around

the city each day for six days. Seven priests carry seven ram's-horn trumpets before the ark, blowing on the trumpets. On the seventh day they march around seven times, the priests trumpeting and the people following them. When Joshua declaims, "Shout; for the Lord hath given you the city," the walls fall down flat. As the war was conceived of as a holy war, the gold and silver, the bronze and iron vessals, are to go into the Lord's treasury, and the inhabitants are to be annihilated, as they are considered dedicated to Yahweh. "And they utterly destroyed all that was in the city, both man and woman, young and old, and ox, and sheep, and ass, with the edge of the sword." *According to the assumptions of the time, this was a religious act.* Rahab and her family are spared, as was arranged. Achan, one of the Israelites, disobeys Joshua's ban on keeping any of the looted treasure, and the Lord is angry. As a result the Israelites' attack on Ai is repulsed. Lots are cast and Achan is forced to confess that he stole gold and silver and a beautiful mantle from Shinar. He and his whole family (the family unit is considered collectively guilty) are stoned to death and then buried. *The hand of the Deuteronomic editor in these two narratives is evident.* In the account of the siege of Jericho obedience results in victory, but here the disobedience of only one Israelite brings defeat.

Conquest of Ai 8. Now that Achan's guilt has been punished, the way is clear for the destruction of Ai. Joshua plans to take the city by surprise. He places one group of his men in ambush close to the city and attacks with a second group, who pretend to run away in order to draw out the defenders. While the defenders attack Joshua's force, the men in ambush quietly fall on the defenseless city, and burn it. Meanwhile Joshua's men turn around, crush the defenders, and capture the king, who is later hanged. "And Joshua burned Ai and made it a heap forever, even a desolation unto this day." *Perhaps this verse suggests an answer to the problem raised by the excavations.* Like Jericho, Ai was not occupied in Joshua's time; indeed, it had been destroyed about a thousand years before. But the word "Ai" can mean "heap of stones," and perhaps the ruin inspired the teller or writer to attach to it a story originally told of a nearby city, perhaps Bethel, which *was* destroyed during the Conquest. The D editor tells how, after the battle, Joshua builds an altar, offers sacrefices, writes the law on the stones (again in imitation of Moses), assembles the people before the ark, and reads them "all the words of the law."

The Gibeonites 9. While the Amorites and other tribes are forming an alliance to fight the Israelites, the men of Gibeon trick the latter into making a covenant by pretending to come from a long distance. They claim that their bread is moldy, their wine bursting its skins, and their clothes and shoes worn out. Joshua fails to ask directions of the Lord and when he finds out the Gibeonites are from near by, he makes them, "hewers of wood and drawers of water" for the Israelites, thus turning their obsequious phrase "your servants" into reality.

Defeat of Southern Kings 10. The Amorite king assembles his allies, other southern kings, and they attack Gibeon. The Gibeonites call on their new allies, Joshua makes a forced march by night from Gilgal, and attacks the confederacy. The Lord helps by putting them in a panic and sending down hailstones. The famous spell, "Sun, stand thou still upon Gibeon; and thou, moon, in the valley of Ajalon," is pronounced by Joshua. The heavenly bodies stand still and the destruction of the enemies is accomplished. *This is a fine poetical tribute to Yahweh's power, and pseudo-scientific attempts to explain it are beside the point.* The five kings are found in a cave, killed, and thrown back into the cave. A list of Joshua's conquests in Southern Palestine follows. The conquest is represented as complete, in direct contrast with the account in Judges 1. Here the D editor thinks of Joshua as completing the conquest of the whole area.

Conquest of Northern Palestine 11-12. Aroused by Israel's conquests, Jabin, king of Hazor, assembles his allies, and encamps near the waters of Merom to fight with Israel. Joshua drives them back and destroys Hazor with fire. *Parts of this account may be of considerable antiquity, perhaps J or JE, and the destruction of Hazor is supported by archaeological evidence. However, the account of the conquest of the north is otherwise brief and inadequate, and Jabin, supposedly killed here by Joshua, survives into the book of Judges.* The rest of Ch. 11 and Ch. 12 lists kings' cities taken by the Israelites, but the picture is an idealized one.

Distribution of Land 13-22. The land was precious, because it was the gift of God, and Israel naturally treasured the lists of places and boundaries which are found in this section. *However, this does not exclude the possibility that the lists were conflated, added to, and in other ways changed over the centuries. The list in 13:1-7 (probably from D) of places yet to be conquered shows that the conquest was far from complete. It is also probable that it was much slower than the early chapters of Joshua imply and that the federation of the tribes* was also very gradual. Other lists and allotments are vague; for example the allotments to Manassah and Ephraim (Chs. 16-17) are not clear. In the latter part of Ch. 17 they are treated as one tribe, Joseph.

Ch. 20:1-9 tells how six small cities of refuge are set up where persons who have killed may be protected from the blood vengeance of near relatives of their victims until the authorities have had time to judge the case. The killer may have killed by accident.

There is a great deal of confusion about the Levites, perhaps because the term was later confused with the "sons of Levi," the professional priests. The D editor seems to have believed (13:14) that the Levites were given no land, but were distributed among cities held by the other tribes. Another account in Ch. 21 assigns 48 cities to the Levites but this was probably a paper scheme, as it is unlikely that the Levites actually controlled these towns. It is more likely that they served as priests there. The landless state of the Levites may explain why they are classed with widows and orphans in Deuteronomy.

Joshua's Farewell 23. Now an old man, Joshua summons the elders, the judges, and all the people. He reminds them that God has fought for them and given them the land. "Therefore be very steadfast to keep and do all that is written in the book of the law of Moses" (RSV). He warns them that if they stray from the law, for example in making foreign marriages, they will perish. *This whole speech is by the D editor, who knew later generations would stray from the law.*

Assembly at Shechem and Joshua's Death 24. This seems to be an appendix, since the book could properly end at Ch. 23. Joshua assembles all the tribes at Shechem, a city-fortress near the grave of Joseph and Jacob's well. He summarizes the whole of Israel's history from Abraham through the Conquest and challenges the people either to serve Yahweh faithfully or to serve the foreign gods.

And if it seem evil unto you to serve the Lord, choose you this day whom ye will serve, whether the gods which your fathers served that were on the other side of the flood [the Euphrates], or the gods of the Amorites [the Canaanites], in whose land ye dwell: but as for me and my house, we will serve the Lord.

To this eloquent appeal the people reply, "We will serve the Lord." Three times they make their vow, reaffirming the covenant made at Sinai and, if Anderson (p. 93) is right, accepting as members the Leah tribes, Reuben, Simeon, Levi, and Judah, who had not been involved in the Exodus and the wanderings in the desert. To such "converts" the challenge to choose between the false gods and the true one would be especially poignant. Joshua sets up a great stone, as a sign of the covenant, under an oak, probably a sacred oak. Once more he urges the people to be faithful. Now that his work is done, he dies and is buried in the hill country of Ephraim.

Judges

Introduction. The English title "Judges" is misleading. The Hebrew word *shofet* more often means champion, deliverer, or military leader. Only Deborah is represented as "judging" in the modern sense. The six important leaders whose stories are told here all emerged in some time of crisis, such as an attack by the Ammonites or the Moabites or the Philistines. They are imbued by God with charismatic power ("charisma" means "gift") so that they can successfully lead the resistance. Six minor judges are included, perhaps to provide at least one judge for all the Northern tribes. *A compiler put the stories together so as to suggest a continuous succession of national leaders, but in fact the "judges" overlapped chronologically and were in most cases only of local importance.* The stories of the "judges" are most probably very old and many of them reflect a barbarous period, for example, Jael's violation of the law of hospitality, the murder of Gideon's sons, the killing of the males of Shechem, the razing of that city, the sacrifice of Jephthah's daughter, and Samson's adventure with the Philistine harlot. *On these crude and often cruel tales, the Deuteronomic editors have imposed their characteristically moral interpretation of history by adding opening and closing formulas.* Look, for example, at Ch. 2:11-16. The people do evil, follow foreign gods, arouse Yahweh's anger, and are punished. Eventually Yahweh takes pity on them and raises up a new "judge" to deliver them. He is victorious and the land has rest for "forty years," a round number meaning quite a long time.

When read in isolation, the narrative in this book gives the impression that the tribal organization is still very loose and unstructured. On occasion, however, the tribes do unite, to worship at Shiloh, for example, or to revenge the rape and murder of the Levite's concubine. In the main, however, the various judges seem to have operated independently.

Conquest of Canaan 1-2:5. The first chapter summarizes the efforts of the tribes to complete the conquest. The accounts come from various early sources, but are not all of the same date. In general the picture is less optimistic than that in Joshua, in that it describes a piecemeal and only partially successful operation. In many cases the Canaanites remain in the area and it is made clear that one reason for their strength is that they have chariots of iron. The first few verses of Ch. 2 are editorial and explain the failure as the result of disobedience to God.

The D Introduction 2:6-3:6. Joshua's death is described again, much as in Josh. 24, but is used here as a link between the end of Joshua and an introduction to the narratives about the judges. Different reasons are given for the Israelites' defeat. Vs. 3:2 suggests that God allowed them to be defeated so that they might learn the art of war. This was probably an earlier idea. More characteristically Deuteronomic is the statement that they ran after the foreign gods and refused to listen to the judges. Even when they did listen and were saved, they usually fell back into sin after the death of the judge. Because of their disobedience, their worship of false gods, they will be tested by their various enemies.

Othniel 3:7-11. "And the children of Israel did evil in the sight of the Lord, and served Baalim [and Ashtaroth]," so he sells them into the hands of the king of Mesopotamia. After eight years, the Israelites cry to the Lord and he raises up a judge, Othniel, who frees them from Mesopotamia.

Ehud 3:12-30. Again the people do evil and are defeated by Eglon, king of Moab. When they cry to the Lord, he raises up Ehud, who takes a tribute to Eglon and, under the pretence of telling him a secret, contrives to be alone with him and kills him with a sword which he has cleverly fastened to his *right* thigh — an unexpected place. The sword sinks deeply into the fat stomach of the king, and he is not discovered for some time because his servants think he is "relieving himself in the closet of the cool chamber" (RSV — the KJV has "Surely he covereth his feet," a *euphemism*). Ehud escapes and the Israelites kill the Moabites in large numbers. "And the land had rest fourscore years."

Shamgar 3.31. This almost forgotten "judge" slays the Philistines with an ox-goad. Like Samson, he used whatever came to hand as a weapon. The LXX, probably rightly, places this verse after Ch. 16.

Deborah 4, 5. This famous story is told in both prose and verse versions, with slightly different details. Ch. 4 combines two stories of enemy kings, which have been fused so that the second king, Sisera, becomes the general of the first, Jabin. Deborah, a prophetess, calls on Barak to lead his men against Sisera. She promises success. Barak does overcome Sisera, in spite of the latter's "nine thousand iron chariots." Sisera flees *on foot* — this seems to indicate that Barak's victory was a very complete one — and is invited into Jael's tent. She gives him milk, makes him comfortable, and when he is asleep drives a tent-peg into his head. *(No comment is made in either version on this violation of hospitality.)*

The poetic version, Ch. 5, called "the Song of Deborah," though it is about her rather than by her, is so impressionistic and so intense in feeling that many scholars think it is contemporary with the event, c. 1125 B.C. This would make it the oldest substantial passage in the Bible. Basically a victory celebration, it includes other elements such as blessing, curse, and taunt.

It is full of effective contrasts. For example, Yahweh's march at the head of his people is contrasted with the former helplessness of Israel. "The earth trembled and the heavens dropped... The mountains melted from before the Lord," as Yahweh shows his power. "Awake, Deborah ... arise Barak," cries the singer. The unresponsive tribes are condemned, the loyal tribes praised. The battle, when "the stars in their courses fought against Sisera," is briefly described. The ugly death of Sisera is mockingly and ironically contrasted with the picture of his mother awaiting his triumphant return loaded with booty. *Parallelism, the chief feature of Hebrew poetry, is effective also in the KJV translation:*

She put her hand to the nail,
and her right hand to the
workmen's hammer;
....
The mother of Sisera looked out
at a window,
And cried through the lattice.

This victory poem is superior in intensity and poetic quality to all known contemporary victory odes of Assyria and Egypt.

Gideon 6-8. Again the people of Israel fall into sin and are overcome, this time by the Midianites, and Gideon is raised up to lead them. Called by an angel, he first purges his own family of Baal worship, then chooses a select group of warriors, those who lapped up water like dogs *(perhaps the most primitive men and so the readiest to fight?)*, arming them with trumpets and torches in jars. The Midianites are surprised at night with trumpet blasts and lights and perhaps driven out to meet the rest of the army *(two accounts have been combined here and the exact sequence of events is not clear)*. Gideon then captures Succoth, tortures its leading men, plunders the city, and eventually kills the Midianite leaders. His followers wish to make him king, but he refuses.

Abimelech 9. This account has no transition formula. Abimelech's mother was from Shechem and he gained power there. *The story incorporates a rare fable in which various talking trees try to choose a king, as the "cedars of Lebanon" (presumably the ruling house of Shechem) cannot rule.* Abimelech is chosen, razes the city, scatters salt so that nothing will grow, but is killed in a siege.

Tola and Jair 10:1-5. These are brief references to otherwise unknown leaders.

Jephthah 10:6-12:7. The editorial preface, 10:6-18, indicates that the enemies punishing the Israelites for their sins this time are the Ammonites. Jephthah, "a mighty man of valor," thrust out by his half-brothers because he is the son of a harlot, is recalled by them when the Ammonites are threatening. He agrees to fight with them provided he is made the leader. He promises Yahweh that if the Ammonites are delivered into his hands, he will offer up as a burnt offering whatever comes forth to meet him when he returns from battle. *The He-*

brew wording indicates that a human sacrifice is intended. The spirit of the Lord comes upon him, so he smites the Ammonites with "a very great slaughter." Unluckily, it is his only daughter who comes to meet him "with timbrels and with dances." He rends his garments, but knows he must keep his vow: "I have opened my mouth to the Lord and I cannot go back." The daughter accepts the situation completely: "My father, if thou hast opened thy mouth to the Lord, do to me according to that which hath proceeded out of thy mouth; forasmuch as the Lord hath taken vengeance for thee of thine enemies." She asks only that she may bewail her virginity for two months upon the mountains. The fact that she dies childless would make her death seem more tragic to the Israelites.

This is the only instance where human sacrifice is justified in the Bible, except for the near-sacrifice of Isaac. Elsewhere the practice is condemned (see Lev. 20:2). The story emphasizes the necessity of keeping vows made to God. *The sacrifice of a young girl in the cause of military victory has a parallel in Greek legend, the sacrifice of Iphigenia by Agamemnon, the subject of two plays by Euripides.*

The war with the Ephraimites is of little interest except for the use of the test word "shibboleth" (means literally "ear of corn" or "stream") to determine which stragglers were from the enemy. The Ephraimites evidently pronounced the initial consonant differently from the men of Gilead. Those who gave themselves away in this manner were stopped at the river Jordan and killed. *Thus the word "shibboleth" has come to mean a party criterion or slogan. It is of interest that during the first World War, Arabs stopping strangers at the Jordan could detect Turks by their pronunciation of certain words.*

Ibzan, Elon, and Abdon 12:8-15 are other minor judges of whom little is told.

Samson 13-16. *Samson has several characteristics which are common among folk heroes.* He is brave, and exceptionally strong, like Hercules. He has a certain native shrewdness and wit which is expressed in his riddles and aphorisms. He acts at times with a boisterous wildness that reminds us of Paul Bunyan and other American folk heroes — in fact the account of his carrying away the enormous Gaza gates to Hebron forty miles away is a sort of tall tale. He has a weakness for women and is betrayed by them. The dedication of Samson as a Nazarite seems to contradict his folk-hero quality, but it is clear that the only vow he keeps is to let his hair grow. *It is possible that someone who worked over the story added the idea of presenting Samson as a Nazarite and interpreted the final episode, the pulling down of the Philistine building, as Samson's way of making his peace with God after failing to keep his vows.*

A word may be said about the Philistines here, since they play such an important part in the Samson story and in the subsequent history of Israel. They were "sea people" who raided the coasts of North Africa and Palestine and who settled near the southwest coast of the latter country, c. 1200 in five cities: Ashkelon, Ashdod, Gaza, Gath, and Ekron. *Artifacts discovered by archaeologists show that they were of Cretan or Greek origin, and that their level of civilization was in most aspects superior to that of the Israelites.* They seem at some point to have had a monopoly of the smelting of iron, as Biblical references and remains of smelting furnaces show. Politically, they were organized like Greek city-states, separately fortified and ruled, but uniting for attack or defense in war. They ultimately absorbed the Canaanite language and religion and gave their name "Philistia" (Palestine) to the whole area.

Like several other leading characters in the Bible (e.g., Isaac, Samuel, John the Baptist), *Samson is born of a woman long childless.* His mother is told that he is to be a Nazarite, i.e., he must let his hair grow long, forswear strong drink and unclean food, and avoid contact with dead bodies, but not much is said of this in subsequent episodes, where he appears as a self-willed, high-spirited warrior and mischief-maker. Against his parents' wish he takes a Philistine wife, kills a lion (using his God-given strength), finds honey in its carcass, and asks a riddle (14:14) which the Philistines cannot answer; they persuade his wife to coax the answer out of him. When his wife is given to another man, he revenges himself by tying torches to the tails of foxes and thus setting fire to the grain. When the Philistines retaliate by killing his wife and her father, he slays them "with a great slaughter," and flees. Handed back to the Philistines and bound, he uses his great strength to break his bonds, which to him are "as flax that was burned with fire," and slays still more Philistines with a new (i.e., fresh) jawbone of an ass. (Either this is a tall tale or he used a weapon resembling the bone.) When he goes to a harlot at Gaza, the men of Gaza lie in wait for him, but he eludes them, taking the gates of the city with him (*another tall tale,* since the gates were huge).

In the final episodes Samson appears as more sinned against than sinning. His wife, Delilah, is bribed to find out the source of his strength. Three times he lies his way out of the trap and breaks his bonds, but finally, worn down with her importuning, he admits that his strength lies in his long hair. His hair is cut off when he sleeps and he is taken captive, blinded, and forced to grind corn and "make sport" for the Philistines. This time he prays to God for strength "that I may be at once avenged of the Philistines for my two eyes." Leaning on the two pillars of the building and using all his power, he pulls down the building, killing more Philistines in death than he did in life. The chapter ends incongruously with the formula "And he judged Israel twenty years."

Note: Chs. 17-21 contain accounts of the Danite cult and of the war between Israel and Benjamin. They do not seem to belong to the rest of the book.

Ruth

Introduction. *This idyllic pastoral story is one of the most charming in the Bible.* In the Hebrew text it is included among "the Writings," but in the LXX it was placed after Judges and before Samuel because, according to the genealogy in Ch. 4, Ruth was David's grandmother. There is no other evidence that David had Moabite ancestry. The phrase "in the days when the judges ruled" has a "once-upon-a-time" flavor and perhaps the author used an old version of the story. He does show some familiarity with the *customs of that ancient time, such as the merry-making accompanying the harvest, the gleaning after the reapers, the obligation to keep land in the family, and the custom of levirate marriage, by which the next of kin, called the "goel" or redeemer, had two obligations, to buy the land to keep it in the family and to marry the widow.* In this case the next of kin is willing to do the first, but not the second, so Boaz, who is next in order of kinship, offers to do both.

Many historians think the present version was composed to combat the exclusive policies of Ezra and Nehemiah, especially their condemnation of mixed marriages. This is an attractive theory, but it cannot be proved, nor does the story read like a piece of propaganda. Perhaps it is best to stress Ruth's loyalty to her new family and her unselfishness toward Naomi in particular. The liberal point of view toward other nations is similar to that in Jonah. The book is post-exilic, but otherwise variously dated.

Ruth's Decision 1:1-22. Because of a famine, Elimelech with his wife Naomi (means "my pleasant one") and their two sons went to dwell in Moab, where Elimelech dies and the sons marry Moabite wives, Ruth and Orpah. This marriage to foreign women is noted without disapproval. Ruth means "friend," "companion," and sometimes "rose." The meaning of Orpah is less certain. "Stiffnecked" and "rain cloud" have been suggested. After about ten years the sons also died and the three widows set out for the land of Judah. Naomi shows her concern for her Moabite daughters-in-law by trying to persuade them to return to their mothers' homes. As they have treated her well, she hopes they will marry again and prosper under the Lord's blessing. She is bitter, not only on her own account, but because of the ill fortune of her daughters-in-law. Orpah is finally persuaded to return, but Ruth clings to Naomi and exclaims, "Entreat me not to leave thee, or to return from following after thee: for whither thou goest, I will go, where thou lodgest, I will lodge: thy people shall be my people and thy God my God." She and Naomi return to Bethlehem in time for the barley harvest, usually in late April or early May.

Ruth and Boaz 2-3. As a poor girl Ruth exercises her right to glean in the fields, i.e., to pick up what the reapers have left behind. When she comes to the field of Boaz, a kinsmen of Naomi's husband, he expresses his admiration for her loyalty to her mother-in-law. He invites her to eat and drink with him and his reapers, and even tells the latter to leave stalks for her. She returns to Naomi with an "ephah" (about half a bushel) of barley. Naomi sees at once how the family names may be preserved and the property retained. On her advice, Ruth washes and anoints herself and returns to the threshing floor, where she lies down quietly at Boaz' feet. When something startles him, she appeals for his protection: "I am Ruth thy handmaid. Spread therefore thy skirt over thy handmaid, for thou art a near kinsman" — i.e., in effect, she asks him to marry her. He is pleased and blesses her, particularly for preferring him to the younger men, but acts with propriety; the next of kin must be consulted first. He gives her more barley to take home, perhaps as a guarantee of his good intentions.

Marriage and a Son 4. The next morning Boaz chooses ten elders to sit in on the case. *(Later it was thought necessary to have ten men in order to have a synagogue service. This incident may have provided a precedent. Among the Essenes, too, ten was considered a quorum.)* In the presence of the elders, he asks the next of kin if he wishes to buy the land held by Naomi and marry Ruth. The man is willing to buy the land, but not to marry Ruth, saying "I cannot redeem it...lest I mar my own inheritance," meaning perhaps, that there would be less property for his other sons. *(The situation is not entirely clear.)* Before the elders and people, Boaz announces that he has bought the land of Elimelech and his sons and acquired Ruth as his wife, "that the name of the dead be not cut off." He thus becomes Ruth's "goel," her redeemer. Ruth bears a son, Obed, and the women who asked scornfully on her return "Is this Naomi?" now congratulate her on her grandchild, a restorer of life and a comfort in her old age.

I Samuel

Introduction. Originally one, but divided because of length, *the two books of Samuel* recount the interrelated careers of Samuel (who gave his name to the whole), Saul, and David. They trace the shift from charismatic leadership by Samuel to David's establishment of a dynastic monarchy. The unstable Saul was unsuccessful both as a charismatic leader and as a monarch.

The most recent scholarly studies have discerned a number of independent units which formed the sources of the books of Samuel. Some of these centered around sanctuaries such as Mizpah, Gilgal, and especially Shiloh. Others focused on traditional stories about Samuel, Saul, and David. There are groups of stories about the ark in both books of Samuel which emphasize its sacred character. Different from all of these, because it was most probably written by a contemporary eye-witness, is the *Court History of David*, sometimes called *the Succession Document*, comprising most of II Sam. 9-20 and I Kings 1-2. Some think the account of the Ammonite War in II Sam. 10 and 12 is also by an eye-witness or at least a contemporary. Embedded in the narrative are *four poems*, the best known of which are the Song of Hannah and David's Lament for Saul and Jonathan.

Two rather conflicting schools of thought are discernible in the first book of Samuel, often designated by scholars the Early (or Saul) Source and the Late (or Samuel) Source. For the reader's convenience, their characteristics may be set down below.

Early Source

Pro-monarchy: sees it as divinely ordained.

Pro-Saul: sympathetic to him; gives him a tragic quality.

Pro-David, who is the real hero of the books.

Shows Samuel as a local charismatic figure who anointed Saul.

Reasonably reliable, straightforward history.

Probably 10th C., perhaps in the reign of Solomon.

Late Source

Anti-monarchy: sees the decision to choose kings as a terrible mistake.

Anti-Saul:

While anti-monarchy, admits David deserved God's favor.

Shows Samuel as the judge and real leader of Israel.

Tends to be homiletic in tone.

Probably c. 750-650 B.C.

The two narratives and their differing points of view account for the many doublets in I Sam., some of them mutually contradictory. II Sam. probably continues the Early Source in the main, and incorporates the Court History mentioned above. The tenth-century authors of these histories wrote graphic, convincing narrative, presented vivid, life-like characters, and avoided moralizing and an excess of religious comment. *They probably have a better right to be called the fathers of modern history than Herodotus, who wrote five hundred years later.*

The D editors made only slight revisions in Samuel, for example in I Sam. 12, which they inserted or rewrote so as to bring out the importance of divine retribution.

Birth and Boyhood of Samuel

1:1-4:1. These stories are all associated with the shrine at Shiloh. Long childless, like Sarah, Rebekah, and Rachel, Hannah pours out her grief before the Lord at Shiloh, promising that if she bears a son she will dedicate him to God. The priest Eli comforts her and in due time the child Samuel is born and taken to Shiloh. Like other sons born to women long barren, he may be expected to have special qualities. *The Song of Hannah (2:1-10) is a hymn of praise to Yahweh, inserted here at a later time. It should be compared to the Song of Mary, usually called the Magnificat (Luke 1:46-55), which it influenced.*

Eli's sons are described as sinful, for they treat the sacrificial offerings with contempt. Their father's reproach is not effective, for Yahweh has already decided that they should die. Meanwhile the child Samuel is ministering to the Lord before Eli. (Compare 2:26 with Lk. 2:52.) One night, as he lies in the shrine near the ark, he hears a voice calling him by name. At first he goes to serve Eli, but finally the old man realizes that it is Yahweh calling, and at the third call the boy replies as Eli has instructed him, "Speak, Lord, for Thy servant heareth." Yahweh tells him that he plans to destroy Eli's house. Samuel becomes known as a prophet throughout all Israel.

Capture of the Ark 4:16-7:2. *(The Early Source probably begins here.)* In this section, attention focuses on the sacred ark or wooden chest symbolizing the power of Yahweh which is carried into battle. Even the Philistines are afraid of it, but even so they manage to capture it and kill Eli's sons. When the runner brings the news, the aged Eli falls backward, breaking his neck. Eli's daughter, hearing of the deaths of her father and brothers, goes into labor and dies. Her child is called Ichabod, meaning "The glory is departed from Israel" — i.e., the ark. However, the ark still has its power. The Philistines take it to Ashdod and place it in the temple of Dagon, a fertility god (the name derives from the word grain). In the morning they find Dagon flat on his face before the ark. The next morning the hands, feet, and head of the image are cut off. The Lord sends a plague to Ashdod and the frightened Philistines move the ark to Gath, which in its turn is afflicted with the plague. At Ekron the arrival of the ark causes a panic and after seven months the Philistines decide to return the ark with a guilt offering. This was in the form of five golden mice and five tumors, *which shows that the connection between the tumors of bubonic plague and the rats that carried the disease was understood.* There are five of each object to represent the five cities of the Philistines. The ark is returned to Kirjath-jearim, nine miles northwest of Jerusalem, since Shiloh had been destroyed by the Philistines. Eleazar is put in charge of it.

Samuel as Judge of Israel 7:3-8:20. (Late Source and D.) Samuel is presented here as the last and greatest of the judges who addresses "all the house of Israel," bidding them to put away foreign gods. Because of his power, according to this source, the Philistines are subdued and the cities and lands returned to Israel. *(This statement is a glorification of Samuel and is contradicted in subsequent accounts.)* Samuel judged "all Israel," going in a circuit to Bethel, Gilgal, and Mizpah, and home to Ramah. But as his sons are evil, the elders beg him to appoint a king to rule over them, so that they will be "like all the nations." Samuel warns them of the evils of monarchy. They will be slaves, and their property will be taken away. (The picture reflects the rule of a despot.) The people do not listen to Samuel, however, but insist on having a king who will rule them and fight their battles.

The Choosing of Saul 9:1-12:25. *Early and late Sources alternate here.* The first account (Early, 9:1-10:16) tells how Saul, a tall, handsome man in the prime of life, loses his way in looking for his father's asses and seeks out Samuel for directions. Samuel, a seer (i.e., he has second sight), has foreknowledge of the visitor and has kept food ready for him. He tells him not to worry about the asses, and makes a bed for him on the roof *(flat and commonly used for sleeping in dry weather).* The next day, following Yahweh's command, he anoints Saul prince of Israel and tells him to look out for a number of signs which will confirm the act. For example, he will meet three men carrying provisions for a sacrificial meal, one of whom will give him two loaves of bread; he will also fall in with some ecstatic prophets and will himself be touched by the spirit. All turns out as the seer predicts. "And the spirit of God came upon him and he prophesied among them" — i.e., he speaks ecstatically in a sort of initiation rite. However, in reply to queries, he only says that the asses are found, but remains silent about the secret anointing. These events take place c. 1020 B.C. *The writer of this account is favorable both to Saul and to the monarchy, which is represented as a gift of God.* Samuel is favorably disposed both to Saul and the monarchy.

In vs. 17 *the Late narrator resumes the story,* another account of the choosing of Saul, this time by lot. Now Samuel speaks disparagingly of the people who have rejected the Lord and insisted on a king. However, he assembles the tribes and he himself casts the sacred lot, presents Saul to the people as their king, and announces his rights and duties. Some historians believe that this record of the tribes assembling at a shrine for such an important occasion reflects the existence of an amphictyony, a perhaps loose confederation of tribes based on a common religion.

With Ch. 11 *the Early document picks up the account,* which logically follows 10:16. Now Saul gets a chance to show his potential. When he hears that Jabesh-gilead is threatened by the Ammonites, he is filled with charismatic power. "And the Spirit of God came upon Saul ... and his anger was kindled greatly." He hews a pair of oxen in pieces and sends messengers with them all over Israel, saying, "Whosoever cometh not forth after Saul and Samuel, so it shall be done unto his oxen." This brings results. "The dread of the Lord" falls upon the people, who turn out in large numbers and cut the Ammonites to pieces. Saul, ascribing the victory to Yahweh, is crowned king at Gilgal. *Ch. 12 was evidently written or rewritten by the D editors.* Samuel asserts his integrity and summarizes Yahweh's saving acts through Moses, Gideon, Jephthah, etc., concluding with himself; the D view was that he was the last of the great judges.

Saul and the Philistines 13:1-14:52. (Early Source.) Now Saul is faced with more dangerous enemies than the Ammonites, the Philistines. The latter have the advantage of iron both for their weapons and for farming tools. Also, their forces greatly outnumber Saul's. Jonathan, Saul's son, together with his armor-bearer, manages to climb through a rocky pass, and up to the Philistines, believing that the Lord will deliver their enemies into their hands. The Philistines are so astonished at their appearance that they panic, and Jonathan and his companion kill about twenty of them.

Meanwhile Saul orders the people to fast until evening, as fasting was considered pleasing to God, but Jonathan, who has not heard the prohibition, eats some honey and is refreshed. He observes that the soldiers would be stronger for battle if they had eaten. They are, in fact, faint with hunger, and when they take cattle and sheep from the Philistines, they fall upon them, eating the flesh with the blood. It is evening, so the veto on eating is no longer in force; but "eating with the blood" was forbidden (Lev. 19, Deut. 12) and Saul, whose religious piety is apparent throughout this episode, is upset. He has a great stone rolled out to serve as an altar, so that the animals can be properly slain. He wanted to follow up his advantage by attacking the Philistines that night. The priest consults the oracle, and when there is no answer, they cast lots to determine who has sinned. The lots (Urim and Thummim) point to Jonathan as the guilty party, whereupon he confesses that he ate the honey. Saul vows, "Thou shalt surely die," but the people protest, "Shall Jonathan die who hath wrought this great salvation in Israel?" He is forthwith ransomed (presumably an animal is sacrificed). Saul continues his war against the enemies of Israel, Moabites and Edomites as well as Ammonites and Philistines. "When Saul saw any strong man, or any valiant man, he took him unto him."

Rejection of Saul 15:1-35. *(Mostly Late Source.)* As is characteristic of the Late author, Samuel is central in this episode and the monarchy is represented as a mistake. Samuel calls upon Saul to wage a holy war against the Amalekites, to "utterly destroy" them and all they have. Saul does defeat the Amalekites, but spares the king, Agag, as well as the best of the sheep and cattle. Samuel is outraged: "I repent me that I have set up Saul to be king, for he is turned back from following me, and hath not performed my commandments." When Saul asserts that he has, Samuel demands grimly, "What then is this bleating of sheep in my ears and the lowing of oxen which I hear?" Saul protests that the people have saved the beasts to sacrifice to Yahweh, a false argument since all the cattle are under Samuel's ban. His reply is a classic statement of the prophet's position.

Behold, to obey is better than sacrifice,
And to hearken than the fat of rams.

Because Saul has disobeyed God, God has rejected him. Saul's prompt admission that he has sinned does not placate Samuel. He summons Agag, who comes cheerfully (RSV; KJV has "delicately," NEB "with faltering step"). "And hewed Agag in pieces before the Lord God in Gilgal." The act would be conceived as a ritual sacrifice, not an atrocity. The Lord repents having made Saul king and we hear of no more meetings with Samuel.

Anointing of David, his Arrival at Court 16:1-23. *Two different accounts* of David's entry into the story are related here, one emphasizing his position as a humble shepherd boy who has to be recalled for his work with the flocks, the other stressing his talent as a musician. In the first story, probably from the Late Source, Yahweh tells Samuel not to grieve over Saul, whom he has rejected, but to seek out a new king from the family of Jesse at Bethlehem. The search is full of suspense as seven sons of Jesse pass before Samuel but are pronounced not the chosen one. Finally, as often in folklore, the least likely person turns out to be the right one. The youngest son, David, a handsome, ruddy (perhaps red-haired) boy with beautiful eyes, is recalled from watching the flocks. Samuel anoints him at once "in the midst of his brethren," and the Spirit of the Lord (charismatic power) comes upon him.

The second story (*Early Source*, vss. 14-23) tells how the Spirit departs from Saul and he is tormented by an evil demon. A servant suggests that David, an able musician as well as a prudent man of valor, may comfort him with his music, which was supposed to be therapeutic. Saul is indeed refreshed and is delighted with David, who becomes his armor-bearer.

David and Goliath 17. *This famous narrative presents several problems.* It offers still another account of David's debut, and contradicts the end of Ch. 16 in that David is not known to Saul (vs. 55). *Also it is not certain whether it is Early or Late or a combination of the two. Moreover, in II Sam. 21:19, Goliath is said to have been killed by Elhanan, one of David's soldiers, which suggests* that the story may have later become attached to the more famous name of David. What is very clear is that in the writer's eyes, David is the agent of Yahweh and in his hands. Goliath's prowess and weapons are described in epic terms. His spear is like a weaver's beam and the head of it weighs almost twenty pounds. Saul's terrified men cannot produce a champion until David, who comes to bring food to his brothers and their leader, offers to take up the challenge: "Who is this uncircumcised Philistine, that he should defy the army of the living God?" He argues and takes off the armor they have put on him, arming himself only with his sling and five smooth stones. As is usual in single combat, the contestants make defiant speeches, Goliath swearing to give David's flesh to birds and beasts of prey, David's eloquent reply emphasizing that he is Yahweh's warrior: "Thou comest to me with a sword and with a spear, and with a shield: but I am come in the name of the Lord of hosts, the God of the armies of Israel." Using his slingshot, he fells Goliath with a well-armed stone and cuts off his head with his own sword. Seeing their champion dead, the Philistines flee, pursued by the Israelites.

David and Jonathan 18:1-5. "And the soul of Jonathan was knit to the soul of David, and Jonathan loved him as his own soul." They make a covenant, the more highly ranked Jonathan giving David his own garments, armor, and weapons. *This gift may have symbolized the adoption of David into the tribe.* The loyalty and friendship of the pair is proverbial. Saul makes David a captain.

Saul's Jealousy of David 18:6-27:12. The next few episodes are somewhat confusing to read, since *Early, Late, and independent sources are intermingled. There are as a result several doublets, some* contradictions, and some episodes out of order. However, it is clear that as David becomes more successful and confident, Saul becomes more jealous, frustrated, and unstable. The total effect is perhaps unjust to Saul. David was probably more of a schemer than he appears.

Saul is naturally angry when the women come out singing,

Saul hath slain his thousands
And David his ten thousands.

He makes various attempts to get rid of David, for example sending him into battle to collect a hundred Philistine foreskins for a bride-price for his daughter Michal. Jonathan tries to defend him and Michal helps him escape after Saul tries to pin him to the wall with a spear. Saul is also jealous of Jonathan's loyalty to David, pointing out that he will never be the heir to the kingdom while David is alive. (Jonathan seems to assume that David will be king; in 20:14-17 he makes him promise to be loyal to their compact "that [he] may not die." Near Eastern rulers often murdered the families they displaced.) David gathers a following of discontented men from Judah and makes himself at home between Judah and Philistia. While Saul broods and rages, David has hair-raising escapes and twice *(the accounts are probably doublets, 24:2-7 and 26:7-16)* spares Saul when he could easily have killed him. Was he truly magnanimous or was he concerned for his "image"? In both accounts Saul breaks down when confronted with the evidence.

Samuel dies and all Israel mourns him. *(This event is treated with surprising brevity. The information is repeated in 28:3.)*

To escape Saul's threats, David decides to serve Achish, king of Gath (Ch. 27; there is a doublet of this, out of place, in 21:10-15), or at least to appear to serve him.

He pretends to make raids on his own people or their allies, while he actually attacks more distant enemies. Achish is quite taken in, saying "He hath made his people Israel utterly to abhor him." Playing this dangerous double game, David awaits his chance.

Saul and the Witch of Endor 28:3-25. Meanwhile Saul is desperate. *(This narrative of his last days is mostly from the Early Source and pictures him as a noble and tragic figure.)* Though he himself had condemned necromancy, when Yahweh does not answer him by normal channels, "by dreams ... by Urim, nor by prophets," Saul in disguise now resorts to a medium at Endor. She fears a trap, but when he importunes her, she "brings up" Samuel. In agony Saul cries, "I am sore distressed; for the Philistines make war against me, and God is departed from me, and answereth no more." The answer is an appalling one. Saul is still being punished for his disobedience in the Amalekite war. *(Some see the hand of a moralistic editor here.)* "Therefore the Lord hath rent the kingdom out of thy hand and given it to ... David ... Tomorrow shalt thou and thy sons be with me," i.e., in Sheol. Saul falls to the earth in terror and weakness. The woman pities him and she and the servants persuade him to eat. With tremendous courage he pulls himself together and makes his way back to Mt. Gilboa.

David's March 29:1-30:31. With his usual good fortune David is not forced to make an open choice between his countrymen and the Philistines. The Philistine commanders distrust him, so Achish is obliged to dismiss him. David happily protests how faithful and honest he is, assuredly with his tongue in his cheek. When he and his men find Ziglag burned and the people, including David's two wives, taken away captive by the Amalekites, David is threatened with stoning by his own men, for he had left the city unguarded. With the help of the priest, Abiathar, he consults the ephod (oracle), and Yahweh advises him to pursue the Amalekites. *(Note that David, unlike Saul, does receive a reply.)* By a forced march, eighty miles in three days, David and his men reach the brook Besor, where a third of the men are too exhausted to go on. An abandoned Egyptian gives them information and leads them to the Amalekites, who are feasting and rejoicing in their conquest. David falls upon them and recaptures people and flocks. There is a quarrel about the division of the spoils. David protests against such selfishness: "For as his share is who goes down into the battle, so shall his share be who stays by the baggage" (RSV) — a very modern recognition of those who serve behind the lines. David also tactfully sends some of the spoils to the elders of Judah.

Saul's Last Battle 31:1-13. The Philistines overcome Saul and his men. Jonathan and two more of Saul's sons are killed, and Saul himself is badly wounded. He asks his armor-bearer to kill him, but when he refuses, he kills himself and his man follows suit. *(Suicide, though uncommon in the Bible, is common in most heroic periods.)* The Philistines cut off Saul's head, put his armor in the temple of Ashtaroth and his body and those of his sons on the walls of Bethshan. The dead in the *Iliad* are sometimes similarly dishonored. The men of Jabeshgilead, in gratitude for Saul's aid to them, cut down the bodies, burn and bury them.

II Samuel

Lament of David over Saul and Jonathan 1:1-27. Second Samuel begins with a different account of Saul's death. A young Amalekite claims to have killed him in pity for his anguish. Possibly he was lying in order to curry favor with David. However, David has him killed and laments over Saul and Jonathan. The elegy was preserved in the lost "Book of Jasher," and there seems no reason to doubt David's authorship. The poem has no religious allusions, but is full of deep feeling and lyric power. Notice the repetition of "How are the mighty fallen" and the use of synonymous parallels in, for example,

> Tell it not in Gath,
> Publish it not in the streets of
> Ashkelon.

David curses the mountains of Gilboa, where the leaders fell, and praises their bravery. In life and death Saul and Jonathan were not divided. He calls on the women of Israel to weep over Saul, while he personally grieves over his brother Jonathan.

> Thy love to me was wonderful,
> Passing the love of woman.

He concludes with a variant of the refrain:

> How are the mighty fallen,
> And the weapons of war
> perished!

David's Anointing and Wars with House of Saul 2:1-4:12. With Yahweh's approval, David goes to Hebron and is anointed king of Judah (1008/9). He promises protection to the men of Jabesh-gilead, perhaps being eager for their recognition. Presumably he already has his eye on Israel, but he has to

scheme for over seven years. The Northern tribes are nominally under the (weak) rule of Ishbosheth (really Ishbaal; some copyists substituted "bosheth," meaning "shame," for the name of the god), but the real power is the general, Abner. The Philistines evidently assume David is still their vassal. At any rate they give no trouble at this point.

The conflict between the houses of David and Saul appears to be touched off by a contest by the pool of Gibeon. In the battle which follows, Abner kills David's nephew. Angered by Ishbosheth, he threatens to go over to David. Part of the arrangement is that David will get back his first wife, Michal, Saul's daughter, which would give him a better claim to Saul's throne. Joab, David's ruthless general, kills Abner, ostensibly in revenge for the nephew, but he was probably not sorry to eliminate a rival general. David mourns Abner in order to dissociate himself from any guilt for his death. Ishbosheth is killed by two of his own men who bring the head to David, expecting a reward, but he quickly has them executed. Thus in two strokes David gets rid of two leaders of Judah without incurring blood-guilt.

David King of Israel 5:1-7:29. The tribes of Israel treat with David on the basis of his kinship with them, his military success, and the Lord's promise that he will be the shepherd of Israel. The elders anoint him king of Hebron (1002/1 B.C.). David's great need now is a capital which will be acceptable to both South and North. He finds it in the Jebusite fortress, Jerusalem, which is conquered in a surprise attack. *The account is full of obscurities, but if David's men* *really gained entrance through the wa021tershaft (now called Warren's shaft), it was a remarkable achievement which must have impressed his followers.*

According to 5:11-12, David obtains cedar and workmen from Hiram king of Tyre, commences a building program, and establishes himself in Jerusalem with his wives and concubines. He makes Jerusalem a religious center as well as a secular one by bringing in the sacred ark with ceremony and rejoicing, also the ephod, and perhaps the sacred serpent of the Levites. The awesome power of the ark is emphasized when a man who accidentally touches it is killed. David takes part in the ceremony, sacrificing an ox and dancing before the Lord, an act which impresses us with its religious spontaneity, but which earns him the scorn of his wife, Michal. Ch. 7, which is either late or composite, explains why David never built a temple. The argument offered by the prophet Nathan is that Yahweh has never had a "house" since the Exodus. *(The writer has forgotten the shrine at Shiloh.)* Yahweh promises to establish David's kingdom forever.

David's Wars 5:17-25, 8, 10. Meanwhile, the Philistines must have realized that David was no longer their ally or vassal. Indeed, he eventually managed to contain them, confining them to their five cities on the coastal strip. He defeated Moab, Ammon, Edom, Amalek, and Syria, in effect surrounding himself with a ring of buffer states. Much of this was possible because the Assyrians and Egyptians were absorbed with internal affairs. Even so, his accomplishment was impressive. His empire stretched from the mountains of Lebanon to the gulf of Akaba and from the Mediterranean to the Arabian desert. Under David, Israel was at the peak of her power.

Court History of David. It is ironical that the accounts of David's success as a conqueror are followed by the devastatingly frank Court History which shows David's weaknesses as a father and eventually as a leader, though it also displays his magnanimity, honesty, and depth of feeling. This narrative comprises II Sam. 9-20, with two short breaks, and I Kgs. 1-2. *Since much of it concerns who shall succeed David, some historians call it the Succession Document. It is so graphic in its detail that most authorities believe it is a firsthand account, perhaps even by a participant in the events. Ahimaaz, Nathan, Gad, and Zadok have all been suggested. Whoever its author, it is a masterpiece of historical biography.*

David's Kindness to Mephibosheth 9. Mephibosheth (Meribaal), Jonathan's son, had been crippled in a fall when his nurse fled with him after the battle of Mt. Gilboa. He had escaped, apparently, the destruction of Saul's descendants by the Gibeonites, permitted by David (see Ch. 21, which should be placed *before* Ch. 9). When he bows before David and calls himself a dead dog, David promises him that he shall eat at his table. This both fulfills his vow of loyalty to Jonathan and makes it possible for him to keep an eye on a not very likely focus of disaffection.

David and Bathsheba 11. *This famous story is told with astonishing truth and psychological insight. David's adultery and, in effect, murder are not glossed over. (The Chronicler omits the entire episode.)* The background is the Ammonite War in which Uriah is a hired soldier. It is perhaps noteworthy that David does not accompany the army. Seeing the beautiful Bathsheba bathing, David sends for her, but when later he finds she is pregnant by him, he dishonestly tries to make it appear that Uriah is the father by sending him home after the battle. As a participant in a religious war, Uriah must remain celibate and very properly remains at the palace gate. Upon further persuasions from David, Uriah makes a dignified stand: "The ark, and Israel, and Judah, abide in tents, and my lord Joab, and the servants of my lord, are encamped in the open fields; shall I then go into mine house to eat and to drink, and to lie with my wife? as thou livest and as thy son liveth, I will not do this thing." When even drink fails to persuade him, David orders Joab to place Uriah "in the forefront of the hottest battle." When he is killed and Bathsheba has completed her period of mourning, David takes her into his house and she bears him a son. "But the thing that David had done displeased the Lord."

Nathan's Parable 12. As the representative of the Lord, the prophet Nathan tells David a parable *(a short tale designed to convey a moral or religious message).* A rich man has many flocks, but a poor man has only one ewe lamb, which is a family pet, eating and drinking with its owner and lying in his bosom like a child. But the rich man, too mean to use one of his own flock, takes the lamb and makes a meal of it for a guest.

David responds warmly, "The man that hath done this thing shall surely die." Nathan turns his answer on himself: "Thou art the man." *(Vss. 7b-12 are editorial.)* David admits, "I have sinned against the Lord." His honesty and spontaneity are in keeping with his character. When he is told that his son will die, he prays and fasts, but when the child actually dies, he washes, changes his clothes, and eats, contrary to Eastern custom, saying, "But now he is dead, where-fore should I fast?...I shall go to him [i.e., in Sheol], but he shall not return to me." As a sign of God's forgiveness, Bathsheba bears another son, Solomon.

Rape of Tamar, Absalom's Revenge and Return 13-14. This sin and its consequences remove two of David's sons from the succession, Amnon and Absalom. Amnon is in love with his beautiful sister Tamar. Pretending to be ill, he lures her to his room, forces her to lie with him over her very reasonable protest, then casts her off in disgust. In her despair, for as a violated woman she can never hope to marry, she turns to her full brother, Absalom, who is furious with Amnon, but bides his time. David, although also indignant, takes no action. Two years later, at a sheep-shearing feast, Absalom has his men kill Amnon, after which he and his brothers flee. David, though reconciled to Amnon's death, continues to mourn at Absalom's absence and makes no attempt to punish him. As king and father, he should have dealt with both these crimes.

Joab, realizing that David is longing for Absalom, prompts a wise woman of Tekoa (near Bethlehem, David's home territory) to tell the king of her son, whom she wishes to be spared, although he killed his brother. Her story operates like a primitive parable. Though David recognizes the hand of Joab in the little plot, he also recognizes that he really wants Absalom back, and tells Joab that he may return, though he will not be received at court. Absalom's beautiful hair, said to weigh two hundred shekels (four to five pounds!) when cut, is described. After two years of exclusion from court and after failing to make Joab visit him, Absalom gets attention by having his men set the general's barley field alight. Under pressure, Joab persuades David to receive his son, and the two are reconciled.

Absalom's Revolt 15-16:14. Absalom must have long been planning a coup d'état. Now he rides in state in his chariot and horses, with fifty men running before him, and poses as a sympathizer with citizens whose cases are not properly represented saying,, "O that I were made judge in the land!" His actions imply criticism of David's failure to establish a working judiciary system. "So Absalom stole the hearts of the men of Israel." After four years he sends secret messengers throughout the tribes to say "Absalom reigneth in Hebron." A messenger tells David, "The hearts of the men of Israel are [gone] after Absalom." David immediately flees, with all his household, leaving ten concubines to keep the house. *Did he panic or was he testing his followers, including the mercenaries, who included Cretans, Philistines and perhaps Achaeans? Or did he hope to maneuver more flexibly in the open country?*

His offer to let Ittai the Gittite, a foreigner, withdraw from his forces exemplifies his magnanimity. The return of the ark to the city is an act of faith. If it is the Lord's will, he will see it there again. He weeps bitterly as he climbs the Mount of Olives, barefoot and with his head covered. All the people weep with him. When he hears that Ahithophel has gone over to Absalom, he prays, "O Lord, I pray thee, turn the counsel of Ahithophel into foolishness." This is accomplished through the agency of Hushai, who enters the city at the same time as Absalom.

Meanwhile David encounters Ziba, the servant of Mephibosheth, who tells him that his master also is in revolt. David believes him and gives him Mephibosheth's property. Shimei, a member of the house of Saul bitterly curses David and stones him for his treatment of Saul's family. Abishai protests, but David is more tolerant, saying,

"Behold my son ... seeketh my life: how much more now may this Benjamite do it? ... It may be that the Lord will look on my affliction and ... requite me good for his cursing this day."

Absalom and Ahithophel 16:15-17:23. On Ahithophel's advice, Absalom publicly takes over his father's concubines, a gross assertion of his power. He invites the counsel of both Ahithophel and Hushai, who has feigned adherence to him. Ahithophel's advice is obviously sound: he wants to pursue David while he is weary, to kill him only and no one else, and to win the people over to the lawful heir. Hushai counters this with a suggestion designed to gain time for David. He argues that an experienced commander like David will not stay with the army, but will have hidden himself for the night. An attack might result in defeat and panic for Absalom's unseasoned troops. Rather Absalom should wait until he can gather all Israel from Dan to Beersheba and lead them against David. Absalom decides to follow Hushai's advice. Ahithophel, realizing that this spells victory for David, kills himself.

David's Victory and Grief, 17:24-19:8b. Meanwhile, David, met on the other side of the Jordan by Barzillai and other friends with generous supplies, has time to regroup. He sends out three forces, under Joab, Abishai, and Ittai, begging them, "Deal gently for my sake with the young man, even with Absalom." David's experienced men easily defeat his son's forces, especially as the treacherous forest of Ephraim devours more people than the sword. Absalom is caught by his head in the branches of a large oak, where he is left hanging as his mule trots on. The ruthless Joab, disregarding David's order, strikes him with three darts (or clubs?). His men finish him off and throw his body into a pit. *(Note: in art Absalom is usually represented as caught by his hair. Probably the artists thought of his death as an appropriate punishment for vanity.)*

Ahimaaz wishes to carry the news to David, presumably hoping to soften the blow, but Joab insists sending a Cushite (Ethiopian). Ahimaaz outruns him and reports the victory, but is evasive about Absalom's fate. Not so the Cushite, who hopes that all the king's enemies may meet a like fate. Heartbroken, David goes to the chamber over the gate and weeps, crying, "O my son Absalom... would God I had died for thee, O Absalom, my son, my son." But when Joab unsympathetically reminds him that he and his men and the king's household will be annoyed at his neglect, David is forced to pull himself together.

David's Return to Power 19:9-20:26. David must now stabilize a divided and uneasy people. He wins over the men of Judah by appealing to their blood ties with him and by promising to replace Joab by Amasa. (One wonders if David did not feel guilty at profiting so often by the ruthless deeds of his hatchet man.) The men of Judah escort him over the Jordan, earning the jealousy of the men of Israel. The cry of Sheba, a Benjamite, "We have no part in David... to your tents O Israel" show how tenuous the hold of the monarchy really was. Joab, sent to deal with Sheba, treacherously kills Amasa en route and obtains Sheba's head. Again he is in power.

The last few verses of Ch. 20 list David's officers, including chief of forced labor, recorder, and secretary. According to Wright the recorder organized palace ceremonies and mediated between king, officers, and people, while the secretary was a combination of private secretary and secretary of state.

Appendixes 21-24. These include records which should be earlier in the book, e.g., the account of the delivery of Saul's sons and grandsons to the Gibeonites, also records of further wars against the Philistines, of David's census, a plague, and the building of an altar. Inserted later, in accordance with the practice of Hebrew historians, are two psalms, one called "the last words of David" but composed at a much later date.

I Kings

Introduction to I & II Kings. Like I and II Sam., Kings was originally a single book, the last part of the Deuteronomic history of Israel from Joshua to the Exile. However, it contains many more sources than II Sam. and has undergone much more thorough Deuteronomic editing. Among its sources are earlier works, now lost, but named in the text, "The Book of the Acts of Solomon," "The Book of the Chronicles of the Kings of Israel," and "The Book of the Chronicles of the Kings of Judah." There are also temple archives, cycles of stories about Elijah, Elisha, and Isaiah, besides other material on certain kings, such as Ahab and Hezekiah.

It is important to understand how the Deuteronomic editors handled this material. Two principles guided them: 1) *that Yahweh must be worshiped in the temple at Jerusalem, and* 2) *that he rewards the people for fidelity to the Cov-*

enant and punishes infidelity. (This second principle is known as the *doctrine of retribution*). Every ruler is judged by these principles, with an easily recognizable formula such as, "And Ahab the son of Omri did evil in the sight of the Lord above all that were before him." The sins are then particularized which in, Ahab's case included marrying a foreign wife Jezebel, erecting an altar to Baal, and defying Elijah.

All the kings of Israel are condemned, usually for worshiping at the high places (local shrines) or for apostasy; and of the kings of Judah, only Hezekiah and Josiah are praised without reserve. Great stress is laid on obedience to God, which will be rewarded, whereas sin will be punished. This emphasis on retribution sometimes leads the editors to exclude historical material which does not illustrate this principle. For example, the prosperity of Omri and of Jeroboam II is touched on only lightly because it in effect refutes the doctrine of retribution. On other occasions, editors add or elaborate passages emphasizing the importance of obedience to God, and the unhappy results of disobedience. Good examples are David's charge to Solomon (I Kgs. 2:3-4), Solomon's address to the people (8:12-21), and much of Ch. 11 which tells of Solomon's apostasy, resulting in God's anger and the loss of all the tribes but one (note especially vss. 7-13).

On a first reading, the reader may find the editor's handling of the records of the rulers of the divided kingdoms a trifle disconcerting, since he tries to synchronize the reigns in a slightly awkward manner. Each account begins with the following information: ————king of Israel, began to reign in the years of————king of Judah. Details about his age, his parents' names, and the length of his reign follow, and he is evaluated as having served the Lord well or (more frequently) done evil. The editor then gives such facts as he chooses and concludes with the formula, varying only slightly, "Now the rest of the acts of————are they not written in the chronicles of the kings of Israel? So,————slept with his fathers and, his son reigned in his stead." Then the same pattern is followed with a king of Judah.

This "shuttlecock method," as it has been called, does have the merit of keeping both kingdoms in view, but the reader should be warned that the dates and ages are not always accurate and that it is well to keep a modern double-column chronology in front of him.

There are thought to have been two stages of Deuteronomic editing, one before the Exile, perhaps during or close to the reign of Josiah, and one after the Exile, c. 560 B.C., which takes the narrative down to the freeing of Jehoiachin.

The books fall into three sections 1) the succession and rule of Solomon, 2) the divided kingdoms, 3) the survival and final collapse of Judah.

Death of David and Succession of Solomon 1-2. This is the last part of the Court History begun at II Sam. 9. Attempts to revive David's virility by contact with a virgin, Abishag the Shunammite, fail and she serves only as his nurse. Adonijah, David's oldest surviving son, attempts to seize power, but he is foiled by Nathan and Bathsheba, who work on David's feelings so that he supports Solomon. The latter is quickly anointed by Zadok while Adonijah and his followers are prematurely celebrating. Adonijah does obeisance and promises to obey Solomon. (One is a little surprised to find Nathan supporting Bathsheba and Solomon.) David offers his dying counsel to Solomon. He should liquidate Joab and Shimei and reward the family of Barzillai for his help during Absalom's revolt. Then David "slept with his fathers."

Adonijah makes one more attempt to gain power. He persuades Bathsheba to ask Solomon to give him Abishag for a wife. Solomon, probably rightly, interprets this as a threat to his claim. Technically Abishag was a member of David's harem, and we have seen that to claim the harem was an implied claim to the throne. At any rate, Solomon has Adonijah put to death. Abiathar and Joab had also supported Adonijah. Solomon expels Abiathar from his position, but does not kill him because he had shared David's afflictions. Joab takes sanctuary, but in spite of this Solomon orders him killed, since he brought blood-guilt on the house of David by his murders of Abner and Amasa. He is killed even as he holds the horns of the altar and the blood-guilt is supposedly transferred to his house. Three years later Solomon finds a pretext for killing Shimei. Thus through a series of murders which eliminated all potentially dangerous enemies, "The kingdom was established in the hand of Solomon."

Wisdom of Solomon 3, 4:29-34.
Solomon marries Pharaoh's daughter. The editor excuses Solomon (and his people) for worshiping in the high places by explaining that the temple is not built yet. Perhaps also the editor's is the dream-prayer for "an understanding heart" to "judge the people." If Solomon's assumption of humility — "I am but a little child: I know not how to go out or come in" — is genuine it is certainly at variance with his general conduct. His taste for ostentation, his ambitious building program, his squandering of the advantages, material and psychological, left him by David, and his unpopular use of forced labor all argue to the contrary.

One is inclined to agree with Gottwald that Solomon is probably the most overrated figure in the Old Testament. It is difficult, he continues, "to reconcile his reputation for wisdom with his almost total disdain of sound government." He suggests that the compiler solved the problem of the contradiction between Solomon's legendary wisdom and the ineptness of his rule by "grouping the laudatory data in Solomon's youth and early reign ... whereas the condemnatory sources are placed later in his reign, following his apostasy to the foreign gods of his many wives." It should also be recognized that the word "wisdom" in this context refers chiefly to riddles, songs, sayings, and proverbs, rather than to political or philosophical wisdom. It is possible that Solomon himself produced "wisdom literature" of this kind and/or that he patronized those who did. He certainly acquired a reputation for such wisdom: I Kgs. 4. 32 reports that he "spake three thousand proverbs: and his songs were a thousand and five," and in Jewish history and legend he is associated with wisdom as Moses is with law and David with music and the composition of psalms. Solomon's handling of the two harlots who quarrelled over the surviving baby (3: 16-28) is wisdom of a somewhat different order, a quick-thinking shrewdness which is often displayed by folk heroes. The story may well be much older than the rest of the chapter.

Solomon's Administration 4:1-28.
Solomon's officials include a priest, two secretaries, a recorder, the general of the army, the "priest and king's friend" (perhaps a kind of "aide-de-camp"), the chamberlain of the palace, and the officer in charge of forced labor. Perhaps

to break up traditional tribal boundaries, Solomon divided his realm into twelve regions with an official over each. An exuberant and greatly exaggerated account of the size of Solomon's empire and the happiness of his people closes the chapter.

Solomon's Building Program 5:1-9:9. Solomon, who wants his kingdom to be "like the [other] nations," now embarks on an ambitious building program which ultimately takes twenty years. The first building, the temple, begun c. 965, is naturally of the greatest interest to the D historian, and its construction is described in loving detail; there is doubtless expansion and exaggeration. Hiram king of Tyre offers cedar and cypress wood in exchange for wheat and oil. Solomon levies huge gangs of forced labor who quarry and dress costly stones. *The temple, quite small by modern standards (c. 90 × 30 feet) was more a royal chapel than the central place of worship remembered by later historians.* Carved decorations, such as cherubim, were overlaid with gold, as was all of the inner sanctuary. More buildings, including a palace for Solomon and one for his wife, were later added to the complex. The temple was dedicated and the ark brought in. Solomon's prayer and benediction have been added later, as was Solomon's dream (9:1-9), which makes the prosperity of his house depend on obedience and faithfulness. Without these, the temple will become "a heap of ruins" (RSV), a safe enough prophecy after the temple was destroyed in 581.

Solomon and the Queen of Sheba 9:16-10. Solomon has a navy at Ezion-geber in the Red Sea and trades in horses. The Queen of Sheba pays a diplomatic visit which is accompanied by much ceremony and exchange of gifts. She is properly impressed with his wealth and wisdom.

End of Solomon's Reign 11. This chapter was probably put together by the Second Deuteronomist in such a way as to give the impression that most of Solomon's troubles came at the end of his reign and were a result of his marriages to foreign pagan women. However, Solomon's use of forced labor, his costly building program, and his lack of care for his people, are only too clear. The rebellion of Hadad, mentioned here, has already taken place. But according to the present historian, he is latterly influenced by his foreign wives and is troubled with rebellions, notably that of Jeroboam, the man in charge of the forced labor at Ephraim. Solomon dies and the regular D-formula is used: "And the rest of the acts of Solomon, and all that he did, and his wisdom, are they not written in the book of the acts of Solomon? And the time that Solomon reigned in Jerusalem over all Israel was forty years. And Solomon slept with his fathers, and was buried in the city of David his father" (11:41-43).

Divided Kingdom: Early Years 12:1-17:28. From the death of Solomon (c. 931) to the fall of Samaria in 722, the historian has to shift back and forth between Israel and Judah, using opening formulas to match the transitions, thus "Now in the thirty-first year of Asa, King of Judah, Omri began to reign over Israel." Information is given about the king's reign, and he is rated as good or fair or evil by the editor. *The reader who wishes to know more is referred to the chronicles of Israel or Judah.*

Solomon's son Rehoboam, following the advice of his young companions, swears to be ever more oppressive than his father. All the tribes except Judah revolt against him and stone his task-master to death. Meanwhile Jeroboam has been made king at Shechem. Intending to break with the Jerusalem cult, he promotes local shrines, and sets up golden calves at Bethel and Dan and consecrates his own priests. For this he is condemned by the prophets, including Ahijah, who had originally encouraged him. Rehoboam is also in trouble, for Shishak the king of Egypt sacks and loots Jerusalem. The short reign of his successor, Abijam, is condemned, but his son, Asa, reigns for forty-one years, initially as a minor. He is credited with reforms such as putting away the male prostitutes and burning his mother's image of Asherah. There was war with Israel, where Baasha had usurped the throne of Jeroboam's son. There is a series of killings: Elah, who succeeds Baasha, is killed by Zimri, who only reigns seven days, for the army elects Omri, who besieges Zimri's fortress and burns it. Zimri dies in the fire. There is civil war, in which Omri is the victor. *We know from external sources that his reign was prosperous; he conquered Moab and built a new capital at Samaria.* He is given short shrift, however, because according to the D-editor he does "evil in the sight of the Lord," leading the people in idol worship. His son, Ahab, is also an evil-doer, but is given much more space because of his involvement with the prophet Elijah.

Elijah and the Drought 16:29-17:24.

"Elijah" means "Yahweh is God" and this is the theme of this collection of stories. Ahab does evil, particularly under the influence of his Phoenician wife, Jezebel, setting up in Samaria an altar to Baal, the Phoenician and Canaanite god who controlled the rains. To show that Yahweh is stronger, Elijah predicts a terrible drought and, to escape Ahab's wrath, he flees to beyond the Jordan, by the brook Cherith (Kerith) which dries up because the rain has failed. He is fed by the ravens, and later by a poor widow whose meal and oil are miraculously increased. The woman's son dies, but Elijah prays and the boy is restored to life. These miracles or "signs" display the power of Yahweh and tell us that Elijah is a holy man. The widow recognizes this when she calls him "man of God."

Contest with Prophets of Baal 18:1-48.

In obedience to Yahweh, Elijah returns to confront Ahab, who addresses him as "troubler of Israel." Elijah reminded him that he is the true "troubler" because he has worshiped the Baals. He demands that the prophets of Baal and Asherah assemble at Mount Carmel and asks them, "How long halt ye between two opinions? If the Lord be God, follow him; but if Baal, follow him." Pitting himself as the lone true prophet against 450 prophets of Baal, he proposes a contest: "Let them therefore give us two bullocks; and let them choose one bullock for themselves, and cut it in pieces, and lay it on wood, and put no fire under: and I will dress the other bullock, and lay it on wood, and put no fire under: and call ye on the name of your gods, and I will call on the name of the Lord: and the God that answereth by fire, let him be God." The Baalites prepare their bull and call upon Baal ecstatically "from morning even until noon, saying O Baal, hear us." Elijah mocks them, saying. "Cry aloud: for he is a god: either he is talking, or he is pursuing, or he is in a journey, or per-adventure he sleepeth, and must be awakened." In despair, they cut themselves with knives until the blood gushes out.

Finally Elijah assembles them and (apparently) repairing an ancient altar, cuts up his bull and, to avoid any suspicion of trickery, pours water on the offering and into the trench. He prays intensely that Yahweh will make himself known. Suddenly the fire of the Lord strikes the offering and licks up the water in the trench. The awe-struck people fall on their faces, acknowledging that "The Lord, he is God." Elijah has all the Baalite prophets slain, tells Ahab to break his fast, and sends his servant seven times to look toward the sea until the tiny cloud appears which signals the coming of rain. As Ahab returns in his chariot, Elijah, infused with charismatic power, runs before him all the way to Jezreel.

The Call of Elisah 19:1-21. He is met by Jezebel's threat to kill him, and suddenly he is afraid. He goes a day's journey into the wilderness, where he begs God to let him die, until an angel brings him food and drink which gives him the strength to get to Mount Horeb. There he complains. "I have been very jealous for the Lord God of hosts: for the children of Israel have forsaken thy convenant, thrown down thine altars, and slain thy prophets with the sword; and I, even I only, am left; and they seek my life, to take it away." And the Lord was present, not in the strong wind, not in the earthquake, not in the fire, but in "the still small voice" — not, as is sometimes said, the voice of conscience, but literally "the sound of absolute stillness." Yahweh is present, and Elijah wraps his face in his mantle. Directed by Yahweh to initiate a political and social revolution in Israel (see II Kings 9), Elijah seeks out Elisha and casts his mantle on him, as a sign that he is to be his successor.

War with Syria 20:1-43. Benhadad of Syria demands Ahab's silver and gold and his fairest wives. Not satisfied with these, he threatens to pillage the city. Ahab, advised by a (nameless) prophet to attack, defeats the Syrians, but Benhadad

escapes. A second Syrian attack is again beaten back, but Ahab spares Benhadad and even invites him into his chariot. Benhadad promises to return cities captured by Ahab's father and to allow Israelite merchants to have bazaars in Damascus, and Ahab is persuaded to let him go. Thus far, this source is rather favorable to Ahab, but now another prophet accuses him of being too lenient. Benhadad was "appointed to utter destruction" and Ahab will have to pay the penalty.

Naboth's Vineyard 21:1-29. Ahab covets Naboth's vineyard in Jezreel for a vegetable garden, but Naboth does not want to give up his family inheritance. Ahab sulks and refuses to eat. His unscrupulous wife, Jezebel, orders trumped-up charges against Naboth; accused of cursing God and the king, he is stoned to death, and Ahab goes down to Jezreel to take over the vineyard. Elijah confronts him, saying, "Behold, I will bring evil upon thee, and will take away thy posterity... And of Jezebel also spake the Lord, saying, the dogs shall eat up Jezebel by the wall of Jezreel." Thunderstuck, Ahab puts on sackcloth and fasts, and the Lord spares him for the present, promising however, to bring evil upon his house.

Ahab, Micaiah, and Syrian War 22:1-53. Wishing to take Ramoth-gilead from Syria, with the help of Jehoshaphat, king of Judah, Ahab wishes to consult a prophet, but objects to Micaiah, saying, "I hate him; for he does not prophesy good concerning me, but evil." Four hundred dervishes prophesy ecstatically before the two kings as they sit in state, and with one accord are favorable to the war. Micaiah is brought in and ironically mimics the ecstatic prophets, saying, "Go and prosper." Ahab puts him on his honor, and he offers, first a vision of Israel "scattered upon the hills, as sheep that have not a shepherd," i.e., he prophesies that Ahab will die. Ahab is sufficiently impressed to go into the battle disguised, but an arrow pierces his armor and he has to be propped up in his chariot. He dies at sun- set. As the servants wash his chariot, the blood flows out and the dogs lick it up, as Elijah had prophesied. "So Ahab slept with his fathers." Jehoshaphat, who fails to remove the high places, is succeeded by Jehoram, who "made Israel to sin."

II Kings

Elijah and Death of Ahaziah 1:1-18. Ahab's son, Ahaziah, King of Israel, injured in a fall, seeks to know his fate from a local Baal. Elijah chastises him for not inquiring of Yahweh. Ahaziah defies him and Elijah destroys his detachments by fire. Ahaziah dies and is succeeded by Jehoram as he has no son.

Stories about Elisha 2:1-8:29. *The cycle of stories about Elisha has a much larger element of popular miracle tales than the Elijah cycle, though a few of the tales parallel those told about Elijah.* Unlike Elijah, Elisha is frequently associated with the communities of prophets and with the king and his army. However, the political events woven with these stories are somewhat vaguely treated, as the kings involved are often not identified. The emphasis is on Elisha's miraculous powers.

The story of Elijah being taken up into heaven in a chariot of horses and fire and a whirlwind really belongs to the Elisha cycle, since Elisha receives his master's mantle and a double share of his spirit. With the mantle he parts the waters, as Elijah had done, and all acknowledge that "The spirit of Elijah doth rest on Elisha." He cleanses the spring with a pinch of salt and calls forth two bears to eat the mocking boys who mock his tonsured head. The next miracle is told against the background of the war against Moab. The attackers are thirsty, and Elisha, in an ecstasy induced by music, produces water in a dry wadi and correctly prophesies the defeat of the Moabites. Subsequently he miraculously produces a large supply of oil for a widow, raises the son of a wealthy Shunammite woman from the dead (both these tales parallel those told about Elijah), cleanses the poisoned food of a band of prophets, their loaves, and heals the leprosy of Naaman, a military commander of Syria who then recognizes that Yahweh is the true God. Apart from the floating of an iron axehead, several miracles which follow involve Elisha's second sight. Through this gift he perceives that his servant has deceived Naaman into giving him two talents. The servant is appropriately afflicted with leprosy as a punishment. Second sight is also useful in the war with the Syrians, for Elisha knows all their plans and tells the king of Israel (not named), besides temporarily blinding the Syrians, so that they are easily captured. They are feasted, restored to sight and sent home, and the war is supposed to be over. However, Benhadad (perhaps the son of Hazael) besieges Samaria. When high prices and cannibalism result, the king of Israel inexplicably blames Elisha and sends a man to murder him. Again warned by second sight, Elisha fastens the door and when the king himself arrives, foretells that the siege will be lifted, that the prices will be normal, and that a captain who doesn't believe him will die. Next day the Syrians flee in a panic, prices go down, and the skeptical captain is trampled to death. Now Elisha once more helps the Shunammite woman whose son he had restored to life. She returns from Philistia after seven years to find her property confiscated, but thanks to Elisha's influence, her property and its produce are restored. With the exception of this last tale, which at least hints that the demands of social justice must be met, these miracle stories will probably strike the modern reader as the reverse of edifying. Nevertheless, they must have delighted an audience who saw in the miraculous the proof that Elisha was a holy man and that the Lord was with him.

Elisha is also involved in Syrian affairs, when Benhadad, who is ill, sends Hazael to learn his fate of Elisha, sending forty camel loads of goods as a fee. Elisha knows that Benhadad will die and that Hazael will succeed him, and so it falls put when Hazael smothers the king and takes over the throne. Elisha weeps, because he knows what damage Samaria will do to Israel, as a punishment for her sins. Now the historian gives brief accounts of the reigns of Jehoram of Judah, who is married to Athaliah, Ahab's daughter, and their son Ahaziah (not to be confused with Ahaziah of Israel, her uncle). Jehoram does evil and his reign is marked by the revolt of Edom. His son joins with Joram (i.e., Johoram) of Israel to attack Hazael. Jehoram is wounded in the battle and goes to be healed in Jezreel.

Revolution of Jehu 9:1-10:36. The Omri dynasty is over, the Jehu dynasty is to be initiated. Both the accession of Hazael and the anointing of Jehu were anticipated in God's directions to Elijah in

I Kings 19:15-18. Now Elisha sends a young prophet to anoint Jehu. That an ecstatic prophet anoints the new king indicates the religious nature of the revolution. Proclaimed to the sound of trumpets, Jehu rides to Jezreel, murders Joram (Jehoram), pursues and kills Ahaziah, and returns to Jezreel where Jezebel is painting her face and arranging her hair. "Who is on my side?" Jehu asks the eunuchs, and without a pause, orders, "Throw her down." Her blood splatters the wall and the horses, and when Jehu (having solaced himself with food and drink) orders her to be buried, only scraps are left. The editor puts into his mouth a comment that Elijah himself prophesied that the dogs would eat her up. Jehu continues his purge by demanding the heads of the seventy sons of Ahab (which are brought in in baskets), by killing all the other members of his house, and by exterminating the kinsmen of Ahaziah of Israel. Assembling the devotees of Baal, he pretends he is about to offer a great sacrifice to the god. When all is ready for the sacrifice, his men slay all the worshipers, to a man, burn the pillar of Baal, and destroy the entire temple. After all this slaughter, presumably for the sake of a purer cult, we are surprised to read in the commentary, 10:28-31, that Jehu, despite his loyalty to Yahweh, was not careful to walk in the way of the Lord, who allows his house only four more generations of rule. Finally he "slept with his fathers" and is succeeded by Jehoahaz.

From Reign of Athaliah to Death of Uzziah 11:1-15:7. When Athaliah (Ahab's daughter and a worshiper of Baal) hears of her son's death, she kills all the male heirs except the baby Joash (Jehoash), who is hidden by the priests and instructed by them. Athaliah in her turn is killed, along with the priest of Baal, at the instigation of the priest Jehoiada, who has the seven-year old Joash crowned king of Judah. The ceremony includes a renewal of the covenant between Yahweh and his people and a covenant between king and people. He is rated a good king, though he did not remove the high places. He exerts himself to repair the temple, evidently in a very bad state, but fails to drive back a Syrian attack, which penetrated as far as Gath. Israel also is subjected to Syrian raids under Jehu's heir, Jehoahaz, but recovers most of the towns under her king Joash, who defeated the Syrians three times.

Two odd tales here complete the collection of Elisha stories. When Joash visits the dying Elisha, the prophet tells him to shoot an arrow and strike the ground three times. By sympathetic magic this ensures the defeat of Syria. Elisha dies and is buried; later a dead man is revived by accidentally touching his bones. Meanwhile, Amaziah becomes king in Judah and is so successful against the Edomites that he decides to challenge Joash of Israel to battle. Joash compares him to a thistle challenging a cedar, but he will not be warned and is beaten and presumably taken prisoner, while his son Azariah takes over. Meanwhile Jeroboam II becomes first co-regent, then king of Israel, c. 782-53. The historian records only that he extended his borders from near Mount Lebanon to the Dead Sea. *We know from the book of Amos and from archaeological sources that his reign was one of great prosperity and consequent economic injustice.* There was trade with Phoenicia, Syria, and Arabia, and Samaria became a very wealthy city. Excavations at Meggido and Samaria have turned up evidences of the luxury condemned by Amos, the "houses of ivory," beads, rings, and other ornaments, the winter and summer houses, besides strong fortifications and other buildings. Amos was active in Israel in the later part of Jeroboam's reign and was expelled from Bethel c. 755. Hosea also began preaching at this time.

When Jeroboam became king, he evidently released Amaziah of Judah from prison. He lives another fifteen years and is succeeded by Azariah, more commonly called Uzziah, who rules for over half a century, c. 792-740. The historian tells us little about him. Like his father, he does right in the eyes of the Lord but fails to remove the high places. When he becomes a leper, his son Jotham is made co-regent. We know from other sources that he increased the size of his army and made conquests in Philistia and on both sides of the Jordan. Judah, like Israel, was successful and prosperous at this time. Amos and Hosea preached during Uzziah's reign, and Isaiah received his call in the year of his death (see Isa. 6).

Decline and Fall of Israel 15:8-17:41. In Israel the death of Jeroboam is followed by civil war and bloodshed at home and danger abroad. Zecheriah, the last king of the house of Jehu, is killed after six months and his assassin, Shallum, only lasts a month. During the ten-year reign of Menahem, Pul — better known as Tiglath-Pileser of Assyria — invades Israel and takes tribute. Pekahiah, the next king, is assassinated after only two years by Pekah, the captain of a Gileadite band. Tiglath-Pileser invades again, and records in his annals that when Israel overthrew Pekah, he sets up Hoshea, Pekah's assassin, as king. Hoshea was to be the last king of Israel.

In Judah, Ahaz becomes Jotham's co-regent in 735. It is recorded that he did not do right in the eyes of the Lord, indeed he even made a burnt offering of his own son. *This horrible act was probably his terrified response to a threatened* attack by Pekah of Israel and Rezin of Damascus. The account here needs to be supplemented from the account of Isaiah, who encounters Ahaz as he is inspecting the water supply with a message from Yahweh, "Fear not, neither be faint hearted" at those "smoking fire brands," Rezin and Pekah, who will soon burn out. But Ahaz is afraid to trust the Lord. He appeals for help to Tiglath-Pileser, and he has to rob the temple of gold and silver and bronze ornaments to pay tribute.

In Israel, Hoshea refuses to send tribute and is attacked by the new Assyrian king, Shalmaneser V, who imprisons him and lays siege to Samaria until it falls, 723/2. The prophet Micah had prophesied the city's destruction. Ch. 17:7-23 is D-editor's explanation for the fall of Israel. *These events mark the end of the Northern kingdom, which from now on is populated with a mixed group of immigrants who contaminate the religion of Yahweh with foreign cults. The inhabitants, soon to be called Samaritans, are regarded by the people of Judah as outsiders down to New Testament times.*

Threat from Assyria 18:1-21:26. Hezekiah, who succeeds Ahaz in 716/15, is given a glowing report by the Deuteronomic editor. "He did that which was right in the sight of the Lord ... He removed the high places, and broke the images, and cut from the groves, and broke in pieces the brazen serpent... after him was none like him among the kings of Judah." His purpose was to purify the worship of Yahweh and to center it in the temple. In this he prepared the way for the Deuteronomic reform under Josiah. His reforms also had a political significance, in that it was a defiance of the power of Assyria.

The political events of Hezekiah's reign are related in the wrong order, but if Ch. 20:1-19 is placed before 18:7, the account makes more sense, particularly if read with the appropriate chapters in Isaiah. Hezekiah was not alone in wishing to defy Assyria. As early as 711, Isaiah had opposed a rebellion against Assyria led by Ashdod and encouraged by Egypt. The visit of Merodach-baladan of Babylonia to Hezekiah (Ch. 20) signaled another move against Assyria and again Isaiah opposed it, though Hezekiah's enthusiasm for the cause is indicated in the pride he shows in his resources. Eventually an anti-Assyrian coalition included Philistia, Moab, and Edom, as well as Judah. The king of Assyria, Sennacherib, acted swiftly, first to defeat Merodach-baladan, then to advance through Samaria and Judah toward Jerusalem (see Micah 1:10-16.) His annals tell how he took forty-six fortified cities, shut up Hezekiah "like a bird in a cage," and sent a delegation, led by the Rabshakeh (deputy?), to demand Hezekiah's surrender, 18:17f. They meet by "the conduit," presumably the Siloam tunnel, which Hezekiah had built to ensure a safe water supply during a siege. The speaker taunts the king with trusting too confidently in his god and the people for trusting in their king. In obedience to the king, the people are silent.

Hezekiah rends his clothes, puts on sackcloth and ashes, and goes to the temple to seek the advice of Isaiah. The prophet counsels him not to be afraid, for Yahweh will entice the king back to his own land. In a second mission, the Rabshakeh urges Hezekiah not to trust in Yahweh, who cannot help him. Hezekiah "spread[s] it before the Lord" in a "complaint prayer," while Isaiah utters a taunt song in the name of Yahweh. In a more modest prose oracle, he claims that "The remnant that is escaped of the house of Judah shall yet again take root downward, and bear fruit upward." *The concept of the remnant is a common one in Isaiah's thinking.* The story has a surprising and dramatic conclusion. "And it came to pass that night, that the angel of the Lord went out, and smote in the camp of the Assyrians a hundred fourscore and five thousand: and when they arose early in the morning, behold, they were all dead corpses. So Sennacherib king of Assyria departed, and went and returned, and dwelt at Nineveh" (II Kings 19:35-37). There he was assassinated by two of his sons.

What really happened? From this mixture of history and prophecy, legend and miracle story it is hard to tell. A story in Herodotus tells how the bowstrings and other equipment of the Assyrian army were destroyed by mice. This has led to the suggestion that Sennacherib's soldiers were the victims of bubonic plague. For some reason, Sennacherib did abandon the siege of Jerusalem. Some historians think that Isaiah 22:1-14, at least in part, describes the rejoicing in the city after his withdrawal. Incidentally, the assassination of Sennacherib, vs. 37, took place about twenty years later, supposing the siege of 701 was the only one.

Manasseh must have been co-regent with his father for ten or so of his fifty-five years. The Deuteronomist sees him as the worst king Judah had ever had. He reverses his father's reforms by rebuilding the local shrines and setting up an Asherah; in addition he builds altars "for all the hosts of heaven" (i.e., the sun, moon, and stars), and encourages Baal worship, soothsayers, mediums, and wizards. These trends all reflect the influence of Assyria, which now dominated the whole fertile crescent in religious matters as well as political. Manasseh even burns his son as an offering, as well as shedding much innocent blood. His son Amon is equally evil and is assassinated after only two

years, when his little son Josiah succeeds.

Josiah and Deuteronomic Reform

22:1-23:30. Josiah is the favorite of the Deuteronomists, because of his extensive and thorough reforms. The way for these was prepared, not only by the good work of Hezekiah, but by a resurgence of prophecy. Zephaniah's attacks on paganism, and his announcement that "the day of Yahweh" was at hand were heard early in Josiah's reign. Jeremiah's call came in 628. Also, since Assyria's power was on the wane, Josiah's religious reforms were accompanied by a revival of nationalism.

Josiah's reign begins in 641/40. When the temple is being repaired in 623/22 "the book of the law," i.e., either the book of Deuteronomy or part of it, is discovered by the priest, Hilkiah. It is possible that Hilkiah knew about the book and "discovered" it when the time was ripe. When the secretary reads the book to Joshua, the king rends his garments, a sign of acute dismay, presumably at the warnings against syncretism in Dt. 6:13-15 or at the frightening curses on those who disobey the law in Ch. 28. The prophetess Huldah, consulted to find if disaster can be averted, foretells that because the words of the book have been disregarded, Yahweh will make Jerusalem "a desolation and a curse." However, because Josiah is penitent and humble, he will die in peace, before he can see the evil to come. Josiah assembles the people and reads the book to them, after which king and people make a covenant together "to walk after the Lord and keep his commandments." We are reminded of the covenant at Shechem in Josiah's time, and, of course, the covenant at Sinai.

The ceremony is followed by a drastic series of reforms by which Josiah helped to avert the disaster prophesied by Huldah. The account of his actions incidentally provides an illuminating catalog of pagan cults and practices. The Baalism of Canaan, the Assyrian astral cult, the worship of Chemosh, the abomination of Moab and Milcom, the abomination of Ammon, and Moloch, the recipient of burnt offerings of children, all are abolished. The cult objects associated with these religions, such as the vessels of Baal and the horses dedicated to the sun, are thrown out and in some cases defiled. Thus the Asherah image is burned, beaten to dust, and thrown on gravel. Sacred prostitution, necromancy, and child sacrifice are done away with and the heathen priests deposed. The high places where Solomon built altars for his foreign wives are defiled. Even the shrine at Bethel is smashed and defiled by burning bones from nearby tombs on its altar. Bethel was in what had been the Northern kingdom, now officially under Assyrian rule.

It is a measure of Assyria's weakness at this point that Josiah could destroy the Assyrian astral cult at Jerusalem and carry his crusade into an Assyrian province. Power was, in fact, quickly passing to a neo-Babylonian empire. In 612 Nineveh, the Assyrian capital fell to a combination of Babylonians, Scythians, and Medes. The prophet Nahum had prophesied its fall. Pharaoh Necho went to Assyria's aid, probably hoping to gain Syria and Palestine for himself. Unfortunately Josiah, perhaps helping to revive the united kingdom under his rule, plotted with the Babylonians, but was killed in the battle of Meggido in 609. His reforms, along with international politics, were fatal not only to himself, but to Judah. His reforms do not seem to have survived him long, but the Deuteronomic writers continued their work after his death and after the Exile.

In bringing the account of Josiah to a close, the second Deuteronomic editor notes that in spite of the king's reforms, Yahweh will still cast off Jerusalem. Josiah himself, however, is given a high rating: "And like unto him was there no king before him, that turned to the Lord with all his heart, and with all his soul, and with all his might, according to all the law of Moses; neither after him arose there any like him" (II Kings 23:25). The editor forgets that the claim of uniqueness was also made for Hezekiah. Still, many historians would agree that Josiah was the greatest king since David. All Josiah's successors are said to have done evil in Yahweh's sight and indeed the end of the nation is near.

Last Years of Judah 23:31-25:30. In the dozen years between Josiah's death and the first deportation the distraught Judeans were trapped between the stronger powers, Egypt and Babylon, subjected first to one and then the other. *It is extraordinary that the prophet Jeremiah is not mentioned in II Kings, for he was very active during this terrible period and had been since about 628. He preached his famous Temple Sermon after Josiah's death. Habakkuk who began to prophesy c. 607, is likewise ignored.*

After only three months' rule (609), Josiah's son Jehoahaz, evidently the head of an anti-Egyptian party, is imprisoned by Pharaoh Necho, who makes Jehoiakim, another son of Josiah, king and an Egyptian puppet. He takes suitable gold and silver as tribute. In 605 Necho is severely defeated by the Babylonians at the battle of Carchemish and Judah becomes a Babylonian province. We hear a great deal more about Jehoiakim from Jer. 34-6 where he appears as an arrogant, greedy, selfish king who restored child sacrifice and worshiped Ishtar, Queen of Heaven. His attitude to the prophet is evident in the famous episode where he cuts the scroll of Jeremiah's oracles into pieces and throws them into the fire. As far as we know, he is the only Judean king who ever had a prophet killed. He rebels against Babylon and dies under mysterious circumstances.

His young son Jehoiachin (called Coniah in Jer.), succeeds in 598/7. Three months later Nebuchadrezzar besieges Jerusalem, which falls on March 16, 597, according to Babylonian records. The king, his mother, his officials and his chief men, together with the prophet Ezekiel, are taken away to Babylon. This is the first deportation.

Zedekiah, the king's uncle, is made regent. The last descendant of David to rule, he is well-intentioned but meek. On occasion he consults with Jeremiah (see Jer. 37-39 for more details of this period), who endorses submission to Babylon, but the pro-Egyptian party evidently persuades Zedekiah to rebel and withhold his tribute. The inevitable renewal of the siege begins January 588, the walls being breached thirty months later. The Lachish Letters give a good picture of the tensions during this period. In the following month Jerusalem is destroyed. The palace, temple, and great houses are burned, the temple equipment broken up and taken away. The ring leaders of the revolt are executed and more of the upper class are de-ported. Jeremiah's famous vision of the good and bad figs probably relates to this second deportation. The best figs are the superior classes whose future is with the Exile, while the bad figs are the poor peasants who are left to till the land. Zedekiah himself flees, but is picked up on the plain of Jericho, forced to watch the execution of his sons, and blinded. Gedaliah, a friend of Jeremiah and a widely respected man, is appointed governor and a new capital is set up in Mizpah. He apparently intends to cooperate with the Babylonians, in accordance with Jeremiah's policy, but is assassinated with all who were with him at Mizpah. A number of the people take refuge in Egypt, accompanied by Jeremiah.

Wishing to end the book on a note of hope, the second Deuteronomist records that Nebuchadrezzar's successor, Evil-merodach, released Jehoiachin from prison, gave him a seat above other noble captains, and made him a regular allowance. *By an extraordinary chance, archaeology has confirmed this statement, for excavations have found tablets recording rations of oil and grain paid to the Judean king.* The Second Deuteronomist evidently received the news that the king was still alive in time to end the book with a glimmer of hope for the house of David.

I Chronicles

Introduction. *It is widely held that the two books of Chronicles are part of a larger history which included Ezra and Nehemiah.* The similarities in style and vocabulary, the extensive use of genealogies and lists, the striking interest in the Jerusalem temple and in the functions of the Levites, all argue a single-minded group and most probably a single author. *Ezra picks up exactly where II Chronicles leaves off, repeating, indeed, the last two verses, without which the rest of Chronicles would make no sense. Thus the narrative in the four books is continuous,* since Chronicles gives the history of the nation from Adam through David and Solomon to the Captivity, ending with Cyrus' decree releasing the Jews, while Ezra and Nehemiah describe the various stages of the return of the exiles to Palestine. The author, called simply the Chronicler, was probably a Levitical priest, perhaps a singer, certainly deeply involved in the Jerusalem temple, its functions, its personnel and its history. His purpose in writing his historical work was to affirm the divine origin of the Davidic dynasty and of the temple, which he saw as inextricably linked embodiments of God's rule on earth.

The Chronicler made use of a number of other Old Testament books from Genesis to Ruth, but particularly Samuel and Kings, which he quotes extensively verbatim (naturally without acknowledgment, for plagiarism is a modern concept). About half his material is from these books. In addition, he refers to fifteen to twenty other works, such as "The Acts of Nathan," "The Acts of God the Seer," "The History of Uzziah by the Prophet Isaiah," "The Acts of Jehu," and a "Commentary on the Book of Kings." It is not really known whether these were separate sources or parts of a larger history, perhaps "The Book of the Kings of Israel and Judah," which is also mentioned. The writer also had access to reliable Aramaic sources, to official lists and registers, and probably to oral traditions.

Much of his narrative, then, parallels earlier Old Testament histories, but is written from the point of view of a Levite in the service of the post-exilic temple. His special interests were the temple, the liturgies, the priests, and the temple officials. He is concerned to demonstrate the legitimacy of the temple in Jerusalem and of the worshiping community there, as opposed to the claims of the rival Samaritan cult. This is one reason why he includes so many genealogies. He deals only briefly

with the early history of the nation, because his real interest is in a theocracy — "rule by God" — through his chosen leaders, of whom David is the first and greatest. David is in fact much more important to the Chronicler than Moses. Hence the (to us) disproportionate space given to David, but it is not the David known to us from the early narratives and the Court History. The Chronicler views David as a great king and military leader, of course, but primarily as the spiritual founder of the temple. *David's character is necessarily idealized.* Emphasis is placed on his piety, his detailed plans for the temple and its furnishings, and the funds and materials which he left to Solomon for its construction. Among the episodes omitted are his early adventures under Saul, the adultery with Bathsheba, and the revolt of Absalom. The death-bed instructions to Solomon to kill off Joab and Shimei are replaced by a beautiful farewell prayer of praise and thanksgiving. *Solomon, too, is somewhat whitewashed, his misgovernment and idolatry being glossed over. This is not history as we understand it, but history in the service of theology.* There was no intention on the part of the Chronicler to deceive. This was merely his way of teaching what he believed.

The date of Chronicles is disputed, but on internal evidence it cannot be much earlier than 400 B.C. Some historians would date it later, c. 250, well into the Greek period. There are signs that it was accepted late into the Canon and it is placed last in most printed editions of the Hebrew Bible.

Genealogies and Lists 1-9. The period from Adam to Saul is covered chiefly by a series of genealogies. Particular attention is paid to the house of David. At the end are lists of prominent residents of

Jerusalem in the post-exilic period and lists of the temple staff. The Chronicler is particularly interested in the gatekeepers and in the singers, who are on duty day and night.

Reign of David 10:1-22:1. Saul's death is briefly described, and the failure of his rule attributed to his disobedience to God and his dealings with the witch (medium) of Endor. His failure is used as a foil to the brilliant reigns of David and Solomon. David becomes King of Israel and captures Jerusalem. *His difficulties and his struggle with the house of Saul are omitted.* Mighty men from all the tribes flock to make him king, forming a great army, "like an army of God." Hiram, King of Tyre, sends workmen and cedar wood for David's house. Eventually the ark is brought in procession to Jerusalem, carried by the Levites and accompanied by Levitical singers. *This shows one of the special interests of the Chronicler; however, Levites did not really exist as a separate group in David's time.* A service of dedication and thanksgiving is held with appropriate offerings. *The account is very different from that in II Sam. 6. David's dancing before the Lord would be considered unseemly in the Chronicler's day and is not mentioned.* David plans to build a temple, but is told through Nathan that God intends instead to build him a "house" — i.e., a dynasty. The accounts of David's military successes follow those in Samuel closely, except that the Chronicler attempts to harmonize the two accounts of the slaying of Goliath by mentioning his brother. An interesting change is made in David's decision to number the people, for whereas in Samuel his decision is attributed to "the anger of the Lord," here he is incited by Satan (means "The Adversary"), for by the Chronicler's time a discreditable act could not be attributed to God's intention. David purchases a threshing floor as a site for the temple, paying six hundred shekels instead of the fifty mentioned in Samuel. Fire from heaven burns up the sacrifice, signifying God's approval.

Plans for the Temple; David's Death 22:2-29:30. *There are no equivalent passages in Samuel or Kings.* The Chronicler wants to establish David's position as the founder of the temple, if not as its actual builder. We have heard that he bought the site. Now we hear that he provides dressed stones, nails, bronze, cedar timber, and enormous quantities of gold and silver, saying, "Solomon my son is young and tender, and the house that is to be builded for the Lord must be exceeding magnificent, of fame and glory throughout all countries." David gives a solemn charge to Solomon to build the temple and commands all the leaders of Israel to help him. He counts the Levites and organizes them in three groups. The priests (the sons of Aaron) are organized into twenty-four divisions and, to match, the temple musicians are also organized into the same number of divisions. Players of cymbals, harps, and lyres are mentioned and also those skillful in singing. Levites also serve as "doorkeepers," responsible for the treasuries of the temple and the gifts made to it. The reorganization of the army of twenty-four thousand men into twelve divisions again reflects the Chronicler's fondness for arbitrary even numbers, here probably suggested by the twelve tribes, which are also mentioned here, though their identities had long been lost. Supervisors of the king's treasuries, over the fields, vineyards, olive and sycamore trees, camels and flocks are also appointed, together with a scribe and a counselor. David assembles the leaders of the people, explains that God will not let him build the temple because he is a warrior who has shed blood, and appoints Solomon as his successor. No mention is made of the rivalries, intrigues, and violent deeds that formed so large a part of the Court History. David explains that though he cannot build the temple, he has prepared for it as carefully as possible. He presents to Solomon the elaborate plans which he has worked out in accordance with God's will. They include the vestibule, treasuries, upper and inner chambers, and the room for the mercy seat, i.e., The Holy of Holies. He has also provided gold, silver, bronze, onyx, multicolored and precious stones and marble. From the leaders he asks generous free-will offerings toward the building of the temple. They give generously, gold, silver, bronze, iron, and precious stones.

David's final speech is in the form of a prayer which expresses praise, thanksgiving, humility, and faith in God. It begins with the beautiful doxology still used today: "Blessed be thou, Lord God of Israel our father for ever and ever. Thine O Lord, is the greatness, and the power, and the glory, and the victory and the majesty: for all that is in the heaven and in the earth is thine; thine is the kingdom, O Lord, and thou art exalted as head above all. Both riches and honor come of thee, and thou reignest over all; and in thine hand is power and might; and in thine hand it is to make great, and to give strength unto all. Now therefore, our God, we thank thee, and praise thy glorious name." We are strangers and sojourners on earth, he continues, "our days on earth are a shadow, and there is none abiding." God tries us and takes pleasure in an upright heart. "O Lord God of Abraham, Isaac, and of Israel, our fathers, keep this for ever in the imagination of the thoughts of the heart of thy people, and prepare their heart unto thee: And give unto Solomon my son a perfect heart, to keep thy commandments, thy testimonies, and thy statutes, and to do all these things, and to build the palace, for the which I have made provision." *In this beautiful prayer the Chronicler expresses the noblest religious ideas of his time.*

Solomon is made king, and the leaders swear allegiance to him. The book closes with a summary of David's reign.

II Chronicles

Reign of Solomon 1-9. *Much of the material in this section is taken from I Kings.* Solomon's wisdom, his wealth and power, his building of the temple and its dedication are recounted as in the earlier history, with occasional changes and additions which reflect the interests and views of the Chronicler. For example, the conclusion of Solomon's prayer in 6:40-42 has been altered, two verses of a psalm praising David and the temple being substituted for reference to Moses and the Exodus. Also, a bronze platform is provided for Solomon to kneel on. God's satisfaction with the temple and the burnt offering is signified, as in David's case, by fire from heaven. Solomon's dream, his building activities, his reception of the Queen of Sheba and his death are taken from I Kgs. with a couple of small changes and some very important omissions. The Chronicler has it that Hiram (i.e., Hiram of Tyre) gave many cites to Solomon, whereas the reverse was the case, and that Solomon would not allow his foreign wife in the house of David "because the places are holy, whereunto the ark of the Lord had come." The omissions show the tendency of the Chronicler to idealize Solomon, for he makes no mention of the intrigues preceding his succession, his marriages to Pharaoh's daughter and other foreign women, his worship of their gods, his troubles with his enemies at the end of his reign, and the prophecy of Ahijah that ten tribes would be lost because of his apostasy (see esp. I Kgs. 11). The last chapter, lifted from I Kgs. 10, describes Solomon's wealth in colorful details, leaving us with a positive impression.

Kings of Judah 10-36. Unlike II Kgs. this section of II Chronicles concentrates on Judah, because the Chronicler considers that the Northern kingdom has sinned in rejecting the line of David. It is only mentioned when there is a close connection or conflict with Judah. As generally, the Chronicler is hostile to the "Samaritans." He has expanded the accounts of several rulers dealt with in II Kgs., using material from other sources or giving his own interpretations. There are additions to the accounts of several kings, e.g., Asa, Joash, Uzziah, Jotham, and Manasseh. In Uzziah's case, the Chronicler explains his leprosy as a punishment for defying the priests in burning incense on the temple altar. Manasseh, depicted in II Kgs. as the very worst king of the Davidic line, is allowed to repent

and purify Jerusalem, for which he is rewarded with a long life. The Chronicler is particularly interested in Jehoshaphat, Hezekiah, and Josiah, because they are righteous kings in the tradition of David and Solomon. Jehoshaphat's care for religion, his legal reforms (theocracy in action), his appointment of priests and Levites to teach the law, all win the Chronicler's approval, and he gives a moral interpretation to the destruction of Jehoshaphat's navy, which he attributes to the King's alliance with the evil Ahaziah of Israel. Hezekiah is regarded, as in II Kgs., as one of the great rulers of Judah, but where the author of Kings summarizes Hezekiah's reforms in one verse (18:4), the Chronicler expands this into three whole chapters, describing in elaborate detail how Hezekiah has the Levites purify themselves, then remove the filth of idolatry from the temple, how he holds a great celebration for the reopening of the temple and a great passover festival, after which the people go out spontaneously to destroy cult objects in the surrounding cities. Compared with this liturgical section, the space devoted to Sennacherib's invasion is very small. In the case of Josiah, the account is much the same as in II Kgs., except that the passover and Josiah's death are described in greater detail. Like II Kgs., Chronicles ends with the capture of Jerusalem and the Exile, but as in Kings, a note of hope is struck in the last few verses, which record the decree of Cyrus of Persia permitting those who wanted to return to Jerusalem.

Ezra and Nehemiah

Introduction. Ezra-Nehemiah was originally one book and is a continuation of Chronicles I. It concerns the return of some of the exiles to Palestine after Cyrus'

decree liberating the peoples conquered by the Babylonians. It is the only Biblical work dealing with the Persian period, 546-334. During this era, the Greeks won their great victories against the Persians, Marathon in 490 and Themopylae and Salamis in 480.

As was his custom, the Chronicler used a number of different sources, the most important being the memoirs of Nehemiah and of Ezra, partly in the first person. There are also lists, genealogies, and temple records, besides Aramaic sources, notably Cyrus' decree and some correspondence between the hostile Samaritans and the Persian court. The Chronicler's preoccupation with the temple, the priests, the services and the worshiping community, which we saw in I and II Chronicles, are in evidence here.

At some point, parts of the texts become displaced so that material about Nehemiah appears in the present Ezra and vice versa. The exact order is disputed. In the summary which follows, I follow the order suggested in the Oxford Annotated Bible, which makes good sense and eliminates repetitions. The editors distinguish four stages: (1) a return under Cyrus (538 B.C.) led by Sheshbazzar, with an attempt at rebuilding the temple that had to be abandoned; (2) a return under Darius I (521-485) led by Zerubbabel and Jeshua, who completed the temple with the encouragement of the prophets Haggai and Zechariah; (3) a return under Artaxerxes led by Nehemiah (464-423) who rebuilt the walls of Jerusalem and tried to establish religious purity but returned from a trip to Persia to find his reforms neglected; and finally, (4) a return under Artaxerxes II (404-338) led by Ezra, who read to the too often faithless people "the book of the law of Moses."

Return of Sheshbazzar and Zerubbabel Ezra 1-6. In the first year that Cyrus rules over Babylon (538), Yahweh implores him to allow Sheshbazzar to rebuild the temple at Jerusalem. Cyrus thought of Yahweh as a local deity and his decision was in line with his tolerance of the other religions under his rule. He restores to the exiles the sacred vessels taken by Nebuchadrezzar and other gifts are made by the community to the returning exiles. However, they do not succeed, and the attempt is taken up again by Zerubbabel and Jeshua, who build an altar, offer a sacrifice, and lay the foundations of the temple. Unfortunately the Samaritans, a mixed people who, however, consider themselves followers of Moses, resent the exiles. They do offer to help build the temple, but only if the Jews recognize the validity of their religion. The Jews' obsession with religious purity and exclusiveness prevents this and the hostility between the two groups hardens. Meanwhile, spurred on by the prophets Haggai and Zechariah, the exiles complete the temple. (The narrative is interrupted by quotations from correspondence with the Persian cult, including a Samaritan protest of a later date.)

Return of Nehemiah, Neh. 1-13 (with some rearrangement and omissions). Nehemiah, the kings' cupbearer, tells how he heard that the exiles in the homeland were in terrible trouble. He prays on behalf of his people and appeals to Artaxerxes to let him return to his ancestral sepulchres. He really intends to restore the walls, inspects them by night, and encourages the people to "rise up and build." As before, the Samaritans, especially the governor Sanballat, interfere with the work, and the workers are obliged to carry arms and sometimes to work at night. There are also complaints from the exiles about their economic plight. Nehemiah rouses them with a spirited speech, and they complete the walls. There is a break in Nehemiah's narrative after 7:5. It resumes in Ch. 11 with a census list. The walls are dedicated, the ceremony being accompanied by "procession of Levites and musicians," sacrifices and purification so dear to the heart of the Chronicler. Nehemiah has to visit Persia. While he is gone, the priest Eliashib, related to Sanballat, allowed an Ammonite to move into a temple chamber, in defiance of the law against forgiveness. On his return, Nehemiah is very angry, throws out the Ammonite, has the room purified, and encourages the Levites and singers who had fled to return. The people bring tithes of grain, wine, and oil to support the temple. Nehemiah gives instances of breaking the Sabbath, e.g., by merchants who want to sell their wares, and of marriages to foreign women, which horrify Nehemiah to the point of violence: "And I contended with them, and cursed some of them, and plucked off their hair." Reminding them of Solomon, he makes them foreswear the practice. He defines the duties of priests and Levites and appoints times for wood offerings and first fruits, concluding "Remember me, O my God, for good."

The last verse of Ch. 9 and the whole of Ch. 10 should probably be placed at this point. The leaders, priests, and Levites set their seal to the covenant and swear to keep themselves separate from the foreigners and to make the expected offerings to the temple.

Coming of Ezra, Ezra 7-10; Neh. 8-9:37. In the reign of Artaxerxes II, Ezra, a scribe skilled in the law of Moses, comes to Jerusalem with a letter from Artaxerxes (in Aramaic) giving him the authority to make enquiries and to set up a new government with a religious basis. Like Nehemiah he abhors foreign marriages, for he believes that they contaminate the chosen and holy people of God. Like Nehemiah, he prays on behalf of the people, "weeping and casting himself down before the house of God." The people are assembled and eventually a list of those who have contracted foreign marriages is compiled. (The narrative is picked up in Neh. 8.) At a later date, the people are assembled again in the square before the Water Gate to hear Ezra read from the law of Moses. It is in Hebrew, so Ezra has to interpret it in Aramaic. At first the people are dismayed and weep, but Ezra comforts them and orders a feast, saying, "Go forth into the mount and fetch olive branches, and pine branches, and myrtle branches, and palm branches, and branches of thick trees, to make booths, as it is written." Apparently the feast of the booths (Succoth) prescribed in Lev. 23:33-43 had not been forgotten, though the ritual described here is somewhat different. The feast is kept for seven days. On the seventh day, at a great assembly, there is a solemn fasting, at which the people confess their sins. Ezra gives a short account of their history from the time of Abraham, and the covenant is renewed with "the great and might and terrible God, who keepest covenant and steadfast love" (RSV).

Esther

Introduction. The book of Esther is read at the feast of Purim in the month Adar (early spring) and purports to explain the origin of that feast. In actual fact the feast was perhaps a spring festival which was taken over by the Jews of Persia and gradually spread westward. In various periods it has been celebrated by feasting and merrymaking, together with exchanges of gifts and charity to the poor. It has sometimes involved a Purim play and/or the burning of Haman in effigy. The name comes from the "Pur" or lot used by Haman to determine the most propitious day for his massacre of the Jews. It is set in the reign of Xerxes I, here called Ahasuerus. During the latter's reign there was an official called Maduka, but not much is known about him; the story is legendary. The date is disputed. Some scholars suppose it was written about the middle of the fourth century by a Jew living in Persia. This would explain the many Persian words and the knowledge of Persian court life. Other scholars connect the tale with the latter period of the Maccabees because of its ruthless attitude to enemies of the Jews. It was certainly very popular in that period.

The author took the trouble to provide a historical background for the hostility between Haman and Mordecai. Haman is supposed to be descended from the house of Benjamin. As early as Moses' time, the Amalekites were troublesome to the Israelites, and there was a confrontation between Agag, king of the Amalekites, and the Benjaminite Saul. In the Esther story, the feud is rounded off by the execution of Haman's sons, the last of the Amalekite tribe.

This dramatic but ruthless story has several peculiarities. *There is no mention of God or religious practices, and the exaltation of vengeance is certainly contrary to the teaching of the Pentateuch.* Moreover, Esther becomes Xerxes' concubine before she is his wife and, of course, marries a non-Jew. These facts gave rise to considerable controversy about the inclusion of the book in the Canon. Many rabbis opposed it as late as the third century A. D. Eventually its popularity and its association with the joyous feast of Purim won a place for it.

Fall of Vashti and Rise of Esther 1-2. Ahasuerus is holding a great feast for his people at his winter palace at Susa. He commands his queen, Vashti, to come and display her beauty. When she refuses to come, the king's counselors warn him that she is setting a bad precedent and must be removed, lest other ladies defy their husbands. An empire-wide beauty contest is held to find beautiful young virgins for the king. Mordecai, a descendant of the Babylonian exiles living in Susa, had adopted as his daughter his beautiful young cousin, Hadassah or Esther, and he now puts her in the hands of the official (probably a eunuch) who is in charge of the king's maidens, charging her not to reveal her Jewish origin. She finds favor with all, including the king, and eventually is made queen. Meantime, Mordecai overhears two eunuchs plotting to kill the king. Through Esther, the plot is revealed to Ahasuerus and the plotters are hanged. The affair is recorded in the official chronicles.

Haman's Plot 3. Ahasuerus now raises Haman, the descendant of Agag, to a position higher than all the other princes and gives him his signet ring. Haman is furious because Mordecai, the Benjaminite, refuses to bow down to him. He plans to destroy, not only Mordecai, but all Jews. By pointing out to the king that dispersed all over his realm is a whole people who set themselves apart and do not obey the laws of the land, Haman persuades his royal master to give him authority to have the Jews exterminated. He has already set the date by Pur (the lot) on the thirteenth day of Adar which falls in March-April. Letters are sent by Xerxes' famous fast couriers to all parts of the empire.

Mordecai and Esther 4-7. Mordecai, like the rest of the Jews, rends his clothes and puts on sackcloth and ashes (the traditional expression of grief). He mourns by the king's gate. Esther sends clothes, but he responds by sending her a copy of the decree and begging her to entreat the king to save her people, reminding her that if the execution is carried out, she too will die. The strict security precautions forbade anyone to approach the king, so Esther is fearful. Even so, she asks Mordecai to gather all the Jews of Susa together and fast, while she makes the attempt. "If I perish, I perish." Notice that the author avoids mentioning prayers which would normally accompany the other manifestations of woe. The possibility of help "from another quarter" (RSV) is mentioned, but God is not specifically named. *(Prayers by both Esther and Mordecai are added at this point in the apocryphal additions to the book.)*

On the third day, Esther in her royal robes enters the inner court. To her relief, the king holds out his golden sceptre to her, and promises to grant her request, even to the half of his kingdom. She promises to announce her petition at a banquet to which she invites Haman. But she puts off her announcement — the author is extracting all the suspense he can from the story — until a second banquet. In the interval we see Haman boasting to his wife and friends of his great riches and power, a nice touch of dramatic irony.

Now chance enters in. As Ahasuerus cannot sleep, he has official chronicles read to him, and is reminded of the fact that Mordecai once saved his life by exposing a plot to assassinate him. Anxious to repay Mordecai's loyalty, he asks "Who is in the court?" Haman, eager to display his new power by asking for Mordecai's death, is ready to answer the question "What shall be done unto the man whom the king delighteth to honor?" He assumes (with appropriate hubris) that he is the man and suggests that he be clad in royal robes and should ride on the king's horse through the city. When he is forced to honor Mordecai in this way, he is humiliated. His wife and counselors tell him that the tide has turned against him and indeed at her second banquet, Esther makes her petition that the king should save her and her people, "for we are sold, I and my people, to be destroyed, to be slain, and to perish ... The adversary and enemy is this wicked Haman." The angry king goes out into the palace garden and returns to find Haman "fallen upon the bed where Esther was." Probably Haman was only attempting a common Oriental gesture of supplication, seizing and perhaps kissing Esther's feet, but Ahasuerus interprets it as sexual attack. Haman's face is covered and by the king's order he is hanged on the gallows he had prepared for Mordecai. (The gallows was really a tall pole on which the victim was spiked and left to die. The height, fifty-two cubits, over eighty feet, is exaggerated in keeping with the melodramatic nature of the story.)

Triumph of the Jews 8-10. The reversal is completed when Mordecai is given the signet ring and Haman's position, together with the power to make a new decree, permitting the Jews to take revenge on their enemies. He is dressed in royal robes, and all the Jews, in a mood of "lightness and gladness and joy and honor," feast and make a holiday. Then, aided by the royal troops, who fear the powerful Mordecai, they turn on their enemies with "the sword and slaughter and destruction." Though there is immense slaughter, even in Susa itself, there is no looting, perhaps a reminiscence of the Agag story, where Saul and his men were rebuked for not destroying all their loot. At Esther's special request, the ten sons of Haman are hanged, thus completing the destruction of the Amalekite tribe. *In what may be an appendix (9:20-10:3),* the feast of Purim is established "as a day for gladness and feasting and holiday-making, and a day in which they send choice portions to one another." The holiday is confirmed in writing, important as it is not mentioned in the Pentateuch. Mordecai, concludes the book, "was great among the Jews and popular with the multitude of his brethren for he sought the welfare of his people and spoke peace to all his people."

Introduction to Wisdom Literature

According to Old Testament tradition, Solomon was the father of wisdom, as Moses of the law, and David of the psalms. Over 3,000 proverbs were attributed to Solomon, and Hiram of Tyre and the Queen of Sheba knew of his wisdom. *While no one passage can be attributed to him for certain, he probably played some part in initiating the writing of wisdom literature.* Wisdom literature itself was international in character, as we know both from Biblical allusions to wise men of many lands and from texts unearthed by archaeologists. Babylon, Egypt, Persia, Phoenicia, Edom all contributed wisdom to the Near Eastern pool. In some cases Hebrew proverbs are translations of famous wise men of other lands, notably Amenhotep of Egypt.

The word for "wisdom" has connotations of skill, craftsmanship, know-how, a thing well done. It was expressed in such forms as *proverbs, riddles, fables, and parables* characterized by conciseness, cleverness, and wit.

Wisdom Books. Proverbs is the largest single collection of wisdom literature in the Bible; Job and Ecclesiastes grew out of the movement, but are very unorthodox. There are shorter passages of wisdom in the Pentateuch and in the historical and prophetic books and "wisdom" psalms in the book of Psalms.

Characteristics of Wisdom Writings. One striking feature of the wisdom writers is their lack of interest in the traditional preoccupations of Judaism. They ignore the temple ritual, the covenant, the concept of Israel as the chosen people, and the hope for a messiah. They are sometimes, though not always, hostile to the priesthood. They do assume the omnipotence of God and think of him as the creator and master of nature. Some uphold the idea of divine providence, some think of man as a participant in bringing about justice in the world. Their ethics are based on practical experience, not mystical insight, though they think of God as the ultimate source of wisdom. They are concerned with achieving the good life by wise conduct which includes faithfulness and obedience to parents, concern for the poor, sobriety, honesty, and hard work. Some of the writers tend to oversimplify, to divide men into the wise and the foolish. This notion is elegantly stated in Psalm 1, where the wise man who meditates on the law is "like a tree planted by rivers of water," whereas the ungodly is "like the chaff which the wind driveth away." The inadequacy of this doctrine was apparent to other wise men, who wrestled more profoundly with the riddles of life's meaning. (See Anderson, p. 500.)

Job

Theme. The book of Job has been called the greatest of the wisdom books, but it goes far beyond the practical and prudential advice of much wisdom literature. *It probes the mystery of undeserved suffering and the existence of evil in a world supposedly created by a good and all-powerful God.* The starting point is an old folktale, which had been in circulation since the second millennium B.C. It tells how a blameless man, Job, is tempted by "The Satan" to curse God. Afflicted with disease, stripped of his possessions and his family, Job remains steadfast and in the end is rewarded with new wealth and a new family. *Between the beginning and the end of this story, the author or authors of a later time have composed a magnificent dialogue, including hymns, laments, and prayers, which express different views of the problem of evil and of the relationship between God and man.*

Antiquity of the Theme. The just man who suffers is the subject of several other Near Eastern works. The so-called Babylonian Job is a monologue in which the speaker complains that the Lord Marduk, although he is supposed to be just, allows his followers to suffer. Another Babylonian text has a dialogue between a sufferer and his friend. The sufferer asks, "How have I profited that I have bowed down to my God?" Akkadian and Sumerian texts also deal with the problem of suffering. The Egyptian "Dialogue of the Suffering one," in which the central character speaks to his own soul about his miseries, was written at about the time when the Hebrews were living in Egypt. While none of these works can be shown to have influenced the Biblical Job, they attest to the antiquity of the theme and of widespread interest in it.

Cosmopolitan Author. There is internal evidence that the author of Job was a sophisticated, well-traveled man. He knew the busy life of the town as well as the life of the lonely nomads, who might be in danger from raiding parties. There are a number of references to Egypt, to its palaces and pyramids, to the Nile, canals, reeds, and papyrus, to the crocodiles and the hippopotamus. The writer is also familiar with wild life, with the lion cubs crouching in their covert, the wild goats giving birth to their young, the wild ass wandering on the steppes, the ostrich laying her eggs to be warmed by the sun.

The prose story takes us back to a nomadic period when a rich man's wealth consisted of sheep, oxen and slaves, though the introduction of the Satan belongs to a later period.

Date. The date of the composition of the Job poem is very difficult to determine, except that we know that it as written after the Exile. There are no references to external events. Some historians conjecture a date after Jeremiah but before II Isaiah, since the author of Job makes no use of the idea of vicarious suffering. The place (Uz) is supposed to be Edom and the friends of Job come from northwest Arabia, i.e., they are non-Jewish. It is also of interest that except in the folk story the cult name for God, Yahweh, is avoided, as is Elohim, the general terms for God. Instead, El, Eloah, and Shaddai are used.

Structure. The plan of the poem is clear. After Job's lament, there are three cycles of speeches. Eliphaz, Bildad, and Zophar speak in turn and Job answers. This order is repeated twice, but the third cycle has been disturbed by editors who tried to make Job sound more orthodox. They inserted a poem on wisdom (Ch. 28), in place of Job's speech, and added a new character, Elihu, who is made to upbraid Job at some length from the point of view of orthodox Judaism. The original order is resumed with the interchanges between Job and God. The whole is rounded out with the last part of the folk story.

Prologue 1-2. "There was a man" is the equivalent of our "Once upon a time" and immediately suggests a folktale. Job is pictured as a great personage, rich in large numbers of sheep, camels, oxen, and asses and blessed in his seven sons and three daughters. "Blameless and upright," he regularly makes burnt offerings for his children, in case they should commit some sin unconsciously.

Suddenly we are in the court of heaven, where Yahweh is receiving the angelic beings in the manner of an Oriental monarch. Among these is the Satan, literally "the Adversary," not the adversary of God, the Satan of later Jewish and Christian thought, but an angel whose task was to look into earthly affairs. Yahweh is boasting about his servant Job, "There is none like him in the earth, a perfect and upright man, one that feareth God and escheweth evil." The Satan suggests that Job would not be so pious if he were not so happy and prosperous, "But put forth thine hand now and touch all that he hath, and he will curse thee to thy face." Yahweh allows him to be put to the test. "Behold, all that he has is in thy power, only upon himself put not forth thine hand." A series of catastrophes follows. Nomads steal the oxen and asses.

The servants are consumed by fire from heaven. Chaldean raiders take the camels. The sons and daughters are killed in a whirlwind. Job tears his garments and shaves his head, Eastern manifestations of grief, but worships God saying, "The Lord gave and the Lord hath taken away; blessed be the name of the Lord." Dissatisfied, the Satan gains permission to take Job himself, "his bones and his flesh." Job's whole body is afflicted with "loathsome sores" (RSV) which he has to scrape with a bit of broken pottery. His wife urges him to "curse God and die," but he remains steadfastly patient. He is so disfigured that the three friends who come to visit him do not at first recognize him. They tear their garments, sprinkle dust upon themselves and sit with him for seven days (the usual time for mourning) without speaking.

Job's Lament 3. In an anguished lament, Job curses his birth and wishes he had been stillborn. Then he would have been in Sheol, where all alike find peace:

There the wicked cease from troubling;
And the weary are at rest.
There the prisoners rest together
They hear not the voice of the oppressor.

First Cycle of Speeches, 4-14. Eliphaz' Rebuke. Eliphaz speaks courteously, offering the traditional Hebrew answer to the problem of evil. *Suffering is punishment for evil.* "Whoever perished, being innocent?" Job, who has strengthened the weak in the past, should not so easily give way to despair. "Yet man is born to trouble, as the sparks fly upward." If God is chastising him, it is for his own good, and he should commit his cause to God.

Job's Complaint. Job does not now answer Eliphaz directly. He speaks of his isolation and of his disappointment in his friends, saying, "Oh, that my grief were thoroughly weighed" and "To him that is afflicted pity should be showed for his friend." They offer him no affection or sympathy, but speak only cold words and to "one that is desperate." He speaks with anguish of the brevity of life:

> My days are swifter than a
> weaver's shuttle
> And are spent without hope.

In this brief life, God is an ever-present tormentor, who haunts Job even when he is trying to ease himself with sleep, frightens him with bad dreams, and does not even give him time to swallow in peace.

> And why dost thou not pardon
> my transgression
> And take away more iniquity?
> For now I shall sleep in the
> dust;
> And thou shalt see me in the
> morning, but I shall not be.

Bildad's Speech. Impervious to Job's anguish, Bildad reasserts the justice of God, who only casts away the sinner.

> If thou wert pure and upright,
> Surely now he would awake
> for thee.
>
> Behold, God will not cast away
> a perfect man,
> Neither will he keep the evil-doers.

Job's Reply. "How should a man be just with [i.e., before] God?" asks Job. God is all-powerful; he can remove mountains and command the sun; he is elusive, breaking Job with a storm and multiplying his injuries. "He destroyeth the perfect and the wicked...he will laugh at the trial of the innocent." Job longs for a confrontation with God, an accounting at which he would demand justice

fearlessly, an umpire who won't judge between him and God — but God is not man and cannot be brought to count. Why has he fashioned Job with such care, only to destroy him like clay, to pour him out like milk? God seems to be unceasing in his anger toward him, and Job longs for a little peace before his brief life is over.

Zophar's Speech. Zophar is annoyed by Job's presumption and garrulousness. He wishes God *would* speak to Job and tell him how wicked he is. God is inscrutable and cannot be besieged with anger such as Job has shown. If he will put away iniquity and stretch out his hands toward God, he will rest in safety.

Job's Defense. Job replies ironically, "No doubt but ye are the people and wisdom shall die with you." He has, he asserts, his own brand of wisdom which is based on experience, not merely on received dogma. He knows as well as his friends, who are "worthless physicians" (RSV), that God is the creator of all nature and the master of men and nations. "Surely I would speak to the Almighty," he claims, "and I deserve to reason with God." Even if God slays him, he wants to defend himself, arguing that a godless man will not dare to come openly before God, and that if God will hear him, he will be vindicated. Once more he muses on the brevity of life. "Man that is born of a woman is of few days and full of trouble." He is gone as quickly as a fading flower or a shadow. A tree which is cut down can bud again. But "man dieth and wasteth away, yea, man giveth up the ghost and where is he?... If a man die, shall he live again?" Momentarily a note of hope breaks into his bleak pessimism. Perhaps God would hide him in Sheol until his wrath is past, and set a time for remembering him.

All the days of my appointed
time I will wait
Till my change [turn] comes
Thou shalt call, and I will
answer thee
Thou wilt have a desire to the
work of thine hands.

But the hope is brief and soon
destroyed. God prevails against
man and he passes from this earth,
not knowing the fate of his sons
and conscious of only his own pain.

**Second Cycle of Speeches, 15-21;
Eliphaz' Second Speech.** Eliphaz
no longer tries to be polite. In
caustic terms he accuses Job of
undermining religion by his arrogance and blasphemy. He drinks
iniquity as if it were water and
will suffer the fate of all wicked
men to be cast out and stripped
of everything.

Job's Reply. "Miserable comforters
are ye all," replies Job, who feels
that both friends and God have
turned against him. God has torn
him, gnashed his teeth at him,
slashed at him, and given him over
to the ungodly. He asks that his
blood may find no resting place,
so that it may cry out to a witness
in heaven for his revenge. Since
blood (life) belongs to God, he will
be forced to take action. However,
Job soon reverts to deep gloom.
"My spirit is broken, my days are
extinct, the grave is ready for me"
(RSV). He has no past and no future except in Sheol.

Bildad's Second Speech. Bildad
taunts Job for his long speeches
and for tearing at himself in his
wrath. There is no hope for the
sinful man.

Yea, the light of the wicked
shall be put out
And the spark of his fire shall
not shine.

Bildad describes the progress of
the wicked man. He is entrapped,
he suffers terror, he loses confidence and strength, he has no offspring, and finally only the appalling memory of his fate remains.

Job's Reply. "How long will ye
vex my soul and break me in pieces
with words?" Job is wearying of
his friends' attacks, as they are of
his rebellious words. He insists
that God has wronged him and
that he cries out for justice in
vain. His family, his friends, his
servants have all forgotten him, yet
paradoxically he begs his friends
for pity. He wishes his words were
written down, so that succeeding
generations might vindicate him.
Again, he has a moment of faith
that he will be vindicated. "I know
that my Redeemer liveth and that
he shall stand at the latter day
upon the earth." *(Perhaps "Redeemer" should be translated "Vin-
dicator.") The next verse, 26, is
corrupt and obscure, but it seems
clear that Job, who has already
longed for an umpire in court (9:
33) and a witness in heaven, (16:
19), now longs for someone who
will vindicate his honor before God,
or perhaps secure the confrontation
he so much desired.*

Zophar's Second Speech. Zophar,
much troubled by Job's intransi-
gence, tries to show that the wealthy
and powerful get their pleasure
from their riches and power. God
will take away their prosperity and
heaven and earth will rise up a-
gainst their iniquity.

Job's Reply. Job's answer is a re-
futation of the whole doctrine of
retribution. "After I have spoken,
mock on," he begins, and points
out that, contrary to what they
have all been saying, *the wicked
do prosper, keep their possessions,
live to old age in safety and wealth,
enjoy their children. (Some verses
expressing orthodox views have been
inserted here.)* He repudiates belief
in hereditary guilt. He observes

that anyone may "in a moment go down to the grave," and that death is arbitrary, for "one dieth in his full strength being wholly at ease and quiet," while "another dieth in the bitterness of his soul" — "They shall lie down alike in the dust, and the worms shall cover them." The wicked may indeed have an honorable funeral, with a watch kept over his tomb, and a pleasant grave. "How then will you comfort me with empty nothing? There is nothing left of your answers but falsehood" (RSV).

Third Cycle of Speeches 22-31. (Note: as explained in the introduction, the order in this cycle has been disturbed by editors who were troubled by Job's views. There have been many attempts to restore the proper order. The one followed here is that of Samuel Terrien, *Interpreter's Bible*, III, 888.)

Eliphaz' Third Speech. The wise man, says Eliphaz, is profitable, not to God, but to himself. He goes on to list sins for which Job might be punished, the sins of social injustice emphasized by the prophets, neglect of nakedness, thirst, hunger, the widow and the orphan. Eliphaz recommends that Job should humble himself now and make his peace with God; then he will be saved.

Job's Reply. Job pays no attention to these comforting suggestions. He continues his anguished search for God: "Oh that I knew where I might find him, that I might come even to his seat (presence). I would order my cause before him and fill my mouth with arguments." This momentary confidence soon disappears as Job's search fails. He insists that he has been obedient to God, but that now he is terrified in his presence. Yet the wicked go free. Job's catalog of wicked actions includes the deprivations forced upon the poor — hunger, nakedness, cold, thirst. The passage is full of vivid pictures, e.g., of the poor, soaked with rain, clinging to the rocks for shelter. Murder, adultery, theft are the sins of those who "rebel against the light." Through God's power, the wicked survive for a while, but soon "wither and fade like the mallow."

Bildad's Third Speech. Since power and fear are with God, how can a man be righteous before him, asks Bildad? Job thanks him ironically for his help and counsel. Bildad speaks further about the power of God over the earth, the clouds, the moon, the sea. (Some critics think this portion, 25:4-14, is an insertion.)

Job's Reply. Job asserts once more that he will cling to his integrity so long as the spirit of God is in him. The rest of the chapter, 27:13-23, is a conventional picture of the ephemeral prosperity of the wicked which seems to belong to one of the friends. *Ch. 28 is a hymn, in praise of wisdom, of a later date, beautiful in itself but inappropriate here since it is out of key with Job's rebellious, anguished spirit.* Man can successfully mine for gold and silver, but only through God can he find true wisdom.

Job's Final Defense 29-31. In these three poems Job contrasts his past happiness with his present misery and makes a final assertion of his integrity. He thinks first of the past when God preserved him.

When his candle shone upon
my head,
And when by his light I walked
through darkness . . .
When the Almighty was yet
with me,
When my children were
about me.

Then he was respected by young and old; and through him the orphan was blessed, the widow's heart sang for joy, the blind and the lame were helped, the wicked were despoiled of their prey. "My glory was fresh in me," he recalls, "Unto me men gave ear and waited, and kept silence at my counsel."

Now in his present misery, he is mocked by youths whose fathers he despised and even by outcasts who live like animals in the caves and bushes of the wilderness. In his good days he wept for the poor and the unfortunate, but now no one hears his cries for help. He is a companion of jackals and ostriches, his skin blackens and falls off, his bones burn with the heat. *(Much in this chapter is obscure, but the general sense is that Job feels alienated and in pain.)*

The last verse is a quiet and solemn disavowal of sins, sometimes called a *"negative confession." It has some parallels in the Egyptian Book of the Dead and is evidence of the very high ethical standards of the author. In a series of oaths, Job curses himself if he is guilty of any of the sins he mentions.* For example,

If mine heart have been deceived by a woman,
Or if I have laid wait at my neighbor's door;
Then let my wife grind unto another,
And let others bow down upon her.

i.e., let her be a slave. With great vividness of expression, Job claims that he has not looked upon a virgin, he has avoided falsehood and deceit, he has been fair and considerate to his servants, he has shared food and clothing with the poor, he has not been over-proud because of his wealth, he has avoided pagan worship, he has been generous to his enemies and hospit-

able to wayfarers. "Oh that I had one to hear me!" he cries, "Here is my signature. Let the Almighty hear me... Like a prince I would approach him" (RSV).

Speeches of Elihu 32-37. Job's challenge to God at the end of Ch. 31 seems to anticipate the Lord's appearance in Chs. 38-42. But now there is an interruption by one Elihu, who claims to speak because he is more upright than Job. He is a young man, but since his elders have failed, he would like to present his own arguments. *Most scholars agree that Elihu's discourses by a speaker so far unmentioned and in quite a different style are a later interpolation by a poet who had new points to make.* He is also more sympathetic than the previous speakers. He insists that God does have ways of answering men, through dreams or visions, even through suffering itself, which may chasten the sufferer and prepare him for repentance and divine mercy. To Job's complaint that his God is unjust, Elihu replies that God's justice is above human pretensions and that he afflicts both the righteous and the unrighteous. *(This is a contrast to the retribution doctrine of the friends.)* If only the sufferer accepts the affliction in the right spirit, he will learn from it *(a theme common in Sophocles' plays).* Elihu's passages on God's power as displayed in his creation, in lightning and storm anticipate Job's own speeches, but instead of letting creation speak for itself in all its majesty, Elihu tells Job that the crashing of lightning may convey God's wrath at iniquity, the raincloud may bring "correction" or "love" (RSV, 37:13). He concludes:

The Almighty—we cannot find him;
He is great in power and justice,

And abundant righteousness
he will not violate,
Therefore men fear him;
He does not regard any who
are wise in their own conceit.

God's Confrontation of Job 38-42:6.

This should probably follow Job's final challenge at the end of Ch. 31. *God speaks out of the whirlwind, a traditional setting for a theophany.* "Who is this that darkeneth counsel?" he asks, "Gird up thy loins like a man!" But instead of answers to his urgent questions, Job is bombarded with God's questions, beginning "Where wast thou when I laid the foundations of the earth?" God does not pity Job, does not even try to be civil to him, nor does he reproach him for his faults. He announces how he measured the earth at the dawn of creation, "when the morning stars sang together and all the sons of God shouted for joy." He controlled the sea and commanded the dawn, he knows where light and darkness dwell, and the secrets of snow and storm. "Can you bind the chains of the Pleiades, or loose the cords of Orion?" (RSV), he asks, reminding Job of the grandeur of the universe. With further questions, he points out the variety of the animal kingdom, the lion, the raven, the mountain goat, the wild ass, the wild ox, the horse, the hawk, and the eagle. Can Job create, feed, and direct such creatures?

Doth the hawk fly by thy wisdom,
And stretch her wings towards the south?
Doth the eagle mount up at thy command,
And make her nest on high?

He concludes:

Shall he that contendeth with the Almighty instruct him?
He that reproveth God, let him answer it.

Job, who challenged God as a prince, is stunned by the revelation of the creator's power. "Behold," he acknowledges briefly, "I am of small account. What shall I answer thee? I lay my hand upon my mouth" (RSV).

God again speaks to Job from the whirlwind, telling him again to gird up his loins like a man. "Wilt thou condemn me, that thou mayest be righteous?" Evidently he felt that Job was not really convinced, for he speaks next of Behemoth and Leviathan, enormous creatures of the deep, based on the hippopotamus and the crocodile, but described in semi-mythological terms. Behemoth is a sort of Rabelaisian beast who can drink up the Jordan, while the Leviathan's sneezes flash light and his mouth emits flames of fire. The fanciful, grotesque description suggests that God delights in *all* his creation, even in these strange beasts.

In there any comfort in this for Job? Certainly his demands for justice are not met, indeed they are ignored, but so is the God of retributive justice of the friends, who seems utterly puny and unbelievable. God has not, as Job hoped, justified him as a pious man, but he has come to him in person and shared with him the joy and power of his creation. Job acknowledges this.

I know that thou canst do all things,
And that no purpose of thine can be thwarted...
Therefore I have uttered what I did not understand,
Things too wonderful for me, which I did not know (RSV).

Comforted by the majesty of the creator, Job realizes how little he can accomplish and perhaps his claims for vindication seem irrelevant. He has experienced the presence of God.

I have heard of thee by the hearing of the ear,
But now mine eye seeth thee.

Describing himself as nothing, he repents in dust and ashes. *(The word translated "repent" here has connotations of deep sorrow and self-depreciation.)*

Epilogue 42:7-17. Here the folk story resumes. The Lord reproaches the three friends for misrepresenting him and orders them to make burnt offerings. Job is to pray for them, and they will not be punished for their folly. After he has prayed, the Lord restores his wealth and children. His brothers and sisters reassemble to eat with him, and the Lord gives them money and a gold ring. Job receives double the number of sheep, camels, etc., that he had before.

Again he has seven sons and three daughters, Jemimah, Kesiah and Kere-happuch. Their names quaintly suggest beauty: "dove," "cinnamon" and "horn of eye-paint." Job, presumably healed of his disease, lives to a great age and sees "his sons and his sons' sons, even four generations. So Job died, being old and full of days."

Interpretations of the epilogue vary. Some critics regret that the poet retained it, since it contradicts the poem. Job's piety *is* rewarded and the doctrine of retribution *is reaffirmed.* Others point out, however, that Job's reward follows his prayer for his friends, and that he is restored to his true selfhood only after a confrontation with the deity. Few would disagree with the judgment that the book of Job "speaks to our condition" as no other Biblical book speaks.

Psalms

Introduction. The Book of Psalms is an anthology of 150 religious poems. In its present form it is divided into five books, each marked off with a closing doxology. These divisions do not classify the psalms according to author, form, or topic, but are an artificial and late arrangement made in imitation of the five books of the Pentateuch. Psalm I is a prologue to the whole collection and Psalm 150 provides a concluding doxology.

The book as we have it is the work of the post-exile period, but many of the psalms are pre-exile in origin. A number are attributed to David in much the sense that the law is attributed to Moses and wisdom to Solomon. The "sweet singer of Israel" traditionally sang and played, and may indeed have composed psalms, though no one psalm can certainly be attributed to him. "*A psalm of David*" may

mean "*in David's style" or "dedicated to David."*

Our knowledge and understanding of the psalms has been greatly enriched both by archaeological and literary studies in the last half century. Hymns from Egypt, Babylon, Assyria, and Canaan show us that the Israelite psalmists were borrowing both stylistic devices and vocabulary from their neighbors, though they often surpassed them in spirituality and in majesty of expression. "Form criticism," the classification of literature by literary types, was applied to the psalms by the German scholar H. Gunkel and the Norwegian Sigmund Mowinckel. Gunkel (in books published in 1926 and 1933) distinguished *five large categories of psalms: hymns, communal laments, individual laments, royal psalms, and individual expressions of thanksgiving.* His *minor categories* included *pilgrimage psalms, communal songs of thanksgiving, wisdom psalms,* and *liturgies.* Gunkel also showed that the psalms had a vocabulary of their own, in which certain words and phrases constantly recurred. Though he acknowledged that the psalms were used in the Second Temple, he tended to think that the most spiritual psalms had been shaped or reshaped by prophetically oriented individuals influenced by the culture as a whole, more than by temple worship. Mowinckel, who had more temperamental sympathy with ritual, was inclined to stress its influence in the development of the psalms. This was particularly strong in the case of the enthronement psalms, which Mowinckel associates with an annual enthronement festival, along the lines of the Babylonian celebration of the victory of the god Marduk over chaos. Psalm 93, for instance, celebrates Yahweh's enthronement after victory over the chaotic floods. Gunkel and Mowinckel agree, however, in placing the origin of many psalms before, sometimes long before, the Exile. Some historians would place a few psalms as early as the time of David or even earlier.

Before studying the psalms, the reader is advised to review the section on Hebrew poetry in the chapter "Literary Forms in the Old Testament." The devices described there are used in the psalms.

A description of some characteristic psalms follows.

Hymns. These psalms commonly begin and end with praise or a call to praise. Psalm 8, for example, begins and ends with "O Lord our Lord, how excellent is thy name in all the earth," while the verses praise God for his creation of the heaven and of man, who has dominion over nature. Psalm 100 begins with a call for "a joyful noise unto the Lord," and closes

"The Lord is good, his mercy everlasting, and his truth endureth to all generations." The middle reminds us that God made us all; "we are his people and the sheep of his pasture." Other hymns in this category are 103 and 104, both of which begin and end, "Bless the Lord, O my soul." Psalm 150, the last in the collection, praises the Lord for his "mighty acts" and his "excellent greatness," calling on a number of musical instruments to "praise the Lord."

Communal Laments. Good examples are Psalm 60, beginning "O God thou hast cast us off, thou has scattered us," and 74, beginning, "O God, why hast thou cast us off forever? Why doth thine anger smoke against the sheep of thy pasture?" Perhaps the most famous and dramatic is Psalm 137, when the singers gather to weep "by the waters of Babylon," and continue.

How shall we sing the Lord's
    song in a strange land?
If I forget thee, O Jerusalem,
    let my right hand forget her
    cunning.

It ends in a revengeful vein, "Happy be he that taketh and dasheth thy little ones against the stones." Several of these laments express hatred for the enemies of Israel and a longing for their punishment, e.g., "Break their teeth, O God, in their mouth" (Psalm 58); "Pour out thy wrath upon the heathen" (Psalm 79); and "O my God, make them like a wheel; as the stubble before the wind" (Psalm 83). Sometimes the congregation reminds God of his care of them in the past ("Lord, thou hast been our dwelling place in all generations" Psalm 90) and begs him, "Turn us again, O Lord God of hosts, and cause thy face to shine and we shall be saved" (Psalm 80).

Individual Laments. One of the best known of the laments is Psalm 22, as the opening words were quoted by Christ on the cross, "My God, my God, why hast thou forsaken me?" The speaker recalls that God delivered his people in the past, but dwells particularly on his own present anguish. "I am a worm and no man," he claims; he is mocked by all those around him, who deride him for trusting in God. "I am poured out like water, and all my bones are out of joint," he exclaims. "My heart is like wax, it is melted in the midst of my bowels... I can tell all my bones." His enemies are so sure he is near death that they are dividing up his garments. He vows that if he recovers, he will offer a formal thanksgiving "in the midst of the congregation." He finishes with a vision of "all the families of the nations" (RSV) turning to God.

One of the most beautiful personal laments is to be found in Psalms 42-3, *mistakenly divided into two.* The mood and style of both parts is the same, and the refrain beginning "Why art thou cast down, O my soul?" occurs in both. The poem begins with the beautiful image, "As the hart panteth after the water brooks, so panteth my soul after thee, O God" an image full of meaning in a land which is often hot and dusty.

However, water itself could be used as an image of overwhelming despair, as in Psalm 130.

Out of the depths have I cried
unto thee, O Lord
Lord, hear my voice.

Even as he says this, the Psalmist reasserts his faith in forgiveness, and continues,

I wait for the Lord...
My soul waiteth for the Lord
More than they that wait for
the morning.

In God is mercy, for the singer and for all Israel.

Royal Psalms. From the time of Solomon on, the temple and the palace, the rule of God and the rule of the king were closely associated. The king was regarded as God's deputy. He was often crowned at the New Year Festival, and every year his coronation was celebrated at the New Year. Psalms 2, 21, 72, 101, 116, and 132 all relate to this custom. Psalm 72, for example, prays that the new king may judge his people righteously, deliver the poor and the needy, and be victorious over his enemies. It contains the graphic simile, often transferred to God, "He shall come down like rain upon the mown grass." Psalm 110 may have been used at a coronation festival. The Lord invites the king to sit at his right hand (this would probably be spoken by a priest), and the congregation replies. "The people shall be willing in the day of thy power." The king makes his vow and the people respond again, asserting that he is both a priest and a military leader. Other royal psalms are 2, 132, 144.

Thanksgiving Psalms. Most of these psalms look back upon a period of misery and thank God that he has raised his people up. Psalms 30 and 32, for example, are thanksgiving hymns after an illness and were perhaps sung in fulfillment of a vow made during the illness. In 32, the illness is associated with an undeclared sin, which had to be confessed. The writer probably thought of the illness as a punishment for sin. In Psalm 92, the writer praises God's power and steadfast love, which have delivered him from evildoers. Psalms 65 and 67 give thanks for good harvests and are certainly corporate. Psalm 65 describes particularly God's part in the success of the harvest.

Thou visiteth the earth, and
waterest it:
Thou greatly enrichest it with

the river of God, which is full
of water:
Thou preparest them corn,
When thou hast so provided
for it.
Thou waterest the ridges thereof
abundantly;
Thou settlest the furrows
thereof:
Thou makest it soft with
showers:
Thou blessest the springing
thereof.
Thou crownest the year with
thy goodness;
And thy paths drop fatness.
They drop upon the pastures
of the wilderness:
And the little hills rejoice on
every side.
The pastures are clothed with
flocks;
The valleys also are covered
over with corn;
They shout for joy, they
also sing.

Psalm 124 gives thanks that "the
Lord...was on our side," "when
men rose up against us," i.e., in
war.

Our soul is escaped as a bird
Out of the snare of the foulers.

Perhaps the happiest, most exultant of psalms of thanksgiving
is Psalm 136, which has a whole
catalog of mercies to be grateful
for. Every line is followed by a
refrain.

O give thanks unto the Lord
for he is good:
For his mercy endureth forever.

(For "mercy" the RSV translates "steadfast love.") The poet
praises the Lord in detail for his
creation and for his goodness to
Israel throughout history.

**Pilgrim Psalms and Psalms of
Zion.** Two psalms in particular, 84
and 122, are associated with pilgrims to Jerusalem for great festivals. The speaker in Psalm 84 is
often said to be rejoicing on his

arrival at the temple, but both the
elegiac style and some of his statements suggest that for some reason he is unable to go, though he
dearly longs to.

How lovely is thy dwelling place,
O Lord of hosts
My soul longs, yea faints for
the courts of the Lord (RSV).

He envies the birds who can live
there freely.

Yea, the sparrow hath found
a house.
And the swallow a nest for
herself,
Where she may lay her young,
Even thine altars, O Lord
of hosts.

He envies the happiness of those
who go "from strength to strength,
to appear before God in Zion," and
declares, "I had rather be a door-
keeper in the house of the Lord
than dwell in the tents of wickedness." In the end he remembers
that God is "a sun and a shield"
to all who put their trust in him.

Psalm 122 seems to describe the
arrival of pilgrims in the Holy
City. The singer looks back to the
exciting moment when someone
proposed: "Let us go to the house
of the Lord" (RSV). They stand
within the gates and admire the
city, "compact together," symbolic
of the tribes' unity in their worship there. Deeply moved by the
sight, the singer calls on his companions to pray:

Pray for the peace of
Jerusalem:
They shall prosper that love
thee.

Psalm 24 is probably a liturgy
used on entering the sanctuary,
bearing the ark, the symbol of
Yahweh's presence. The procession
moves up "the hill of the Lord,"
they declare that "the earth is the
Lord's." The question is asked, Who
is worthy to enter? The answer
is that only those who have clean

hands and a pure heart (i.e., are clean ritually and morally) may enter. Now those in the procession call on the gates to open. Twice they are asked who the king is, and twice reply:

Lift up your heads, O ye gates
Even lift them up, ye everlasting doors;
And the king of glory shall come in.
Who is this king of glory
The Lord of hosts, he is the King of Glory.

Psalm 46 is a magnificent statement of faith in God who dwells in Zion, who triumphs over earthquake and flood, whose voice can melt the earth, whose command can make wars to cease unto the ends of the earth. The refrain, "The Lord of Hosts is with us, the God of Jacob is our refuge," should close each of the three stanzas; *it is missing after verse three.* The opening line, "God is our refuge and strength, a very present help in trouble," inspired Martin Luther's magnificent hymn, "A Mighty Fortress is Our God."

Wisdom Psalms. These are closely related to other Wisdom Literature; see the introduction to that genre which prefaces the book of Job. The main purpose of these psalms is to teach that obedience to God's laws (by now, identified with wisdom) will bring material reward, a premise sometimes defined as moral optimism. Oversimple as this principle is, the wisdom psalms have a serenity and certainty of their own. *At least two of them (73 and 139) raise the same question which the book of Job raises.*

Psalm 1, which introduces the whole Psalter, is a beautifully neat and elegant exposition of a popular wisdom theme, the contrast between the pious man and the wicked man. It is probably a later addition to the collection.

It consists of two short, artificially balanced stanzas. The first defines the condition of "blessedness" or "happiness."

Blessed is the man
That walketh not in the counsel of the ungodly,
Nor standeth in the way of sinners
Nor sitteth in the feet of the scornful (RSV "scoffers")
But his delight is in the law of the Lord,
And in his law doth he meditate day and night.

The stanza ends with a charming simile, comparing the happy (i.e., pious) man to a tree planted near a stream, which bears green leaves and ripe fruit.

The contrasting stanza begins with a brief statement and another simile:

The ungodly are not so:
But are like the chaff which the wind driveth away.

Their fate is briefly described:

Therefore the ungodly shall not stand in the judgment,
Nor sinners in the congregation of the righteous.

The conclusion is inescapable:

The Lord knoweth the way of of the righteous,
But the way of the ungodly shall perish.

The theme of several other wisdom psalms is the same, notably Psalm 112, where the theme is "Blessed is the man that feareth the Lord, that delighteth greatly in his commandments." Psalm 127 praises obedience to God, a safe home and a large family, and praises the harmonious spirit when "brothers dwell together in unity."

Psalm 73 is different in that it raises the same questions as the book of Job raises. "I was envious of the arrogant," says the wicked, "for they have no pangs; their bodies are sound and sleek" (RSV). Pride is their necklace, violence is their garment, they are fat, scornful, malicious, oppressive. The writer wonders why he has troubled to keep himself pure. Eventually he realizes that their prosperity is only temporary, that they will eventually be set "in slippery places," and they will eventually perish. By contrast he realizes that he is always close to God:

Thou shalt guide me with thy counsel
And afterward receive me to glory.

Psalms of Faith. "They that trust in the Lord shall be as Mount Zion, which cannot be removed, but abideth forever" (Psalm 125). This is the mood of the psalms which express complete confidence in God. "God is our refuge and strength," Psalm 46, discussed under the Psalms of Zion, conveys this trust and confidence. Psalms 11, 16, 62, 129, 131, all are psalms of confidence.

The most beautiful and best loved of all is Psalm 23. The first line, "The Lord is my shepherd, I shall not want," sets the tone and states the theme. The hearers, familiar with shepherd life and shepherd imagery would respond to this credo, which is illustrated in three serene but realistic pastoral scenes. The shepherd leads the sheep to green pastures, has them rest peacefully before they drink from a quiet stream. Thus he restores their soul — their life and vitality "for his name's sake," that is, because he is that kind of leader, one who leads the flock in the safest paths. This is not always possible, and sometimes the sheep must walk in "deep darkness" *(the correct translation of vs. 3a)*. Even so, the sheep do not fear, for the shepherd is armed with a stout club and a staff.

The third stanza describes a meal being prepared, and some commentators picture a Bedouin host welcoming his guests, or even a sacred meal preparatory to a sacrifice. Samuel Terrien, however (in *The Psalms and Their Meaning for Today*, pp. 228-236) maintains convincingly that the pastoral metaphor is maintained in all three stanzas. He interprets the third stanza as a picture of the shepherd preparing the pasture by pulling up poisonous weeds, cutting off thistles and cacti, and getting rid of serpents and scorpions. Sheep who are injured in spite of these precautions are anointed with healing oil and comforted with a soothing mixture of fermented grain, honey and herbs. (Terrien translates the last line of vs. 5 as "my cup is intoxicating.") *Terrien's interpretation has the merit of maintaining the same metaphor throughout and of presenting the shepherd as a healer and comforter as well as a wise, gentle man who cares for his sheep.*

Proverbs

Introduction. A proverb or wisdom saying usually is a short, pithy, two-lined observation on human life. Sometimes these lines are parallel in thought *(synonymous parallelism)*, as in the following:

A good name is rather to be chosen than riches
And loving favor rather than silver and gold.

Or the parallel lines may present a contrast *(antithetical parallelism)*:

A wise son makes a glad father;
But a foolish son is the heaviness
of his mother.

Our book of proverbs also contains poems, short moral essays, prayers, and numerical lists. It is didactic, intended for the teaching of the young. Most of the lessons are cast in verse so that they can be easily memorized.

The book is conventionally attributed to Solomon, but while it is possible that he was a patron of wisdom, most of the material is of a later date. "Men of Hezekiah" (eighth century) are mentioned as copying proverbs of Solomon. There are important foreign influences at work, particularly Egyptian and Phoenician. The religious teaching of the book is not particularly characteristic of Israel, but is more universal. The prophets would have agreed that "the fear of the Lord is the beginning of wisdom," and that wisdom is the gift of God, but there is litle allusion to the temple cult or to Israel's peculiar responsibility as God's chosen nation. Most of the proverbs concern sensible, level-headed behavior, hard work, sobriety, clean living, honesty and prudence in business dealings and in choosing a wife. The familiar wisdom distinction between the wise and the foolish man, so clearly set down in Psalms, reappears here in several texts, e.g.,

Scornful men bring a city into
a snare,
But wise men turn away wrath.

and

Reprove not a scorner, lest he
hate thee,
Rebuke a wise man, and he
will love thee.

The book as we have it consists of four collections and an appendix.

Praise of Wisdom 1-9. This section was probably added last, in spite of its heading, "Proverbs of Solomon." It is intended for the instruction of youth and promises long life if the advice is followed. Parental wisdom and true values, as against material success, are stressed. In two passages Wisdom, speaking as a prophetess, denounces scoffers, promises security and ease to her followers (1:20-33), and proclaims her authority as God's first creation. "Blessed are they that keep my ways," she says, but "he that sinneth against me wrongeth his own soul: all they that hate me love death." (8:1-36). In Ch. 9 wisdom invites her followers to a feast and bids them beware of folly, a harlot who leads men only to death.

First "Proverbs of Solomon" 10-22:11. This is a large collection, mostly of two-line maxims, though a few are longer. They praise the more prudential virtues — diligence, self-control, honesty, good sense; also generosity, justice and kindness to women. Some examples follow:

He becometh poor that dealeth
with a slack hand,
But the hand of the diligent
maketh rich.

The lips of the righteous know
what is acceptable,
But the mouth of the wicked
speaketh forwardness.

A false balance is abomination
to the Lord
But a just weight is his delight.

And a neat and famous proverb:

A soft answer turneth away
wrath:
But grievous words stir up
anger.

There is a whole collection of warnings about women, particularly contentious women. One wonders if one of the philosophers, like Socrates, was afflicted with a nagging wife.

As a jewel of gold in a swine's
snout,
So is a fair woman which is
without discretion.

A virtuous woman is a crown
to her husband,
But she that maketh him
ashamed is a rotteness in
his bones.

Better a dry morsel and
quietness therewith
Than a housewife of sacrifices
with strife.

A continual dripping on a
rainy day
And a contentious woman are
alike (RSV).

Other topics are the blessings of
old age — calm and grandchildren,
the blessings of marriage, and the
blessings of friendship ("There is
a friend that striketh closer than
a brother").

Words of the Wise 22:17-24:34.
*A number of the proverbs here
are based directly on the Egyptian
of Amen-em-Opet who may have
lived before 1000 B.C.* "Have I not
written for you thirty sayings?"
(RSV-KJV mistranslates excellent things) recalls the fact that
Amen-em-Opet's book had thirty
chapters. *Only one proverb here
is not based on the Egyptian original.* The admonitions include "Rob
not the poor," "Make no friendship
with an angry man," "Remove not
the ancient landmark," "Withhold
not correction from a child," and
"Look not upon the wine when it
is red." Wisdom is praised: as
honey is to the taste, so is wisdom
to the soul. A particularly fine
saying is

Rejoice not when thine enemy
falleth
And let not thine heart be glad
when he stumbleth.

**Second "Proverbs of Solomon"
25:1-29:27.** *These are said to be the
ones copied out by Hezekiah's
scribes.* Many of the proverbs in
Chs. 25-27 are not very polished
and some are not even in parallel
form. They often show an interest
in rural life and scenes.

As cold waters to a thirsty soul,
So is good news from a far
country.

As snow in summer and as rain
in harvest
So honor is not seemly for
a fool.

The final chapters are much
more like the first of Solomon's
proverbs. They deal with wise rule,
the care of the poor, avarice, the
treatment of servants. There is a
return to the theme of the contrast
between the good and the wicked,
but now the wicked are seen as
a danger to the righteous.

Appendix 30-31. *It is agreed that
the material in these chapters is
different from the rest of Proverbs,
but its origin is disputed. It may
be Canaanite, Phoenician, or Arabian.* The "words of Agur" at the
beginning of Ch. 30 remind us of
Job in that they assert that God in
his creative power and might cannot be known. This is contradicted
in vss. 5-6 and some interpret the
text as a dialogue between a scept-
ic and a believer. The rest of the
chapter is a miscellany of proverbs, some numerical and some not.
The chapter does contain one famous and charming passage:

There be three things which
are too wonderful for me,
Yea, four which I know not:
The way of an eagle in the air,
The way of a serpent upon
a rock,
The way of a ship in the midst
of the sea,
And the way of a man with
a maid.

The "words of Lemuel" (31:1-9) advise kings not to drink lest they forget the law. The rest of the chapter is an acrostic on the ideal housewife, i.e., each verse begins with a letter of the alphabet. It begins "A good wife, who can find her? She is more precious than jewels, the heart of her husband trusts in her" (RSV). She is hard working and responsible, she rises early to direct her masters, she works late at night, spinning her wool, she makes fine linen and scarlet cloth for her household, she buys property and engages in trade. She is good to the poor, "strength and honor are her clothing," and she is blessed both by her husband and her children. The poem makes a pleasant ending to the book.

Ecclesiastes

Introduction. The title comes from the Greek "ecclesiastes," an attempt to translate the Hebrew "Koheleth," meaning "preacher." Like the book of Job, Ecclesiastes takes off from the Wisdom movement, but challenges its optimism. *It is so unorthodox that it probably would not have been included in the Canon if it had not been attributed to Solomon (vs. 1).* In spite of the fact that the author is called a preacher, the book is not really a sermon, but a rather formless discourse on the inscrutability of God and the transcience of human life. The themes remind many readers of those treated by Omar Khayyam in his *Rubaiyat.* As in *The Rubaiyat,* there are passages of great beauty and eloquence.

Vanity of Vanities 1-4.

Vanity of vanities, saith the
Preacher...
All is vanity.

Generation upon generation lives and dies, but "the earth abideth forever," and "there is nothing new under the sun." The preacher has tried without success to make his mark by planting vineyards and making pools, but gets no pleasure out of it. He tried to understand life, but came to hate it. "All is vanity and a striving after wind" (RSV).

To everything there is a season
A time to be born and a time
to die...
A time to kill and a time
to heal...
A time to weep and a time
to laugh,
A time to mourn and a time
to dance...
A time to love and a time
to hate,
A time for war and a time
for peace (RSV).

These times are appointed by God, and the best man can do is to enjoy life while he can. The preacher considers the injustices of the world and the tears of the oppressed, who have no one to comfort them. Envy and greed are self-destructive. "Better a handful of quietness than two hands full of toil and a striving after wind" (RSV).

Maxims for Living 5-11. Bits of advice for getting through life as well as possible are interspersed with statements about its injustices and its futility. In the house of God, man should listen rather than sacrifice, and pray with few words. Vows to God must be performed. Man comes naked from the womb and can take nothing away. God often gives men wealth or many children, but not the power to enjoy them. A series of maxims in verse follows:

A good name is better than
precious ointment,
And the day of death, than the
day of birth ...
Sorrow is better than laughter,
For by sadness of the
countenance
The heart is made glad (RSV).

and many more in the same vein.
The preacher has seen the right-
eous man perishing in the midst of
his righteousness, while the wick-
ed man is rewarded. This denies,
of course, the doctrine of retribu-
tion, as does "as is the good man,
so is the sinner" (RSV). As the
dead have no reward and are soon
forgotten, the reader is advised,
"Eat thy bread with joy, and drink
thy wine with a merry heart, for
God now accepteth thy works...
Enjoy life with the wife whom ye
love, all the days of your vain
life" (RSV). Perhaps the most eloquent of the comments on the ca-
priciousness of reward and punishment is the following:

I returned, and saw under the
sun, that the race is not to the
swift, nor the battle to the
strong, neither yet bread to the
wise, nor yet riches to men of
understanding, nor yet favor to
men of skill; but time and chance
happeneth to them all.

Ch. 10 contains a number of
verse maxims on wisdom and folly.
The speaker admires wisdom, but
sees that it is easily damaged by

folly. A thought echoed by historians is "Woe to thee, O land,
when thy king is a child." Man must
act, whatever the consequences.
"Cast thy bread upon the waters,"
advises the preacher, though one
cannot tell what will prosper. On
occasion, "Light is sweet, and it
is pleasant for the eyes to behold
the sun"; man may live many
years, but "The days of darkness
will be many" (RSV).

Concluding Precepts 12.

Remember now thy Creator in
the days of thy youth, while the
evil days come not, nor the years
draw nigh, when thou shalt say,
I have no pleasure in them.

The heavens are darkened, ter-
rors abound, old age comes, desire
fails, the pitcher is broken at the
fountain, the dust returns to earth.
"Vanity of vanities, saith the
Preacher; all is vanity."

This seems to be the end of Koheleth's work. An editor comments
that the preacher *(he has forgotten*
that he is supposed to be Solomon)
studied to present his thoughts in
pleasing words. "Of making many
books," he comments, "there is no
end, and much study is a weariness
of the flesh." His final words were
intended to modify the impression
created by the book. He asserts
that "God shall bring every work
into judgment ... whether it be
good or whether it be evil."

The Song of Solomon

Introduction. The true title of this
lovely work is "The Song of Songs"
—i.e., "The most beautiful of all
songs." *The nature of the "Song"*
has been disputed for centuries.
There was opposition to its inclu-
sion in the Canon, because of its
secular content; besides, as in Es-
ther, the name of God is not men-

tioned. The book was explained allegorically as representing the love
between Yahweh and his people.
Hosea had used the marriage metaphor for this relationship, though
to him the bride was a harlot. This
theory was Christianized by supposing that the bridegroom and
bride represented Christ and the

church. *This theory survived until modern times.* A variant of it interprets the book as a dialogue between Christ and the soul. Meanwhile, the theologian Origen, in the third century A.D., described the book as "a nuptial poem composed in dramatic form." The Dartmouth Bible uses headings which suggest a little drama, though the editors state clearly that their purpose is to give a dramatic structure to the book which it does not really have. In the late nineteenth century J. G. Wetzstein, a Prussian consul at Damascus, noticed *similarities between the Song and Syrian wedding festivities;* however, no real relationship can be traced. Another modern theory interprets the books as confused *fragments of a fertility rite* which celebrates the union of a god and a goddess, perhaps **Ishtar** and **Thammuz.** Some scholars accept this view, while others wonder how a basically polytheistic book could have won acceptance into the Canon. *The simplest and most common view is that we have here an anthology of love poems,* perhaps by a number of different authors, romantic, colorful, deeply sensitive to nature and frankly rejoicing in physical love, which Hebrew tradition has regarded as one of the gifts of God. *Some of the poems may allude to ancient myths.*

Maiden's Songs 1:2-8. The maiden longs for her lover's kisses, for his love is better than wine. She says she is sunburnt, dark as the tents of Kedar (of goat's hair), but still beautiful. Her brothers are angry because she has lost her heart to a shepherd lover.

Lovers' Dialogue 1:9-2:17. The youth praises her beauty and her jewels; while she compares him to a bag of myrrh and a cluster of henna blossoms. She herself is like a crocus or a lily. The whole has images which suggest fragrance. The maiden goes on to describe how her lover brought her to the bridal chamber.

> He brought me to the banqueting house,
> And his banner over me was love.

But in the next vss., 5-7, it seems that the maiden is still longing for the moment of consummation; perhaps this is a separate lyric. For the KJV "Stay me with flagons," the RSV translates "Sustain me with raisins," and continues "Refresh me with apples, for I am sick with love." *Both fruits were thought to be aphrodisiacs.* The next lines are explicitly and tenderly erotic:

> O that his left hand were under my head,
> And that his right hand embraced me (RSV).

In the next vss. 8-17, again perhaps a separate poem, the maiden speaks of the delights of love in spring, when her lover, leaping like a gazelle, calls her to come out and enjoy the spring.

> For lo, the winter is past,
> The rain is over and gone.
> The flowers appear on the earth,
> The time of singing has come,
> And the voice of the turtledove
> Is heard in our land
> Arise my love, my fair one,
> And come away.

(This is the RSV, which is more correct than the KJV at several points.) The only danger is from the little foxes who spoil the vineyards. "My beloved is mine and I am his," continues the maiden, "until the day breathes and the shadows flee" (RSV).

Bride's Reverie and a Wedding Procession 3. Either dreaming or day-dreaming, the maiden longs for her lover, rises and looks for him in the streets, finds him and takes him to her mother's house. The second half of the chapter describes a wedding procession, supposedly of Solomon; a litter decorated with silver, gold and purple, is accompanied by sixty men.

Bridegroom's Praise 4:1-5:1
Three or four poems may be combined here. A series of similes is based on familiar scenes. Some of them seem odd to us because the point consists in a single similarity. The girl's eyes are gentle like doves, her hair is black like that of mountain goats, her teeth white like sheep, while her neck is slender like David's tower, and so on. The references to the Syrian mountains in vs. 8 suggest to some scholars a connection with the cult of Adonis. Repeating "my sister, my spouse," *a form of address to the beloved found in other Near Eastern literature,* the bridegroom speaks of her as "a locked garden" (a reference to her virginity) and again associates her with sweet-smelling and sweet-tasting plants, henna, saffron (both with spikenard), pomegranates, frankincense, myrrh, aloes, and with fresh streams flowing from Lebanon. He calls upon the winds to waft these fragrances about, while he eats honeycomb and wine and invites his friends to eat and drink.

Maiden's Dream 5:2-6:3.
In her sleep the maiden hears him knocking, calling "Open to me, my sister, my love." She has undressed and bathed her feet, and her heart thrills as she opens the door — but her beloved has gone. She wanders about looking for him, and begs the women of Jerusalem to tell him that she is sick with love for her beloved. He is very beautiful.

My beloved is white and ruddy,
The chiefest among ten thousand
His head is as most fine gold;
His locks are bushy and black as a raven . . .
His mouth is most sweet,
Yea, he is altogether lovely.

Supporters of the view that the Song is connected with a fertility myth point out that certain lines could describe the statue of a god. For example, in vss. 14-15, the lover's arms are described as "rounded gold, set with jewels," his body as ivory, "encrusted with sapphires," and his legs as "alabaster columns" on gold bases (RSV). However, the mood of pastoral love is soon resumed:

I am my beloved's and my beloved is mine;
He pastures his flock among the lilies (RSV).

Bride's Beauty 6:4-7:9.
Next the bride's beauty is described in much the same terms as in Ch. 4. Now she is said to be more beautiful than queens and concubines, terrible in her beauty "as an army with banners," "fair as the moon and clear as the sun." After a visit to the orchard to see if the vines and pomegranates are blooming, the bride is asked to dance, as was often the custom at weddings. Beginning with her graceful feet, the beauty of her body is described, her rounded thighs, her white stomach, her breasts "like two young roes," her neck like a slender tower, her eyes like pools of water, and her flowing locks "like purple." The lover compares her to a fruitful palm tree and her kisses to the best wine.

Her Reply 7:10-8:14.
She invites him to come to the fields, where she will give him her love. She wishes he could always be close, like a brother, with his left hand under her head and his right arm around her. She begs him to be faithful to her,

For love is strong as death;
Jealousy is cruel as the grave . . .
Many waters cannot quench love,
Neither can the floods drown it.

In Ch. 8:9-10 she seems to boast of her chastity. *The chapter concludes with three fragments*, the last one another invitation:

Make haste, my beloved
And be thou like to a roe or
a young hart
Upon the mountains of spices.

Introduction to Prophecy and the Prophets

Our word prophet comes from the Greek word *prophetas*, which means literally one who speaks for another, especially for a god. This Greek word is a fair equivalent for the Hebrew word *nabi*, which denotes a spokesman — one who speaks for God. While prophets did sometimes make predictions (some of which came true while some did not), this was not their only or even their main function, which was to declare the will of Yahweh to the people. Their concern was not for the distant future but for the present and the immediate future. Other Old Testament terms for them indicate their character: keepers, watchmen, men of God, servants of God, and messengers of God. Their function was to assert moral and religious truths at times of national and spiritual crises. *They performed this function with such honesty, acuteness, and power that much of what they say still has value for us today.*

The great prophets of the eighth, seventh, and sixth centuries — Amos, Hosea, Isaiah, Micah, Jeremiah, Ezekiel — are sometimes called *the reform prophets* or *the classical prophets*. They represent the full flowering of Hebrew prophetic genius. They are the end result of a long period of development of which something should be known if the achievements of the classical prophets are to be understood.

Diviners, Seers, and Prophets. Primitive methods of divination were practiced at early stages of Israel's religious development and survived for a long time among the superstitious. Reading the future from dreams, from the entrails of sacrifices, from games of chance, and from unusual happenings in nature was long practiced by seers or diviners. Sometimes these seers, men who could see things which were lost or hidden from common eyes, would for a small sum of money answer questions. These questions could be quite trivial, as we see in I Sam. 9:1-10:16, where Saul and his servant appeal to Samuel to help them find some asses which have gone astray. Early prophets may have performed some or all of these functions; however, at some point a distinction seems to have been made between "seer" and "prophet," the former being noted for his ingenuity in interpreting signs and dreams, and the latter for his gift in "speaking for Yahweh," perhaps in a state of delirium or ecstasy. Similarly, while both priests and prophets were attached to shrines and temples, a distinction of function was made, so that while the priests taught the religious beliefs, took care of the ceremonies, and operated Urim and Thummim (the sacred lots which gave yes-or-no answers to questions), the prophets commented on current events and pronounced the will of Yahweh through their oracles.

Ecstatic Prophecy. Prophecy was frequently associated with possession by the spirit, a sort of frenzy or ecstasy in which the possessed one babbled unintelligibly, cried out as if mad, and performed weird dances and other strange acts. This possession can still be observed to-day in parts of the Near East and indeed in certain sects in our own country. It is the phenomenon of speaking in tongues, described in the New Testament (Acts 2) and discouraged by St. Paul (I Cor. 14:19). Frequently a whole group was seized by the spirit in this way. A good example of this may be seen in I Sam. where, as was often the case, the ecstasy was assisted by music, for the "sons of the prophets" as they were called, came down from the high place to the music of a harp, tambourine, flute, and lyre, and were joined by Saul, who also prophesied (i.e., spoke ecstatically). On another occasion (I Sam. 19) Saul again was seized by the spirit, spoke ecstatically, and afterward lay naked all day and all night. We must remember that these strange seizures and acts probably authenticated the prophet in the opinions of many onlookers. Several references in the Books of Samuel and Kings suggest that eventually there were large numbers of the "sons of the prophets," apparently living in communities, on occasion under royal patronage, otherwise supporting themselves by begging and by fees received for performing cures and wonders. When Amos says "I am no prophet, nor a prophet's son" (1:14, RSV), he is in all probability dissociating himself from such groups.

"The Prophetic Succession." From time to time there were individual prophets who stood out from the crowd, as it were, and who offered genuine religious and ethical judgments. R. B. Y. Scott (in *The Relevance of the Prophets*) traces what he calls "the prophetic succession" right back to Moses, "a man who knew the presence and the moral will of God as an intense experience, who discerned his summons in current events and situations, and who declared that Yahweh demanded obedience and loyal-ty" (p. 63). His loyalty and obedience was expressed by adherence to the covenant relationship and to the Ten Commandments. Scott demonstrates that many of the classical prophets "believed their message was not new, but was a recall to the essential religion of the formative period of Moses" (p. 64). *He distinguishes four stages in the development of the "succession" after the time of Moses. These stages form four convenient groups in which the history of the Old Testament prophecy may be studied.*

(1) Individual prophets from the time of Samuel (about 1050) to Micaiah (about 850). With the exception of Samuel, who was an important leader, these men made only short appearances, but are important because they show that there really was a succession of responsible prophets side by side with the ecstatic prophets. Examples are Nathan, who reproached David for his slaying of Uriah and his sin with Bathsheba; Gad, Shemaiah, and Ahijah who advised kings in various crises; and Micaiah, who bravely contradicted all the prophets who promised victory to Ahab. These men anticipated the classical prophets in making political and ethical judgments. Also, Nathan anticipated the reform prophets by his use of a prophetic "sign" — tearing his garment to represent the disruption of the tribes.

(2) Elijah and Elisha. Elijah appeared (I Kings 17) when recognition of the Phoenician Baal, a fertility god, was undermining Israel's faith in Yahweh. By asserting that Yahweh withheld his rain, Elijah asserted his power over the fertility of the land. The outcome of his dramatic challenge to the 450 prophets of Baal justified his faith and convinced the people to return their loyalty to Yahweh (notice the ecstatic frenzy of the Baalite prophets, who perform a limping dance, mutilate themselves, and "prophesy" in

vain: I Kings 18:27-9). When the king unlawfully got possession of Naboth's vineyard (Ch. 21), Elijah told him that he had done evil and would be punished. Both in asserting absolute loyalty to Yahweh and in demanding absolute justice, Elijah showed that he understood the spiritual and moral demands of the convenant. In this respect he pointed the way to the reform prophets of the next century. Elisha, who was the servant and follower of Elijah and a leader of one of the groups or guilds of prophets, seems not to have been as striking a figure as his master. The stories which survive about him are largely miracle stories, the product of folk-imagination. He is relatively unimportant in the succession.

(3) In the eighth century begins the great age of Hebrew prophecy. Since each figure will be discussed in relation to his book, they need be only briefly mentioned here. The chronological charts should be studied so that historical background is understood. Amos and Hosea preached in Israel about the middle of the eighth century, followed by Isaiah and Micah in Judah. A whole group of prophets may be associated with the years before the Exile, the Exile itself, and the years that follow: Jeremiah, Zephaniah, Nahum, Habakkuk, and Ezekiel. In some cases the dating is disputed.

(4) Last came the post-exilic, post-classical prophets of the Persian period. The anonymous poet who wrote Isaiah 40-55 must be associated with the period of Cyrus, and Haggai and Zechariah with the rebuilding of the Temple in Jerusalem, c. 520-515. Malachi, Obadiah, and Joel probably fall in the next century. (Jonah and Daniel are not really prophetic books at all; see the introductions to these books.) This late period is characterized by much imitation of early prophecy, often anonymously, and by the reinterpreting and editing of earlier

prophets. There was some original work, besides that of the prophets just named, but much of this was inserted in earlier books, notably the beautiful Servant Songs which are included in the Book of Isaiah as we now have it. Toward the end of the period we can discern a shift to a new kind of writing — apocalyptic — such as we find in the Book of Daniel.

Composition of Prophetic Books. The prophetic books contain four main types of literary material: short, pithy oracles, often in splendid poetry; homiletic addresses, sometimes the work of editors; biographical narratives; and first-person autobiographical passages. These units are often put together rather haphazardly without a modern historian's concern for chronology or pattern. The present-day reader who dips into Isaiah or Hosea may be baffled by them at first unless he has some idea how these books developed into their present state.

The term "writing prophets" as applied to Amos and his successors is probably misleading. These prophets may have written down certain passages, and Jeremiah unquestionably dictated to Baruch when prevented from preaching publicly, but it seems certain that in many cases both prophecies and stories about the prophets were circulated orally. Prophets were speakers; they addressed themselves in speech to the people at large, often on special religious occasions or at times of crises, and when their messages seemed especially relevant. If, as many modern scholars now think probable, many of the prophets were associated with cultic shrines, other members of the cult may have played an important part in preserving the records of the prophecies and of historical events connected with them. Disciples or followers of the prophet who were especially impressed with the oracles may have committed them to memory and passed them on to their own followers in turn. While some passages may have been set down in writing, oral transmission probably predominated. We see in Isaiah 8:16 how that particular prophet committed his message to his followers.

In any case, it is clear that adaptations and alterations were sometimes made to make the prophecies relevant to new situations. Collections of oracles might be combined and so substantial additions might be made to the original material. The outstanding example of this is our present Book of Isaiah, where on the scroll containing the work (already edited) of Isaiah of Jerusalem was copied, in chapters 40-55, the work of an anonymous sixth century prophet whom scholars call Second Isaiah. Still later, a miscellaneous collection of oracles which make up the last ten chapters was copied on to the same scroll. There is no prophetic book which has not been edited and enlarged to some degree in this way. After the time of Zechariah, prophecy became imitative and literary and was in all likelihood written down instead of spoken.

We have said that the chief function of the prophet was to speak for Yahweh, to remind the covenant people of the covenant imperatives. Often they did not succeed in this, and in every generation new voices were needed for the task. Eventually the movement lost its freshness and fervor and trailed off into concern for ritual purity, legalism, and the apocalyptic. Yet the lessons of the greatest prophets still remain today and, as a modern historian has claimed, "the existence of the Old Testament, of the Jewish people, of the Christian Church are posthumous monuments to their greatness." (Gottwald, *A Light to the Nations*, p. 281).

Isaiah

Composition of the Book. The "Latter Prophets" of the Old Testament were copied on four large scrolls, roughly the same length — the books of Isaiah, Jeremiah, and Ezekiel, and the book of The Twelve. It is clear enough that the last of these is a collection or anthology of prophetic material. It is not quite so obvious at first sight that this is true in the case of the other three books, but such in fact is the case. Each contains a nucleus of original oracles and narratives by the prophet who gave the book its title, but each has been reinterpreted, re-edited, and ultimately greatly enlarged. We must realize that the circle of disciples and their followers who carried out this process were not trying to deceive the public, but rather to bring their admired teacher up to date and to make sure that his message would seem clear and relevant to the current audience. It is also important to emphasize that these additions are not necessarily inferior to the original nucleus. Some of the most glorious passages in the whole of the Old Testament are from an anonymous sixth-century prophet whose work happened to be copied on to the scroll which we call the book of Isaiah.

This book as we have it contains sixty-six chapters. Most modern scholars agree that Chs. 40-66 are not by Isaiah of Jerusalem, but reflect conditions of about two centuries later. Chs. 40-55 are usually attributed to a sixth-century prophet whose name is not known, but whom scholars call "Second Isaiah" simply because his work is contained in the same scroll as the oracles of Isaiah. Chs. 56-66 are thought to be a disciple or disciples of Second Isaiah.

However, not all the oracles in Chs. 1-39 are original with Isaiah. Chapters 34 and 35, for example, accord more with the thinking of Chs. 56-66 than with that of Isaiah of Jerusalem, and Chs. 24-27 contain material which is probably even later than Second Isaiah. When we turn to the large collection of oracles on foreign nations, Chs. 13-23, we see that some mention nations, such as the Chaldeans and Medes, which were not prominent in Near Eastern history until long after Isaiah was dead. Most of the important additions will be indicated in the summary. For the reasons given by scholars for thinking these passages are additions, consult a standard commentary.

One of the most important finds in the Qumran caves was a complete text of the book of Isaiah.

Introduction to Chs. 1-39: Isaiah of Jerusalem. Isaiah began his long ministry in 740, the year the great King Uzziah died, and was still active at the turn of the century when Sennacherib besieged Jerusalem. He seems to have had court connections and is sometimes thought because of his elegant style, to have been an aristocrat. That he was a man of the city with great respect for kingship and for civic and religious institutions seems clear. His earlier oracles, in Chs. 1-5, condemn religious dishonesty and disobedience, social injustice, and greed. By the time the youthful King Ahaz succeeded (735), the external political situation was a frightening one. Tiglath-Pileser III had made Assyria a powerful enemy of the little countries of the Near East. His invasion of Israel in 742 may ac-

count for the oracle of doom in Ch. 6. When Pekah of Israel and Rezin of Syria planned an attack on Judah, hoping to replace Ahaz with their own candidate, Isaiah advised him to stand firm, trust Yahweh, be tranquil, and avoid entangling alliances. But this Ahaz was not strong enough to do. Even when Isaiah assured him that Israel and Syria would be overthrown, Ahaz was still afraid. In his fear, he appealed to Assyria — successfully, for Tiglath-Pileser attacked and defeated the alliance. But the net result for Ahaz was that Judah became a vassal of Assyria and even took over some Assyrian religious practices. It was at this point that Isaiah apparently decided to withdraw from his public ministry, put his trust in the faithful remnant, and turn over his oracles for preservation by his disciples, looking toward a future day when perhaps his message would be understood.

It is not quite certain whether Isaiah really remained silent for the rest of Ahaz' reign (735-715). Some scholars think there are references to the fall of Samaria in 722-1. In any case he seems to have been active again after Ahaz died and was succeeded by Hezekiah. (One theory about the Messianic passages in Chs. 9 and 10 is that they were composed for Hezekiah's coronation.) Some of the oracles against foreign nations were composed at this time. Ashdod and other cities revolted against Sargon II about 714-711 B.C. The last period of Isaiah's preaching coincides with the time when the leaders of Judah were seeking an alliance with Egypt. Isaiah disapproved of this "covenant with death," as he had disapproved of overtures to Assyria. But by now Hezekiah was involved in a revolt against Sennacherib of Assyria. In 701 Sennacherib defeated most of the coalition against him. Hezekiah held out as city after city in Judah fell until he was shut up "like a caged bird" in his own city. Finally he had to submit, at a price, to save Jerusalem from destruction. In this crisis Isaiah's faith remained the same. Perhaps Assyria was the rod of God's anger to punish Judah for her misdoings. Perhaps Sennacherib in his turn would fall. Perhaps Jerusalem would survive. Whatever happened, king and people should wait in tranquility, for Yahweh was Lord of history.

Superscription 1:1. This title covers the contents of the original book through the present Ch. 39, and tells us that Isaiah prophesied under Uzziah, Jotham, Ahaz, and Hezekiah.

Short Oracles on Judah and Jerusalem 1-2:5. In a brief introductory poem, Yahweh calls on heaven and earth to witness that his children are rebels who do not really know him.

Next (vss. 4-9), the prophet reproaches the sinful nations that have despised the Holy One of Israel and whose land and cities lie desolate with only a small remnant left.

In his next oracle (10-17) the prophet emphasizes the point that without obedience to the moral code, the outward acts of religion are hateful to Yahweh. Sacrifices, burnt offerings, vain oblations, new moon festivals, even prayer itself weary him when not accompanied by well-doing. "Wash ye, make you clean; put away the evil of your doings from before mine eyes; cease to do evil, learn to do well; seek judgment, relieve the oppressed, judge the fatherless, plead for the widow." Be obedient and you shall prosper; rebel, and you will fall to the sword. The prophet (24-26) laments that Jerusalem, the faithful city, has become a harlot. Yahweh will smelt away her dross and she will be faithful once more.

This group of oracles closes with the beautiful anonymous poem which also occurs in Micah (4:1-4, where there is an additional verse). The nations shall beat their swords into plowshares and their spears into pruning hooks and war shall be no more.

Day of the Lord and Fall of Rulers 2:6-3:15. *(The text is bad.)* Idolaters are condemned. Foolish and proud men shall be humbled and terrified. Food and water will be short in Jerusalem *(this may predict the Assyrian siege)* and people will attack each other. Jerusalem shall be in ruins, and Yahweh will judge Jerusalem and her leaders, for their greed has ground the faces of the poor.

Daughters of Zion 3:16-4:1. The vain and haughty ladies of Jerusalem, with their outstretched necks and wanton eyes, walk mincingly with tinkling feet. For their pride Yahweh will take away their anklets, bracelets and other jewelry, sashes, perfume boxes, rings, and garments. "Instead of sweet smell there shall be stink; and instead of a girdle a rent; and instead of well-set hair baldness; and instead of a stomacher a girding of sackcloth; and burning instead of beauty." The women will long to be protected by such few men as survive. (An eschatological passage follows.)

Yahweh's Vineyard 5:1-7. Introducing his parable in the manner of a ballad-singer, Isaiah sings his friend's song of his vineyard. His friend cleared the land, planted choice vines, and prepared a wine press; but the land yielded only wild grapes. In his disappointment, the owner of the vineyard says he will take away its hedge and wall and make it a wasteland. In the last verse the friend is identified with Yahweh and the vineyard with Judah. Notice the puns in the second part of the verse:

and he looked for justice
(mishpat),
but behold, bloodshed
(mishpah);
for righteousness (sedhakah),
but behold, a cry (se'akah)!
(RSV)

Woes against the Unrighteous
5:8-30. In a series of strongly
worded reproaches, Isaiah inveighs
against greed, pride, hard-hearted-
ness, and religious apathy. First he
attacks those who acquire property
at the expense of others: "Woe
unto them that join house to house,
that lay field to field." Then he
assaults those who drink all day
to the lyre, harp, and flute, but
do not see what the Lord is doing;
those who in their dishonesty cling
to their sins; those who are wise
in their own eyes; and those who
take bribes. (The rest of the chapter seems to belong after 10:4.)

Call of Isaiah 6:1-13. The open-
ing words suggest that Isaiah's account of his vision is retrospective;
perhaps he dictated it or wrote it
down after his failure in 734 to
persuade Ahaz to trust Yahweh
made the prophet decide to stop
preaching for a time, collect his
various oracles, and add this and
subsequent passages to explain and
authenticate his work.

The passage is one of matchless
beauty and power. The vision evidently comes to Isaiah as he stands
in the Temple, perhaps in his cap-
acity as one of its prophets. Suddenly he is intensely aware that
God is present. Isaiah does not try
to describe him, but conveys a presence of majesty and holiness. God
is on his throne and his train fills
the Temple. The six-winged sera-
phims fly above him (RSV) and
sing "one ... to another" (i.e., anti-
phonally). The smoke of the Temple incense seems like the cloud of
God's glory, and his power shakes
the threshold. Suddenly Isaiah
realizes that he and the commun-

ity of which he is a part are unclean. But a seraph cleanses his
lips with a burning coal, and when
Yahweh asks, "Whom shall I send,
and who will go for us?" the prophet replies, "Here am I; send me."
Then comes the warning that the
mission will be a discouraging one.
The people will be dull-witted, un-
perceiving, unhearing, unresponsive
— "until cities be wasted without
inhabitant, and the houses without
man, and the land be utterly desolate."

Confederacy of Syria and the
Two Signs 7:1-8. Rezin, king of
Syria, and Pekah, king of Israel,
threaten Judah. Fearing a siege,
King Ahaz goes to inspect the
city's water supply, and there
Isaiah, together with his son Shear-
jashub ("a remnant shall return"),
confronts him. The message of
Yahweh is "Take heed, and be
quiet; fear not, neither be faint-
hearted for the two tails of these
smoking firebrands," that is, Rezin
and Pekah. Their plans will fail.
"If ye will not believe, surely we
shall not be established." But Ahaz
evades the issue and will not ask
for a sign. Nevertheless, Isaiah announces the sign; a maiden shall
bear a child, who shall be called
Immanuel ("God with us"), but
before the child is old enough to
tell good from evil, the land whose
kings are now such a source of
terror to Ahaz will be deserted.

Isaiah next prophesies that Yahweh, as Lord of history, will bring
an invasion. The land will suffer
and the people will be very poor.

At Yahweh's behest, Isaiah
gives his next child another symbolic name, Maher-shalal-hash-baz
("speed-spoil, haste-prey"). Before
the child can say "father" or
"mother," the riches of Israel and
Syria will be taken away. Moreover, temporizing with Assyria will
be dangerous, for like a flood she
will cover the land of Judah. Yahweh is the only true sanctuary.

(Ahaz did not become the man of faith Isaiah hoped for. He turned to Assyria, paid homage to Tiglath-Pileser, and set up an Assyrian altar in Jerusalem. It seems to have been at this point that Isaiah decided to give up prophesying publicly and to write down his oracles until they should be attested.) "Bind up the testimony," directs the prophet, "seal the law among my disciples. And I will wait upon the Lord... and I will look for him." (Two brief fragmentary oracles follow.)

The Messianic King 9:1-12:6.

Two passages describing the coming Messiah are interrupted by a collection of oracles. It is disputed whether or not the Messianic passage in Ch. 9:1-6 is by Isaiah and whether or not it describes a real or ideal king. Traditionally it has been applied by Christians to Jesus of Nazareth, called the Messiah or the Anointed One, and this association has been reinforced by Handel's *Messiah* and by the reading of this passage in churches on Christmas Day. While Jesus certainly taught justice and righteousness and some phrases seem to fit him well, it has been objected that he never aspired to be a political ruler such as seems to be intended here. A recent explanation is that the oracle was written for the enthronement of a king. There seems to be no very cogent reason for denying that it is by Isaiah or by a disciple of his. "The people that walked in darkness have seen a great light." The nation rejoices because the rule of the oppressor is broken, the soldiers' boots and the bloody garments of war are no more, and a marvellous king has come. "His name will be called Wonderful Counsellor, Mighty God, Everlasting Father, Prince of Peace."

The oracles in 9:8-10:34 seem to be mostly connected with the Assyrian invasion. Judah should take warning from the disasters which have overtaken Israel. Assyria is God's rod against fatherless nations, but is not aware of it. The remnant of Israel will be destroyed as in a forest fire. A remnant will return, "even the remnant of Israel, unto the mighty God." Zion should be brave, for Yahweh's anger will not last forever and the inhabitants are still His people. God, like a woodsman, will "lop the bough with terror... and the haughty ones shall be humbled."

The description of the Messianic kingdom (11:1-16) should be studied with 9:1-7. From the house of Jesse (i.e., the Davidic family) shall come a new shoot, a new monarch, "And the Spirit of the Lord shall rest upon him, the spirit of wisdom and understanding, the spirit of counsel and might, the spirit of knowledge and of the fear of the Lord." He will judge with discernment, with wisdom and authority and with a sense of justice. His reign shall be peace. "The wolf also shall dwell with the lamb, and the leopard shall lie down with the kid; and the calf and the young lion and the fatling together; and a little child shall lead them." No dangerous creature shall hurt another, "for the earth shall be full of the knowledge of the Lord, as the waters cover the sea." (Vss. 10-16 were almost certainly added later.) God will bring back the remnant from the far corners of the earth.

Two short thanksgiving psalms (12:1-6) have been inserted here to round off this section.

Oracles against Foreign Nations 13:1-23:18.

A number of these are probably by Isaiah, but some are not. The doom of Babylon is from a later period when Babylon is in danger from the Medes. Most of Ch. 14 consists of a dramatically effective taunt on the overthrow of a tyrant. The chapter concludes with two short oracles of doom by

Isaiah, one (vss. 14-27) affirming God's lordship over history and predicting the downfall of Assyria, and the other (28-32) dated in the year of Ahaz' death (715), warning the Philistines that they are in danger from Assyria (the smoke from the north of vs. 31). A long doom against Moab, of uncertain date, follows in Chs. 15 and 16. With Ch. 17:1-6, we are back with Isaiah again, probably in 734, when Judah was in danger from Israel and Syria. The prophet declares that Damascus will become a desolate heap of ruins and that "the glory of Jacob shall be made thin." The rest of the chapter deals with pagan worship of the Asherim (poles or idols representing the goddess Asherah) and of Adonis, a dying and rising fertility god, concluding with a brief analogy between swift storms and swiftly changing events. The splendid doom on Egypt which follows (18:1-7) may well be from Isaiah's own hand. Several other oracles of uncertain date, mostly in Egypt, take us through Ch. 20. After Sargon's underling took Ashdod, God told Isaiah to walk naked and barefoot like a prisoner of war, as a sign that the Assyrians would lead the Egyptians captive. Pronouncements of doom on Babylon (probably c. 540 B.C.), Dedan, and Kedar (Arabian tribes), a reproach against thoughtless carousing when an invasion threatens, a curse on a royal official, and a doom on Tyre and Sidon conclude this collection of oracles.

Eschatological Pieces 24:1-27:13. This collection of eschatological prophecies, interspersed with psalms and prayers, comes from the post-exilic period. Certain apocalyptic motifs occur, such as the feast for all nations, the overthrow of the dragon, the punishment of the rebel "host of heaven," the resurrection, and the judgment, but many apocalyptic features, for example, bizarre symbolisms, elaborate calculations with dates and numbers, and the trick of attributing the writing to earlier authors, are lacking.

The first poem describes withering, desolation, and mourning of the earth as a result of the breaking of the covenant, appended to which is a short song of rejoicing. After a fragment on the fear of the day of the Lord, the violent shaking of the earth, like a drunkard, and the imprisoning of hosts of heaven and kings of earth, the confounding of sun and moon, and the final triumph of the Lord are described. A thanksgiving for the fall of a fortified city is followed by a prophecy that the Lord will hold a feast of wine and fat things for all peoples: "he will swallow up death for ever, and the Lord God will wipe away tears from all faces" (cf. Rev. 21:4 and the final lines of Milton's *Lycidas*). A short doom on Moab which compares that country to a man floundering in a dung pit precedes two linked psalms, one of which celebrates a triumph over a lofty city, while the other is a psalm in which the author expresses his yearning for Yahweh and his faith in his power, even to the resurrection of the dead. The ancient myth of the struggle with "that crooked serpent" Leviathan, "the dragon that is in the sea," is the subject of a short piece which describes how Yahweh will slay him with a "great and strong sword." Isaiah's parable which speaks of Judah as Yahweh's vineyard provides an idea for a short poem in which Yahweh declares his willingness to defend his vineyard from thorns and briars. In the future "Israel shall blossom and bud, and fill the face of the world with fruit." After a confused fragment about Israel's guilt and suffering, this whole eschatological collection ends with the image of the Lord as the great Thresher of the harvest. "And in that day the Lord shall beat off from the channel of the river unto the stream of Egypt, and ye shall be gathered one by one, O ye children of Israel. And it shall come to pass in that day that the great trumpet shall be blown and they shall come which were ready to perish in the land of Assyria, and the outcasts in the land of Egypt, and shall worship the Lord in the holy mount of Jerusalem."

Isaiah's Oracles against Israel and Judah 28:1-32:20.

Most of the material in this section is genuinely by Isaiah and the greater part of it is usually thought to have been written in the closing years of his career, when he tried to persuade Hezekiah not to join the anti-Assyrian revolt. However, the first oracle is probably earlier, since it seems to be before the siege of 724-721. Some verses describing the quickly fading beauty of Samaria are now applied to Jerusalem. Isaiah says that the rulers of Judah, even priests and prophets, "stagger with strong drink" (RSV) and "err in vision" — i.e., perhaps give bad political advice. They reply that he is talking to them as if they were children, but are told that in an alien tongue they will be reproved for not reposing in Yahweh (there are obscurities in the passage) and that they may "go, and fall backward, and be broken, and snared, and taken." Once again the prophet addresses the scoffers who have, he says, made a pact with false gods, and hence a covenant with death. But justice and righteousness will "sweep away the refuge of lies," and the covenant will be annulled.

The attractive parable of the farmer (28:23-29) makes the point that Yahweh has a purpose and is wise and orderly in carrying it out. As the farmer sows each crop in the most appropriate manner and threshes or treats dill, cumin, and grain by whatever method

works best for each particular seed, so Yahweh may be trusted to care wisely for his people.

"Woe to Ariel" (i.e., Jerusalem, 29:1-8) perhaps belongs to 701 when Jerusalem was in fear of the Assyrians under Sennacherib. The city will be besieged and will be like a man lying in the dust and speaking only in a whisper. Yahweh will come with his terrible storm, but suddenly the nations who threaten Mount Zion will disappear as a dream passes.

In a short passage, 29:9-12, Isaiah reverts to the provision made at the time of his call (Ch. 6) that his hearers would hear but not understand, see but not perceive. "Stupefy yourselves ... blind yourselves .. be drunk but not with wine," he cries, "for the Lord has poured out upon you a spirit of deep sleep," so that the prophet's message is like "a sealed book." Following this are two brief poems (vss. 13-17). In the first, Isaiah pokes fun at worshippers who unthinkingly mouth the correct words and reminds them that the Lord can and will do marvellous things. In the second, he reproaches schemers — perhaps those who were putting out feelers for an Egyptian alliance — who hide their schemes from Yahweh and his prophet. The chapter closes with two eschatological passages.

Most of the next group of oracles are concerned with the Egyptian alliance. In the first (30:1-7), Isaiah, speaking for Yahweh, rebukes the rebellious children who carry out their own plan, not his. "Therefore shall the strength of "Pharaoh be your shame, and trust in the shadow of Egypt your confusion." God tells Isaiah to write his oracles in a book that they may be a witness to the future. We are reminded of a previous occasion, during the attack from Israel and Syria, when Isaiah turned over his prophecies to be preserved by his disciples; see Ch. 8. If only pursues Yahweh, the people would trust the Holy One of Israel; "In returning and rest shall ye be saved; in quietness and in confidence shall be your strength: and ye would not." Here an editor, at vs. 18, has inserted a plea to the people who are suffering to wait patiently, for they will be shown the way. The concluding prophecy of the chapter is that "through the voice of the Lord shall the Assyrian be beaten down." "Woe to them that go down to Egypt for help" is the theme of the next oracle (31:1-3). The schemers are reminded that "the Egyptians are men, not God." A confused passage follows, the gist of which seems to be that Yahweh will protect and deliver Jerusalem — evidently in 701.

A splendid picture of ideal kingship (32:1-8) may or may not be by Isaiah. The righteous king will be "as the shadow of a great rock in a weary land." Eyes and ears will be alert, and folly, knavery, and nobility will be seen for what they are. Next (vss. 9-14) the speaker, perhaps now Isaiah himself, rebukes women, not the fashionable women this time (as in Ch. 3), but unthinking, overconfident girls who dance at the harvest festival, not realizing that the harvest will fail and the city be deserted. An eschatological passage which anticipates the pouring out of the "Spirit...from on high" has been linked to the oracle on women.

A Liturgy 33:1-24. Chs. 33 through 35 differ from Isaiah proper in subject matter and style. The liturgy in this chapter is perhaps recited by the prophet-author during the services of worship. The opening "Woe to you destroyer... you treacherous one" is directed against an unnamed enemy, perhaps during the Maccabean struggle. A prayer for salvation is followed by a promise that God will be the deliverer. Further lamentations about the state of the land — "the highways lie waste, covenants are broken, the land mourns" — are answered by the repetition of promise. The heathen nations "shall be as the burnings of life," even the wicked of Israel will be destroyed, the Lord is the King who will save, and Zion will be "a quiet habitation."

Two Eschatological Psalms. 34:1-35:10. The first is a vivid and carefully planned poem on the theme of God's vengeance. The nations and the whole of the earth are called to witness God's wrath against the heathen and specifically against Edom. "The sword of the Lord is filled with blood," and there is great slaughter of lambs, goats, oxen, and bulls. Edom will "become burning pitch" and the land will be taken over by birds of prey, thorns, nettles, thistles, and supernatural creatures. This is the Lord's command and is written in his book.

In complete contrast with this terrible picture is the glorious and moving psalm describing the new Eden which God in his heaven will create and the joyful return of the exiles. "The wilderness and the solitary place shall be glad for them; and the desert shall rejoice, and blossom as the rose. It shall blossom abundantly, and rejoice even with joy and singing." The prophet is told to comfort and encourage the weak and fearful, for God is coming to save them. The feeblest and most helpless of the exiles will be renewed. "Then the eyes of the blind shall be opened, and the ears of the deaf shall be unstopped. Then shall the lame man leap as an hart, and the tongue of the dumb sing; for in the wilderness shall waters break out, and streams in the desert." Where the desert was there will be pools and springs, reeds and rushes. A special high-road will be prepared for the pilgrims returning to Zion, and it shall be called "the way of holiness," safe for all wayfarers and leading to the holy city. "And the ransomed of the Lord shall return, and come to Zion with songs and everlasting joy upon their heads; they shall obtain joy and gladness, and sorrow and sighing shall flee away."

Invasion of Sennacherib 36. King Sennacherib of Assyria captures all the fortified cities of Judah. The Assyrian armies come to Jerusalem, where their commander talks with several high Jewish officials. He tells them to tell Hezekiah that his plan to depend on Egypt for military assistance is doomed to fail, and he offers the Jews a chance to be reconciled with Assyria. If they refuse to pay tribute, then they face disaster at the hands of the Assyrian armies.

Judah Delivered 37. When Hezekiah hears the Assyrian message he is overcome with despair, and he sends to Isaiah for counsel. Isaiah says that the king should not lose heart, because the Lord will defend Israel. The Assyrians renew their threats against Jerusalem, saying that it is foolish to trust in Yahweh. Other nations have trusted in their gods and they have been defeated; the same will happen if the Jews do not come to terms. Hezekiah prays to the Lord to smite Sennacherib. Isaiah again relays the Lord's word, saying that indeed he will defend his people. Then "the angel of the Lord" kills 185,000 of the Assyrian soldiers (perhaps an epidemic broke out in the Assyrian camp), and the remaining forces retreat to their own land.

Hezekiah's Sickness 38. Hezekiah falls deathly ill, and Isaiah tells him that he is about to die. The king prays, asking the Lord to remember that he has been faithful to him. His prayers are granted, and he is given an additional fifteen years to live. The sign that his prayers have been heard is that the sun is reversed in its course by ten degrees.

Hezekiah Receives Envoys from Babylon 39. The son of the king of Babylon sends envoys to Hezekiah to express his joy that the king has recovered from his illness. Hezekiah shows the envoys all the treasures of his palace and of the Temple. Isaiah asks him the identity of his visitors and what he has shown them. When Hezekiah tells him, the prophet replies that the result of his action will be that all the royal treasures, along with the royal family, will pass to Babylon.

Introduction to Second Isaiah. "Second Isaiah" is the name given by many scholars to the anonymous author of Chs. 40-66 of the Book of Isaiah. Other scholars, however, believe that these chapters are the work of several hands, and that it is only Chs. 40-55 (with the exception of certain passages) that can definitely be assigned to Second Isaiah, with the other chapters sometimes thought to be the work of his disciples, sometimes collectively called "Third Isaiah."

Second Isaiah was more than a prophet — he was a very great poet who was able to put his joyous visions of Israel and her future into poetry which some consider to be the greatest in the entire Old Testament. His message was very different from that of First Isaiah, and for good reason. In the 200 years or so that separate the two prophets, circumstances had changed radically for the Hebrews. Whereas First Isaiah wrote before the Babylonian Captivity, when the Israelites still lived in Judah under their own king, Second Isaiah wrote during the Exile, after Israel's punishment had been dealt out to her. Consequently, unlike First Isaiah, he had no need to warn the people of the penalties they pay if they transgress. The nation had already expiated its sins, and Second Isaiah comes not to chastise but to comfort and encourage. God is to turn to the Hebrews in the spirit of forgiveness, and once again gather his people to him and restore them to their homeland. The note of hope which runs throughout Second Isaiah can be better understood against the background of the political events of the time. Chief among these was the imminent accession of the Persians, and of their great king, Cyrus, to supremacy in the Near East (culminating in the fall of Babylon in 539 B.C.). The Hebrews hailed Cyrus as sent by God to deliver them, as he was indeed to do (see Ezra and Nehemiah). Cyrus was an extremely benevolent king, whose goodness was all the more extraordinary when compared to the evil perpetrated by most conquerors of the time. And although his humaneness had not yet been demonstrated on a large scale, the quality of the man was evident; as he rose, so did the hope of the Israelites. (Some scholars feel that Second Isaiah wrote immediately after the Persian capture of Babylon, rather than during Cyrus's rise to power.) Perhaps the most well-known part of Second Isaiah is what has come to be called the "Servant" poems. Their fame is due not only to their exceptional beauty but also to the fact that Christianity has seen in them an Old Testament prophecy of the coming of Christ. The traditional Jewish interpretation sees the Servant as the Hebrew nation, Israel. Scholars do not agree on whether these poems are the work of Second Isaiah or a later addition to the book.

The Lord's Comforting Words to Zion 40. The first words of Ch. 40 sound the keynote of Second Isaiah: "Comfort ye, comfort ye my people, saith your God." He speaks to the people, wretched in their exile, and tells them that God will relent in his harshness toward them. A new day is dawning, one in which the Lord will once again favor his people. Most of Ch. 40 is a hymn of praise to the greatness of the Lord. There is nothing that can compare to his greatness and majesty.

God's Assurance to Israel 41:1-20. God, speaking in his own voice, reassures the people that he is with them: "... thou, Israel, art my servant ... I have chosen thee, and not cast thee away. Fear thou not; for I am with thee; ... for I am thy God: I will strengthen thee ..."

The Lord's Challenge to False Gods 41:21-29. The Lord challenges the false gods of the surrounding nations to show their divinity or else be scorned. The obvious implication is that they cannot meet such a challenge, and the chapter concludes with the statement that the other gods are "all vanity; their works are nothing: their molten images are wind and confusion."

The Lord's Servant 42:1-9. Here is introduced for the first time the ambiguous figure of the Lord's (suffering) Servant. The chapters in which he occurs have been used by Christians as evidence that Christ (who is identified with the Servant) is the fulfillment of Old Testament prophecy. Nevertheless, it is not at all clear who or what the Servant is or is supposed to be. Sometimes he seems to be a man (perhaps the prophet?), sometimes the nation of Israel. Some scholars believe that the passages concerning the Servant are parts of a longer work about him which somehow have been included in Isaiah.

Here he seems to be a prophet: "I have put my Spirit upon him: he shall bring judgment to the Gentiles."

Praise for the Lord's Mighty Deliverance 42:10-25. Now the prophet tells the people to praise the Lord for the mighty manner in which he will deliver them from their bondage. The tone changes as Israel is rebuked for having been deaf and blind to the Lord's voice.

The Lord the Only Redeemer 43, 44. Now, however, all that is changed. The Lord has heard the pleas of his people, and he will answer them: "O Israel, fear not: for I have redeemed thee." The Lord reiterates to the people that he is the only Redeemer, the only source of salvation. Even though Israel has wandered from the true path, the Lord freely wipes out the nation's sins and once more takes his people to him. He is the One, the Only, the all-powerful. Ch. 44 closes with still another statement that the Lord is omnipotent and that Israel owes everything to him.

Commission to Cyrus 45:1-7. The Lord announces that he has given dominion over the world to Cyrus, the emperor of Persia. (This is one of the two mentions of Cyrus, part of the evidence that Second Isaiah lived considerably after (First) Isaiah of Jerusalem, for whom the threat was the Assyrians, and for whom the Persians do not even exist.)

The Lord the Creator; the Lord and Babylon 45:8-47:15. The remainder of Ch. 45 is a hymn of praise to the majesty of the Lord, and especially of him as creator of the entire world. He is the center of righteousness; there is none besides him. Babylon has looked to its own gods instead of to

Yahweh, and consequently Yahweh has judged her. No more will she be supreme among nations in power. Her time has come, and she is to be toppled from her eminence (by the Persians, under Cyrus).

Israel's Unfaithfulness Rebuked 48. Israel has been obstinate and has persistently strayed from the path of the word of God; therefore she has been punished severely. Had she not sinned, her place would have been "as a river, and [her] righteousness as a sea." Nevertheless, for all their mistakes, the Lord has redeemed his people, and they may now look forward to returning to their homeland.

Israel the Lord's Servant: the Restoration of Zion Promised 49. Israel, the Lord's servant, shall once again arise and be the object of respect in the eyes of the nations. For the Lord has returned to his people, and will restore them to their now devastated homeland.

The Lord Helps Those Who Trust in Him 50. Trust in the Lord will be rewarded: "Who is among you that feareth the Lord, that obeyeth the voice of his servant...let him trust in the name of the Lord, and stay upon his God."

Words of Comfort to Zion 51:1-52:12. The prophet calls to those among his people who are seekers after righteousness to hearken to him. They must lift up their eyes to the heavens. It is time to awake, to gather strength, for the Lord has redeemed his people. No longer will Israel be forced to drink from the cup of affliction. Her tribulations have come to an end, and now her redemption is at hand. For now the Lord will deliver Zion from her enslavement: "Shake thyself from the dust; arise and sit down, O Jerusalem: loose thyself from the bands of thy neck, O captive daughter of Zion." It is time to "break forth into joy... For the Lord hath comforted his people, He hath redeemed Jerusalem."

Suffering of the Lord's Servant 52:13-53:12.

This passage is another of the "Servant" poems. It sets out, in very affecting language, the trials of the Lord's servant. The servant "is despised and rejected of men; a man of sorrows, and acquainted with grief." He is said to "have borne our griefs, and carried our transgressions." The servant was "oppressed," but he does not complain; he is a lamb brought to the slaughter. Jesus and the writers of the gospels knew the Book of Isaiah well, and especially this chapter; the language describing the servant has been used time and again to describe Christ. Of course, Second Isaiah knew nothing of Christ and was probably describing the sufferings of his people. The servant is nowhere said to be the Messiah.

The Lord's Everlasting Love for Israel 54.

Here is another statement that Israel is to be restored to its homeland. The people's relation to God is likened to that between a wife and her husband. The people are a widow that the Lord has come to marry and raise up. His love is constant and will never change or depart.

Mercy for All 55.

The Lord is merciful, and his mercy is infinite. The Lord is near at hand; seek him and he will slake your thirst with the waters of his mercy.

Rewards for Those Who Keep God's Covenant 56.

The Lord says that those who keep his covenant will be rewarded with his blessing, and in the immediate future: "My salvation is near to come, and my righteousness to be revealed." This is another reference to the restoration of the homeland to the exiled nation.

Condemnation of Israel's Idolatry 57.

The righteous man shall be saved — but what of the evildoer? What will his fate be? The Lord says that he rejects such a man, he who "hast lied, and hast not remembered me." God is always ready to pardon, but those who remain mired in their evil will be punished: "There is no peace, saith my God, to the wicked."

Observance of Fasts and Sabbath 58.

The people complain that they have fasted as a token of their repentance and yet the Lord does not hear their pleas. The Lord replies that their fasting was a sham because it was not done sincerely. In fact, says the Lord, "ye fast for strife and debate, and to smite with the fist of wickedness." This is not what fasting is supposed to be, and therefore it is to no avail. If, however, the people wish to have their fasting mean something to the Lord, then they should "draw out [their] soul to the hungry, and satisfy the afflicted soul"; that is, they should acompany their fasting with some concrete good action to show that their hearts are in what they are doing. Then the Lord will accept the fasting and reward those who fast. Similarly it is with the Sabbath; to find favor with the Lord, one must honor the Lord on the Sabbath and not devote the day to the pursuit of one's own desires and pleasures.

Confession of the National Wickedness 59.

Isaiah looks about him and describes the evil that is widespread in the land. There is no justice to be had; everyone is engaged in the pursuit of evil ("iniquity"). In such a state, living lives completely opposed to the word of God, we can expect no help from him. The Lord is displeased that things are as they are. Isaiah reminds the people that the Lord will provide a champion of justice and righteousness.

Future Glory of Zion 60. Once again the prophet returns to his theme of the coming restoration of the people and their return to Zion. The Lord shall "make of thee [the people] an eternal excellency, a joy of many generations." Israel shall come into a life of peace and prosperity (18). The Lord shall resume his place as the source of light for the nation, and the nation will be exalted. And all this coming soon: "A little one shall become a thousand, and a small one a strong nation: I the Lord will hasten it in his time."

Good Tidings of Salvation 61-62. The Lord has told Isaiah to "preach good tidings unto the meek; he hath sent me to bind up the broken-hearted, to proclaim liberty to the captives ... to comfort all that mourn." Once again the prophet tells the people to be happy because the great day is here. The Lord is about to right the balance and return Israel to the position it should occupy among the nations. Zion shall no longer be forsaken. Jerusalem will once again be the shining place it once was. The Lord has proclaimed: "Say ye to the daughter of Zion, behold, thy salvation cometh."

Lord's Vengeance 63:1-6. The prophet has a vision of the vengeance of the Lord in the form of a man whose clothes are stained red. The prophet asks the man how his clothing came to be this color, and God's vengeance replies that the redness is from treading the winepress of the Lord's wrath: "I will tread them [the enemies of Israel] in mine anger, and trample them in mine fury; and their blood shall be sprinkled upon my garments, and I will stain all my raiment. For the day of vengeance is in mine heart, and the year of my redeemed is come."

The Lord's Kindness to Israel 63:7-14. Isaiah speaks of the love and kindness God displayed toward Israel. But then Israel strayed from his way and fought against him; naturally, this rebellion caused him to punish his people. But then he remembered Moses and the days of old; his heart softened towards them, and he redeemed them once more.

Prayer for Mercy and Help 63:15-64:12. The prophet prays that the Lord restore the nation to its homeland (its "inheritance"). He beseeches the Lord to descend to earth and show himself, in his full power and majesty, to his enemies. The people realize that they are only sinners, and they abase themselves before the greatness of God. Isaiah begs the Lord not to be angry too much longer, and to remember the devastation of Zion and Jerusalem. He finishes by asking "Wilt thou refrain thyself for those things [Zion and Jerusalem] O Lord? wilt thou hold thy peace, and afflict us very sore?"

Punishment of the Rebellious 65:1-16. Isaiah describes what Israel looks like to the Lord. He sees men disobeying his commandments on every hand and he is greatly angered. He is tempted to destroy it but reconsiders because there does exist a small group who are truly his servants. These people will he elevate, and these people will he install in Palestine. But that great multitude who deny the Lord, they shall be annihilated.

New Heaven and New Earth 65:17-25. The Lord says that he is creating a new heaven and a new earth, ones which will make those now existing seem pale by comparison. (That is, the new order that the Lord will establish in Zion will be as different from the present life in exile as night from day.) In this new world there will be no sickness or evil or injustice. This utopian vision concludes: "The wolf and the lamb shall feed together, and the lion shall eat straw like the bullock . . . They shall not hurt nor destroy in all my holy mountains, saith the Lord."

The Lord's Judgments and Zion's Future Hope 66. The Lord promises that those who have trusted in him and followed his way will be vindicated, and that those who have departed from his way will be punished. To the righteous he holds out joy; they are to return to Zion. They are to inhabit the new earth, under the new heaven. The Book of Isaiah closes on a vision of Zion restored, in which the righteous will live and from which the wicked will be cast to their destruction.

Jeremiah

Introduction. Jeremiah lived in times of uncertainty and violence. He was born some time during the reign of Josiah (640-609), whose religious reforms in 622 initiated a mood of national improvement and optimism. Unfortunately, Josiah was killed by Pharaoh Necho in 609, and his untimely death was only the first of a series of shocks for Judah. His successor, Jehoahaz (called Shallum in Jer. 22-11), was deposed by the Egyptians, who made another son, Jehoiakim, a puppet king in his brother's place. Jehoiakim undid much that his father had accomplished. Religious syncretism, social injustice, and political uncertainty marked his reign. For a while he remained faithful to the Egyptians, but after the victory of Nebuchadrezzar at the battle of Carchemish, he evidently decided he would do better with the rising Chaldeans (Babylonians). This led to invasions by the Chaldeans, Syrians, Moabites, and Ammonites in c. 602, and later to the siege of Jerusalem. Jehoiakim died during the siege and was succeeded by his eighteen-year-old son, Jehoiachin (sometimes called Coniah). Jehoiachin capitulated to Nebuchadrezzar in 597 and with the queen mother, many of the nobles, priests, officials, and citizens was taken into captivity in Babylon. Nebuchadrezzar appointed Zedekiah, still another son of Josiah, to rule Judah. He seems to have been a well-intentioned but spineless king. He had several secret interviews with Jeremiah and probably favored his policy of nonalignment, but eventually was won over to the pro-Egyptian faction. When he refused to pay tribute to Babylon, the Babylonians attacked many Judean towns and besieged Jerusalem for over a year and a half. Eventually the city fell in 586, and another group of captives was taken into exile. Gedaliah, a Jew of a good family and an excellent man, was made governor, but was assassinated about 582. Evidently fearful that the Babylonians would retaliate, a large group of Jews fled to Egypt, forcing Jeremiah to go with them.

In the midst of these events Jeremiah spent his prophetic career. Born into a priestly family in Anathoth, a little village north of Jerusalem, Jeremiah grew up steeped in the best traditions of Northern Israel (especially the work of Hosea) and in the life of the countryside. His call to prophesy came when he was a young man (see 1:4-16) and when (according to recent theories) the Babylonians were a rising force. They and not the Scythians (as used to be said) are most probably the foe from the north of which he often speaks. His early oracles (Chs. 2-6 and possibly 8:4-9:1), the Temple sermon, and the calls to repentance, belong to the reign of Jehoiakim. The oracle against Egypt in Ch. 46 is probably connected with the battle of Carchemish, and Zedekiah's burning of Jeremiah's scroll (Ch. 26) and its subsequent re-writing by Jeremiah's scribe, Baruch, probably took place in the same year. Jeremiah's praise of the faithful Rechabites (Ch. 35) and his imprisonment for foretelling the fall of Jerusalem (Ch. 20) may belong to the end of Jehoiakim's reign. Jeremiah's scriptures on the proud and selfish king may be read in 22:13-19.

The vision of the good and bad figs (Ch. 24), the incident of Hananiah and the yoke (Chs. 27-8), and the letters to the exiles belong to the years after the first deportation (598). Many incidents are recounted of the siege years, 588-586. They include, roughly in this order, the warnings to Zedekiah (34:1-7, 37:1-10); the hypocritical freeing of the slaves (34); Jeremiah's arrest, supposedly for desertion (37:11-15); the secret interview with Zedekiah ("Is there any word from the Lord"; 37:16-21); the purchase of the field of Anathoth (32); the attempt of the princes to leave Jeremiah to die in the cistern (38:1-13); and a second secret talk with Zedekiah (38:14-28). After the fall of the city, Jeremiah was released from prison under Gedaliah's guardianship. It seems likely that he would have supported the governor in his efforts to rehabilitate the city. As recounted above, Jeremiah was forced to go to Egypt with a group of panic-stricken Jews after the assassination of Gedaliah, about 592.

Superscription 1:1-3. According to the editor, Jeremiah came from Anathoth and preached under Josiah, Jehoiakim, and Zedekiah, until Jerusalem was taken and the people exiled in 586. Actually, the book contains material written by Jeremiah several years after 586, besides editorial matter of a still later date.

The Call of Jeremiah 1:4-19. Yahweh tells Jeremiah that he knew him before he was even conceived and appointed him "a prophet to the nations." Jeremiah hesitates to accept such a responsibility — "Ah, Lord God! behold, I cannot speak: for I am a child" — but is told that he must go. However, he should not be afraid, for Yahweh will be with him. Yahweh touches Jeremiah's mouth to purify it, sets him over the nations, and explains that his task is in two parts — to destroy and tear down on one hand and to build and plant on the other. Two signs, the almond rod and the boiling pot in the north (portending danger from that direction), accompany the call. Jeremiah must not be dismayed, for the Lord has made him a fortified city.

Jeremiah's Early Ministry 2:1-6:30. A series of oracles from Jeremiah's early ministry deals chiefly with Israel's faithlessness and failure to repent and with the punishments which may result, including the threat of danger from a frequently mentioned enemy, probably the Babylonians (i.e., here Chaldeans). Jeremiah considers Israel's history since she arrived in Canaan. In the desert she was faithful, but in Canaan she has chased after the worthless gods of Canaan. Priests, specialists in the laws, rulers, and prophets have all been unfaithful. The people have forsaken Yahweh, "the fountain of living waters and hewed out broken cisterns that they can hold no water." As a result they have suffered military reverses (Pharaoh Necho's victory over Josiah at Megiddo, 609, is probably meant). Jeremiah, like Isaiah and Hosea, registers his disapproval of alliances with either Egypt or Assyria. Israel in her sin is compared to a harlot and to a wild, degenerate vine which has unaccountably sprung from good seed, for she worships trees and stones, disregarding punishments sent to warn her, guilty of social injustice — "Also on your skirts is found the lifeblood of the guiltless poor" (RSV). A long plea that Israel, the faithless wife, will repent and turn to Yahweh with a real change of heart (3:1-4:4) is interrupted by some editorial material. A vivid description of the coming of the foe from the north closes with another call to repentance and an account of the prophet's own suffering, of the destruction and desolation which is to come. Jerusalem is spoken of as a harlot who decks herself with paint and ornaments, but whose lovers turn against her and seek her life. In an ironic passage, Jeremiah excuses the poor, who are foolish and ignorant; he will turn to the great, who surely know the Lord's ways. However, the rich are as faithless as the poor, and will be destroyed. There are more hints that punishment will come from the north. (A reference to the Exile in 5:18-19 is probably editorial.) Diatribes against the people who do not realize that Yahweh is creator, against the wickedness of the rich, and against the shortcomings of priests and prophets close the chapter. Ch. 6 consists of miscellaneous threats and complaints. Jerusalem will be besieged. Gleaning the remnant of Israel for good grapes is a thankless task, for the people are corrupt and the leaders greedy and shallow, saying "Peace, peace; when there is no peace." The ancient paths which give rest to faithful souls are useless, for the people say, "We will not walk thereon," and Yahweh's watchmen (prophets) are denied, for the people say, "We will not hearken." The words of the prophets and the law of the Lord are neglected, and therefore offerings and sacrifices are meaningless. In this situation, the prophet is an "assayer and tester" (RSV) of the people; but though he tries to refine the people as metal is refined in a furnace, his efforts are in vain.

Temple Sermon 7:1-8:3. This section contains genuine teachings of Jeremiah, but as it stands is the work of the Deuteronomic editor. It contains Jeremiah's sermon in the Temple in which he denies that Temple rites and sacrifices give men security. Only a righteous life does that. Those who steal, murder, commit adultery, swear falsely, burn incense to Baal, and follow other gods make Yahweh's Temple into a den of robbers. The sins of the people — including making cakes for the queen of heaven (Ishtar) — are so great that the prophet is forbidden to intercede for them. The people have even built high places in the valley of Hinnom "to burn their sons and daughters in the fire" — a reference to child sacrifices, which are abhorrent to Yahweh. Disturbing corpses, thought to be blasphemous, is also mentioned as deserving of terrible punishment.

Miscellaneous Oracles 8:4-10:25. A miscellany of oracles follows. Israel's "perpetual backsliding" is contrasted with the ways of migrating birds, who knew when to fly, while the people do not know the laws of God. They confuse the living law of the Lord with a law that can be written in a book. An invasion is regarded as punishment for sin. The prophet suffers deep grief over some unidentified calamity to the people. He is appalled, on another occasion, by their treachery and deceit. He laments the destruction of Jerusalem and Judah. He declares that the only reason for boasting consists not of wisdom or power or riches, but of the ethical nature of a God who exercises kindness, justice, and righteousness. A somewhat puzzling passage on the punishment both of the circumcised and the uncircumcised perhaps means that the rite itself is unimportant compared with the inner spiritual change of heart which is needed. A satirical piece on idols (10:1-10) is editorial. A dialogue between Jeremiah and Jerusalem speaks of the distress of the siege, the stupidity of the shepherds (i.e., rulers) and the desolation that is to overtake the cities of Judah. A prayer by the prophet, vss. 23-4, concludes this section, for vs. 25 is a late insertion.

Covenant, Sacrifices, and a Plot against Jeremiah's Life 11:1-12:6.

In the strongest terms, Jeremiah is told to urge the people to obey the covenant, or they will be under a curse. It is not certain whether the reference is to the Sinai covenant or whether an oracle from Jeremiah has been reworked to provide support for the Deuteronomic Code. It does not really seem likely that Jeremiah would be in favor of the Code, with its emphasis on ritual and sacrifice. A short poem (vss. 15-17) makes the point that sacrifice cannot ward off God's punishment. In an autobiographical passage Jeremiah tells of a plot against him by his relatives at Anathoth. We do not know what the reasons for this plot were. The experience makes Jeremiah ask the question. "Wherefore doth the way of the wicked prosper?" which Yahweh answers, rather enigmatically," "If you have raced with men on foot, and they have wearied you, how will you compete with horses?" Evidently even worse experiences lie ahead for the prophet.

Israel's Neighbors 12:7-17. Yahweh himself laments Israel's destruction by her enemies. She is his heritage, his beloved, his vineyard. Her destroyers should be ashamed. The rest of the chapter (14-17) may be editorial.

Parables and Laments 13:1-27.

Jeremiah is told to hide a loin cloth in the cleft of a rock and later to go and fetch it again. The loin cloth is spoiled and Yahweh points the moral: "Even so will I spoil the pride of Judah and the great pride of Jerusalem" (RSV). The same pattern is followed in the parable of the jars. The jars are filled with wine; even so, kings, priests, prophets, and people of Jerusalem will be drunken. A short warning against pride may belong to 598, the year of the first deportation to Babylon. A dirge over the king and queen mother was doubtless for Jehoiachin and his mother Nehushta. Next, Jerusalem is addressed as a shepherdess who has left her flock. She will be shamed for the greatness of her sins. The prophet speaks ironically, "Can the Ethiopian change his skin, or the leopard his spots? then may ye also do good, that are accustomed to do evil." For her harlotry and abominations she will be shamed and scattered like chaff.

Laments and Dialogues 14:1-15:4.

Some of the material here is editorial. The collection opens with a vivid description of the horrors of a drought. Noble and farmer alike suffer and even the wild asses pant for air. To a short confession of many backslidings, Yahweh replies that he will indeed remember the many iniquities he has observed. A prediction that false prophets will be the victims of famine and sword is followed by a short but touching lament in which Jeremiah weeps for "the virgin daughter of my people." The people make one more appeal to Yahweh: "we looked for peace, and there is no good; and for the time of healing, and behold trouble." Yahweh's reply (15: 1-4), probably the work of the Deuteronomic editor, declares that even if Moses and Samuel spoke for the people, they deserve only "the sword to slay, and the dogs to tear, and the fowls of the heaven, and the beasts of the earth, to devour and destroy." A lament over Jerusalem, whose widows are more than the sands of the seas, whose mothers mourn their sons slain at noon day, is followed by the prophet's protest that he is suffering persecution and isolation because of his calling. He even questions God's good faith: "Wilt thou be altogether unto me as a liar, and as the waters that fail?" Yahweh's reply is stern, he must speak what is of value and not worthless things; then he will be as strong as a fortified wall and no one shall prevail against him, for Yahweh will be with him to save and deliver him.

Miscellany 16:1-18:17. These chapters contain a collection of threats, promises, prayers and other forms. Many of them are not by Jeremiah. A rather prosy explanation of Jeremiah's failure to marry because of his devotion to his prophetic vocation is followed by a very late prophecy of the return from the dispersion, by a threat of punishment for Israel's sin, and by a post-exilic prediction that all nations will turn to Yahweh. The poem which says that the sin of Judah is written both on the people's hearts and on the horns of the altars, i.e., in their rituals, is probably by Jeremiah. A short psalm contrasting "the man that trusteth in man" with "the man that trusteth in the Lord" reminds us of Psalm 1, and is followed by two proverbs, one on the deceitfulness of the human heart and one on ill-gotten gains. In an unlikely setting, close to a statement on the greatness of the Temple and one on Sabbath observance, is a touching prayer by Jeremiah (17:14-18). "Heal me, O Lord, and I shall be healed; save me and I shall be saved." He has spoken the word of the Lord and been mocked for his pains. He wants his enemies put to shame: "Let them be confounded that persecute me, but let not me be confounded: let them be dismayed, but let not me be dismayed..." The parable of the potter (18:1-12) is effective. As Jeremiah watches the potter rework a spoiled vessel, he hears the word of the Lord, "O house of Israel, cannot I do with you as this potter? saith the Lord. Behold as the clay is in the potter's hand, so are ye in mine hand, O house of Israel." If he threatens a nation and it turns from its evil ways, he will repent of the evil that he intended. But the people say: "There is no hope; but we will walk after our own devices, and we will everyone do the imagination of his evil heart." A short poem on the unnaturalness of Israel's apostasy asks "Does the snow of Lebanon leave the crags of Sirion?" (RSV). How can the virgin Israel make their land "desolate and a perpetual hissing"?

Events in Jeremiah's Life 18:18-20:18. Probably this plot was the culmination of a long struggle between Jeremiah and a group of religious leaders. They plan to "smite him with the tongue," i.e., slander him. Jeremiah is very angry, especially as in the past he has begged God for mercy towards them. Now he asks God for terrible punishments to fall upon them, famine and sword for their children, childlessness and widowhood for their wives, death by pestilence and sword.

A somewhat confusing narrative follows. Jeremiah is told to take a potter's earthen flask and go to the Postherd Gate with elders and priests. Then he is told to make a pronouncement about Tophet and the valley of Hinnom. Only later do we understand the meaning of the potter's flask. Yahweh will break the people of the city as the flask is broken. Apparently as a result of this incident, Pashur, the priest, probably an official responsible for keeping order in the Temple precinct, beats Jeremiah and puts him in the stocks. Jeremiah says that he should be called Terror, that Judah would fall to Babylon, and that he, Pashur, with all his house, would go into captivity. Then he turns to God with a bitter complaint: "O Lord, thou hast deceived me, and I was deceived: thou art stronger than I, and hast prevailed: I am in derision daily, every one mocketh me." In spite of this mockery, he is compelled to speak the word of the Lord by "a burning fire shut up in my bones." Even while he hears his acquaintances whispering about him, watching for his fall, the prophet has not lost his faith in God, who is with him "as a dread warrior" (RSV). "O Lord of hosts," he cries, "Who triest the righteous, who seest the heart and the mind, let us see thy vengeance upon them, for to thee I have committed my cause" (RSV). He praises God and curses the day he was born.

Jeremiah and the Kings of Judah 21:1-23:8. During the siege of Jerusalem (589-587) Zedekiah sends a deputation to ask Jeremiah if the Lord will make him withdraw. Jeremiah replies in the words of Yahweh that he will himself fight against his people, "even in anger, and in fury, and in great wrath." Those who survive pestilence, sword, and famine will be carried away into Babylon. Next follows an oracle against the house of David and one against Jerusa-

lem, and a Deuteronomic appeal to the "house of the king of Judah" to do justice and righteousness. "Weep ye not for the dead" (22:10-12) refers to Josiah, killed at Megiddo, and is addressed to his son, Shallum, i.e., Jehoahaz, who was exiled into Egypt and is probably "him that goeth away: for he shall return no more, nor see his native land." Next (vss. 13-19) is a condemnation of Jehoiakim (609-598) for building a grand palace with spacious upper rooms and neglecting the poor and needy. As a result, no one will mourn for him and he will be "buried with the burial of an ass." After a lament over Jerusalem, whose sufferings in the siege are compared to those of a woman in labor, Jeremiah turns his attention to Jehoiachin (598/97), who succeeded his father during the siege, but was carried into captivity in Babylon three months later. The people ask "Is this man Coniah [a short form of the king's name] a despised broken idol? is he a vessel wherein is no pleasure? wherefore are they cast out, he and his seed, and be cast into a land which they know not?" Jeremiah's comment was "Write ye this man childless, a man that shall not prosper in his days: for no man of his seed shall prosper, sitting upon the throne of David, and ruling any more in Judah." Jehoiachin was not in fact childless, but the second half of the prophecy was accurate, for Zerubbabel, his grandson, though governor of Judah, never really reestablished the throne of David. Woes on false shepherds and promises of the return and of the restoration of the house of David close this section.

Jeremiah and the Prophets 23:9-40. Jeremiah says he is like a drunken man at the spectacle of the adultery of the Lord. Both prophet and priest are ungodly. The prophets of Samaria prophesy by Baal, and the Jerusalem prophets are even worse, for they spread ungodliness all over the land by not honestly presenting the word of Yahweh. Their prophecies are only the reflection of their own dreams. The passage on the burden of the Lord (vss. 33-40) is mostly editorial.

Good and Bad Figs 24:1-10; 25:1-38. In a vision which recalls those of Amos, Jeremiah sees two baskets, one of freshly ripened figs and one of rotten figs too bad to eat. Yahweh interprets the vision. The good figs are those who are sent "into the land of the Chaldeans" (Babylon). "I will set mine eyes upon them for good, and I will bring them again to this land: and I will build them, and not pull them down; and I will plant them, and not pluck them up. And I will give them a heart to know me, that I am the Lord: and they shall be my people, and I will be their God: for they shall return unto me with their whole heart." But the bad figs are "the residue of Jerusalem, that remain in this land, and them that dwell in the land of Egypt." They will be "a reproach and a proverb, a taunt and a curse" and will be cut off by sword, famine, and pestilence.

Warnings to Judah and Yahweh's Wrath 25:1-38. Because of Judah's disobedience, the Deuteronomic editor prophesies her destruction. After seventy years (a vague round number) Babylon will be punished. The list of the nations who must drink the cup of Yahweh's wrath was probably intended to go with the oracles against foreign nations in Chs. 46-51. The chapter ends with a prophecy of the coming of Yahweh in judgment. It has affinities with later apocalyptic literature.

Jeremiah in Conflict with Priests and Prophets 26:1-28:17. At the beginning of Jehoiakim's reign (609) Jeremiah delivered the temple sermon, of which an account has already been given in Ch. 7. The sermon caused an uproar. Indignant at Jeremiah's prediction that Jerusalem would be desolate, the priests and prophets attacked him and he was brought to trial, but the "princes" (i.e., court officials) and many of the people were on his side and denied that he deserved the death sentence. It is clear that the sermon placed Jeremiah in a dangerous position, but that he acted calmly and with dignity, insisting that he did not deserve it, as he was the spokesman of Yahweh.

The next two Chs., 27 and 28, skip to the reign of Zedekiah (597-587), at a time when a revolt against Babylon is being plotted. Putting on a yoke as a symbol of submission and addressing the kings involved in the conspiracy (Edom, Moab, Ammon, Tyre, and Sidon were involved), Jeremiah insists that Yahweh himself has given these lands into the hands of Nebuchadrezzar, who is his agent. To Zedekiah he advises submission to the yoke of Babylon. He tells the priests and people not to listen to the prophets who say that the Babylonians will bring back the cult objects they took from the temple. Hananiah, apparently one of these optimistic prophets, says the cult objects will be returned in two years, and breaks the yoke from Jerusalem's shoulders as a sign that the yoke of Babylon will be cast off. But Jeremiah goes his own way and Hananiah dies that same year.

Letters to the Exiles 29:1-32. Some time after this, Jeremiah composes an open letter to the elders of the exiles in Babylon: "Thus saith the Lord of hosts, the God of Israel, unto all that are carried away captives, whom I have caused to be carried away from Jerusalem unto Babylon: Build ye houses, and dwell in them; and plant gardens, and eat the fruit of them; Take ye wives, and beget sons and daughters; and take wives for your sons, and give your daughters to husbands, that they may bear sons and daughters; that ye may be increased there, and not diminished. And seek the peace of the city whither I have caused you to be carried away captives, and pray unto the Lord for it: for in the peace thereof ye shall have peace." In Yahweh's name, the people are assured that he has plans for them, that he will bring them back within seventy years (a vague round number). (A Deuteronomic passage promises to gather the exiles in from the nations.) The chapter concludes with a fragment of a separate letter about Shemaiah, who had apparently written to Jerusalem to ask Zephaniah why he had not put Jeremiah in the stocks for advising the people to settle down in Babylon. Jeremiah says Shemaiah will be punished.

Book of Comfort 30:1-31:40. Most of these oracles of comfort come from a much later date than Jeremiah. The editor seems to have been influenced by Second Isaiah. Most of the oracles deal with the joyful restoration of Israel. However, the poem in 31:2-6 is widely thought to be Jeremiah's own. It confirms Yahweh's everlasting love for the people who "found grace in the wilderness" and promises that Israel will be restored and will again plant vineyards on the mountains of Samaria.

Jeremiah and the Field at Anathoth 32:1-44. With this chapter we return to the period when Jerusalem is still under siege and Jeremiah in prison. He has an opportunity, as next of kin, to purchase some family land at Anathoth. Astonishingly, he takes the option, signing the deed in prison and having it properly witnessed

and put away in an earthen pot for safekeeping. Thus he vividly dramatizes his faith that "houses and fields and vineyards" will again be occupied in the land. (The prayer in 16-25 is secondary.)

Restoration of Israel 33:1-26. Except for vss. 4-5, which seem to refer to the defenses against the Chaldeans, this chapter consists of late predictions regarding the return, the rebuilding of Jerusalem, and the restoration of the Davidic monarchy and the Levitical priesthood.

Promise to Zedekiah 34:1-7. Through Jeremiah, Yahweh tells Zedekiah that he is giving the city over to the hand of the king of Babylon, that he, the king, will have to go to Babylon, but that he will die in peace. It seems as if a condition — perhaps that Zedekiah should submit — proposed by the prophet has been dropped out. In any case Zedekiah was in fact blinded and taken to Babylon.

Slave-owners of Jerusalem 34:8-22. During the siege, the slave-owners, partly because their slaves were now a burden, partly for what they claimed were religious reasons, vow to release their slaves. When the siege is lifted, they reclaim their slaves. Jeremiah censures them for this piece of hypocrisy.

Rechabites 35:1-19. The Rechabites were a primitive religious group who strove to maintain the "pure" standards of the nomad life, free from the corruptions of Canaan. They lived in tents, did not farm, and refused to drink wine because it was connected with the agricultural life of Canaan. They had been forced to withdraw inside the walls of Jerusalem because of the siege. Jeremiah seems to admire them, regarding their refusal to drink wine as a manifestation of obedience to their code. He holds them up as an example to the disobedient people of Jerusalem.

Burning of the Scroll 36:1-32. In 605, Nebuchadrezzar defeated the Egyptians and the Assyrians of Carchemish. This put Judah, whose King Jehoiakim had been the choice of the Egyptians, in a serious position. Jeremiah chooses this crucial time, when Judah was in danger of "the foe from the north," to publish his oracles. He dictates them to his secretary, Baruch, since for some reason which we are not given, he has been forbidden to enter the Temple area. At his master's direction, Baruch reads the scroll before the prophets. When the princes (court officials) hear of this, they in turn demand a reading. What they hear alarms them so much that they decide that the king ought to know about it, although at the same time they advise Baruch and Jeremiah to hide. The king does not take the scroll as seriously as the officials do. As the reader proceeds, grimly the king cuts piece after piece from the scroll and burns it in the brazier, in spite of the protests of the elders, until the entire scroll is burned up.

Jeremiah then once more dictates the contents of the scroll to Baruch, saying as he does so that the king of Babylon will certainly destroy the land and that Jehoiakim's body will be exposed to the elements. (This prophecy does not seem to have come to pass.)

Siege of Jerusalem 37:1-40:6. After Jehoiakim died and Jehoiachin was taken to Babylon, Zedekiah (597-587) was appointed King of Judah by the Babylonians. Jeremiah is still free to preach at this time, but neither Zedekiah nor the people pay attention to him. Zede-

kiah and the Pharaoh Hophra conspire to rebel against Nebuchadrezzar. This move disturbs Jeremiah, who consistently regards the Babylonian (Chaldean) conquest of Judah as the will of Yahweh. When the prophet tries to leave Jerusalem, at a time when the siege is temporarily lifted, he is arrested as a deserter and imprisoned. The king reveals his anxious state of mind by interviewing Jeremiah secretly and asking him "Is there any word from the Lord?" He may have hoped for good news, but Jeremiah's reply is stern: "Thou shalt be delivered into the hand of the king of Babylon." During the final days of the siege, Jeremiah's enemies complain to the king that he is undermining the morale of the soldiers and obtain the royal permission to put him to death. They cast him into an empty cistern, where he sinks in the mud. Fortunately an Ethiopian eunuch takes pity on his plight and persuades the king to let him rescue the prophet, who is pulled up with ropes. The king interviews him once more, but Jeremiah's stand is unchanged: surrender to Babylon and be spared; continue to fight and neither king nor city shall escape.

Finally, a breach is made in the wall of the besieged city. Zedekiah flees, but is caught and forced to watch his sons killed. Then he is blinded and he and the people are taken to Babylon. Jeremiah is released from the court of the guard and entrusted to the care of Gedaliah. (Much of the rest of this chapter is secondary and so are the first six verses of Ch. 40.)

Gedaliah 40:7-41:18. The authentic narrative resumes at this point. Gedaliah is appointed governor and persuades many of the Jews to serve the Chaldeans. Many fugitives return to Judah to gather the crops and live under Gedaliah's governorship. Unfortunately, Gedaliah, though a promising leader, is too goodnatured for his own safety. When Johanan comes to warn him that one Ishmael is planning to kill him, Gedaliah refuses to take action. Ishmael assassinates him, kills a large number of innocent pilgrims, and captures the people of Mizpah. These people are luckily rescued by Johanan.

Escape to Egypt 42:1-43:7. The rescued citizens of Mizpah and Johanan and his companions consult Jeremiah as to whether they are wise in trying to flee to Egypt. They promise to act according to the word of Yahweh, but when the prophet tells them that Yahweh wishes them to remain in Judah, they accuse him of lying, of following Baruch's advice instead of God's, and of wanting to deliver them into the hands of the Chaldeans. They flee to Egypt, taking with them Jeremiah, Baruch, and the people left in Gedaliah's charge.

Jeremiah in Egypt 43:8-44:30. After his arrival in Egypt, Jeremiah hides some large stones under the pavement at the entrance to Pharaoh's house, as a symbol that Nebuchadrezzar will come and set up his throne in that spot, bringing with him pestilence, captivity, and the sword. Jeremiah further censures the people (much of this is Deuteronomic), but the women insist that their attentions to the queen of heaven (Ishtar) are effective and will be continued.

Oracle on Baruch 45:1-5. Baruch seems to have suffered in Yahweh's service much as Jeremiah suffered, but like his master is told that he must be prepared for even more suffering: "Behold, that which I have built will I break down, and that which I have planted I will pluck up, even this whole land. And seekest thou great things for thyself? seek them not . . . "

Oracles against Foreign Nations 46:1-51:64. Some of these oracles have been added or edited later. Parts of the oracle against Egypt may be original and are perhaps related to the battle of Carchemish. The oracle on Nebuchadrezzar is secondary. An oracle against the Philistines, the historical background of which is uncertain, is followed by an enormously long oracle against Moab, which may be genuine in part, if indeed the Moabites joined the Babylonians in attacking Egypt. A prophecy of war against the Ammonites says that they will be dispossessed and that Rabbah will become a desolate mound. The oracle against Edom reflects the hatred of the Israelites for their kinsmen because they took advantage of the siege and fall of Jerusalem to occupy land in Judah. The same situation is reflected in the Book of Obadiah. It does not seem very probable that Jeremiah was concerned about this particular situation. The oracle against Damascus is probably a late addition. The oracle against the Arab tribes Kedar and Hazor may find its origin in historical events of Jeremiah's time, but the exact circumstances are not known. The substantial group of oracles (50:1-51:64) directed against Babylon seem not to be from Jeremiah, since they are mainly about Babylon's fall and the return of the exiles and since they fail to recommend submission to Babylon, a chief feature of Jeremiah's policy.

Captivity and Release of Jehoiachin 52:1-34. This chapter reproduces II Kings 24:18-25:30, omitting the narratives about Gedaliah covered in Chs. 40-43. No doubt this historical narrative was added to show that Jerusalem fell, as Jeremiah said it would, and to continue the story of the city and the exiles down to the release of Jehoiachin from prison.

Lamentations

Introduction. The word Lamentations means "dirges." We have seen dirges before in the Bible, notably David's lament for Saul and Jonathan (II Sam. 3:33-4) and Amos's for the virgin Israel (Amos 5:1-2). Lamentations consists of five dirges. The first four are alphabetical acrostics, that is, the twenty-two stanzas begin with the successive letters of the Hebrew alphabet. The fifth contains the right number of stanzas, but is not an acrostic; perhaps the author never completed his work. The alphabetical order may have been intended as an aid to memorizing the poems. The reader can get a good idea of the original poetry from the (RSV), where the translator has preserved the Hebrew line division and the break (called a caesura) in the middle of the line.

The book was traditionally ascribed to Jeremiah, but the artificial style is quite unlike his. Moreover, Jeremiah would have repudiated some of the ideas of the author, who admired royalty, advocated an Egyptian alliance, and was concerned with the ritual aspects of religion. Probably the poems were written by a contemporary or contemporaries of Jeremiah (soon after the fall of Jerusalem in 586 B.C.) though some critics would place them later. The dirges are still sung today in synagogues on the ninth day of Ab.

Summary of Book of Lamentations

The first dirge (Ch. 1) describes the grief and suffering of Jerusalem:

How lonely sits the city
that was full of people

How like a widow she has
become, she that was great
among the nations! (RSV)

Remembering all the precious things she has lost, the city weeps bitterly, weeps for the maidens, youths, and children taken captive, weeps for her princes, weeps for hunger, and weeps for the exile of Judah: "Is is nothing to you, all ye that pass by? behold, and see if there be any sorrow like unto my sorrow..." The poet acknowledges that the city's sin is a cause of her suffering. "Jerusalem hath grieviously sinned; therefore is she removed," and "the Lord is righteous; for I have rebelled against his commandment." He holds the city's miseries up before the Lord, praying that his enemies in turn may suffer.

The second dirge (Ch. 2) brings out more clearly the fact that Yahweh's "fierce anger" is the cause of the city's ruin. He has done what he has long threatened. He has destroyed not only the palaces and strongholds of Jerusalem, but also his own sacred places, altar, and sanctuary. "The law is no more," and the prophets receive only fake visions. Children faint from hunger in the streets and even in their mothers' arms.

Should women eat their
offspring, the children of their
tender care?
Should priest and prophet
be slain in the sanctuary
of the Lord? (RSV)

In the third poem (Ch. 3) the poet speaks as an individual who has experienced the sufferings of the siege. Yahweh has walled him about with suffering, has torn him as a bear tears its prey, has driven arrows into his heart. Yet he is resigned in his affliction, recognizing that sin and rebellion are the cause of suffering. He repents his wrong-doing, calls on Yahweh and weeps, and puts his ultimate trust in God's justice and mercy. "Though he cause grief, he will have compassion according to the abundance of his steadfast love" (RSV, 3:32). This is the central message of the book.

The fourth poem (Ch. 4), like the first and second, laments the fall of Jerusalem. It contrasts her past grandeur and holiness with her present state of misery and humiliation.

How the gold has grown dim,
how the pure gold is changed!
The holy stones lie scattered
at the head of every street.
The precious stones of Zion
worth their weight in fine gold,
how they are reckoned as
earthen pots,
The work of a potter's hands.

The princes who were whiter than snow are black and shriveled, the women now eat their children. Better to have perished by the sword. The sins of priests and prophets, who shed the blood of the innocent, are punished, for God has scattered them. The inhabitants of Judah were deeply embittered because their neighbors, the Edomites, joined in the looting of the city, and the poet closes with a threat that their iniquity, too, will be punished. The final dirge is a prayer on behalf of the whole nation. They remind Yahweh that they are now orphans and slaves. The land is conquered, the people are starving, the women ravished, the princes overpowered, the elders insulted, the youths enslaved. "The joy of our heart is ceased; our dance is turned into mourning. For their sins Yahweh has forgotten them." Yet he is king forever, and the final prayer is "Renew our days as of old."

Ezekiel

Introduction. The Exile is a great milestone in the history of the Jewish people. Behind it lies the ancient religion of the Hebrews, while after it appear what we can begin to call Judaism. Ezekiel, the contemporary and disciple of Jeremiah, is therefore an important figure, because he helped to shape what Judaism was to be. Unfortunately, the book which bears his name bristles with difficulties. The text is corrupt and the style turgid, repetitious, and obscure. Critics disagree on important points such as the date of the book and the location of Ezekiel's ministry, whether it took place in Palestine, Babylon, or both. While most scholars agree that the book has un-

dergone fairly substantial editing, probably in the fifth century, the extent of this editing is in dispute. Some scholars think that the editing has been so thorough that the characteristic style of the book, which can be recognized even in translation, is the editor's rather than the author's.

The strange psychological make-up of the prophet adds to the difficulties. To a greater extent than any other classical prophet, he was subject to trances, ecstasies, periods of muteness, and perhaps paralysis. He employed strange symbols, allegories, and eccentric signs to a much greater extent than his predecessors, and some of his visions are much more weird and complex. His claims to have been transported from Babylon to Jerusalem "in the spirit" to see the pagan rites being celebrated in the Temple (Chs. 8-11) have led some historians to suppose that he actually did return there and others to credit him with second sight. Yet despite his eccentricity or perhaps because of it, Ezekiel's strange personality has a certain fascination for those who are willing to work through the difficulties of the book.

According to the traditional account, Ezekiel was deported to Babylon by Nebuchadrezzar with the first group of exiles in 597. Five years after that, in 593, he received his call in the strange vision of the throne-chariot (Ch. 1), and thereafter prophesied in Babylon for over twenty years. Archaeological studies seem to support this, for details in the book display a close knowledge of Babylon in the early sixth century. Perhaps the problems of his knowledge of Jerusalem can be solved by assuming that the exiles frequently had news of their homeland or (less probably) by assuming a return visit to the sacred city.

Ezekiel's task in preaching to the exiles was not an easy one. Many thoughtful Jews must have questioned whether the ancient relationship with Yahweh still held when their country was taken away from them and when the Temple was destroyed. "How shall we sing the Lord's song in a strange land?" asked a poet. Ezekiel's attempts to clarify the position of the exiles seem to be compounded of judgment and promise. He sees the exile and the fall of Jerusalem as the divinely ordained punishment for past sins. But the vision of the valley of dry bones (Ch. 37) shows that he hoped for the miracle of a new beginning for Israel. The bones gained flesh, the wind blew upon them, and "they stood upon their feet, an exceeding great army." So

Israel would become one living nation again and be restored to her homeland. If Chs. 40-48 contain a kernel of Ezekiel's own thinking, he pictures the restored community as an ecclesiastical one, centering on the Temple and its ritual. This would agree with his emphasis elsewhere on the importance of cultic purity, and his distress at the pagan rites in the Temple itself. It must be remembered that Ezekiel was a priest as well as a prophet and therefore emphasized the priestly outlook much more than earlier prophets did. He also emphasized the holiness of God more than his compassion or justice, and even implied that the very act of restoration was an act of self-vindication carried out so that Israel and the nations might know that Yahweh was Lord.

In conclusion we may say that Ezekiel, though perhaps less attractive than his great predecessors, has an importance equal to theirs in the history of religion. His book reflects the thought of a great period of transition. His belief in the restoration of a purified Israel under a Davidic king had important consequences and his emphasis on individualism has been important both in later Judaism and in Christianity. The book in its present form falls into four parts: (1) visions and oracles before the fall of Jerusalem, (2) oracles against pagan nations, (3) oracles and visions on the restoration, (4) the vision of the restored Temple and community.

Superscription 1:1-3. Ezekiel writes that his call came to him in the fifth year of the Exile (i.e., 593) by the river Chebar (a canal which passed through Nippur, a city south of Babylon). *It is not known what he meant by "the thirtieth year."* The editorial comment in vss. 2 and 3 tells us that the prophet was the son of Buzi, the priest.

Call of Ezekiel 1:4-3:27. The first part of Ezekiel, Chs. 1 through 24, deals with events which took place before the fall of Jerusalem in 587. Ezekiel's call is the most elaborate and the strangest of all recorded of the prophets. It seems that the violence of an electrical storm mingled with the prophet's own imaginings to produce an extraordinary vision of Yahweh in glory. The imagery of the vision combines motifs from Hebrew and Babylonian religious symbols. The throne-chariot of Yahweh is borne by four living creatures, each with four faces (a man, a lion, an ox, and an eagle), and four wings. The creatures move harmoniously, animated by the spirit gleaming like fire. Beside each of the creatures is a wheel, with a wheel within it, so that the chariot can move in any direction. The wheels are like topaz, and the rims are full of eyes. The whole chariot symbolizes the all-seeing power, purpose, and majesty of the deity. Above the throne is "the likeness of a firmament," shining like sapphire. The sound of the creatures' wings sounds like the roaring of mighty waters. Above the firmament is the throne and on it a form in human likeness (NEB), who shines like bronze and about whom seems to be something like a rainbow. (Notice how throughout his description of the vision, Ezekiel is careful to say only what it resembles. He wishes to avoid saying that the deity actually appeared in these shapes, yet he wishes to convey the presence of God in mystery and majesty.) Before this vision the prophet prostrates himself. A voice addressing him as "son of man" (i.e., human being, "mortal man" as in AT) tells him to stand to receive his commission. Fearless in the midst of thistles and scorpions, he is to speak to the rebellious house of Israel. As a sign of his calling he is given a scroll covered with lamentations to eat, a scroll which tastes like honey in his mouth. To the sound of wings, the spirit lifts him up, and he dwells "overwhelmed" (RSV) for seven days at Tel-abib by the river Chebar. At the end of the seven days he is told that he is the watchman for the house of Israel; that is, if he does not warn men against wickedness, he will be responsible for their sins. Once again he sees the glory of the Lord on a plain and is told that, bound and mute, he will be unable to prophesy until the Lord opens his mouth.

Fate of Jerusalem and Judah 4:1-7:27. At the divine command, Ezekiel performs a series of acts which dramatize the coming fate of city and people. He draws a sketch or plan of Jerusalem under siege. He lies for 390 days on his left side and 40 days on his right, apparently to indicate how long Israel and Judah would be punished. He prepares emergency rations of coarse bread and water to signify the privations of the siege. He cuts his hair with a sword and divides it into three parts to show the different fates of the inhabitants and Yahweh's anger against them. He inveighs against the mountains of Israel and prophesies the horrors of the days of doom.

Visions of Temple at Jerusalem 8:1-11:25. The spirit takes him by a lock of hair and carries him to Jerusalem where, north of the altar gate, he beholds the "image of jealousy" (RSV "abomination"; a pagan image, perhaps the Asherah, consort of Baal). Penetrating the wall, Ezekiel sees heathen rites performed before pictures of reptiles, beasts, and idols. By the north gate are women weeping for Tammuz (a dying and rising fertility god, somewhat like Osiris or Syrian Adonis), and in the inner court of the Temple are twenty-five men worshiping the sun. Horrified by these abominations, Ezekiel beholds the slaughter of the idolators and the departure from the Temple of the glory of Yahweh by the same throne-chariot in which He first appeared to the prophet. By the east gate he sees twenty-five men, some of whom he names. One of them, Pelatiah, dies, and Ezekiel asks, "will thou make a full end of the remnant of Israel?" He is told (in what may be an editorial addition) that the exiles will return to Israel and will be given a new spirit. "I will take the stone heart out of their flesh, and will give them a heart of flesh." The glory of Yahweh leaves the city and Ezekiel tells the exiles what he has seen.

Prophecies of Doom and Exile 12:1-14:23.

Once again at God's command, Ezekiel performs signs which symbolize the exile. He acts out the hasty packing of baggage and by night digs a hole through the wall, as though fleeing secretly. He drinks water and eats bread trembling, as though in fear. Yahweh promises him that the prophecies will be fulfilled. The prophet denounces prophets who offer their own notions as prophecy, instead of waiting on the word of Yahweh; he also denounces sorceresses, diviners, and idolators. Jerusalem will be punished with the sword, famine, wild beasts, and pestilence.

Four Allegories 15:1-17:24.

Jerusalem is like a useless vine, good for nothing but firewood. She is like a faithless wife, who takes the gifts of her husband to make heathen images, offers her children as sacrifices, builds unlawful shrines, and commits harlotries with Egypt and Assyria. For all these sins she shall be exposed in her nakedness; yet she shall be ashamed and Yahweh may yet resume his covenant with her. As a great eagle plucks the top of a cedar and takes up seed and scatters it on fertile fields near rivers, so Nebuchadrezzar plucks up the king of Judah (Zedekiah) and the people of Judah and takes them to Babylon. To another eagle a well-rooted vine turns for water as Zedekiah turned to Hophra, Pharaoh of Egypt, and for this it shall wither away. Finally comes the allegory of the cedar which is to be planted on a lofty mountain of Israel. The cedar is to be noble and fruitful, and birds of all kinds shall nestle in it. All the trees shall know that Yahweh has power to bring down the high tree, raise up the low, dry up the green tree, and make the dry tree perish. (This final allegory may be a Messianic addition from a later period.)

Individual Responsibility 18:1-32.

This chapter enunciates one of Ezekiel's most important doctrines. He begins by quoting a popular proverb. "The fathers have eaten sour grapes and the children's teeth are set on edge." In the words of Yahweh he repudiates this principle of collective guilt and responsibility. "Behold, all souls are mine." Each man will be held responsible for his own acts. This is illustrated by three hypothetical men. The righteous man who has broken no religious laws and who has been moral and upright in his dealings with neighbors, debtors, and the poor "shall surely live." However, his son may be a robber, murderer, adulterer, oppressor, and idolater, and "he shall surely die; his blood shall be upon him." In turn his son, the righteous man's grandson who re-enacts his grandfather's religious and moral piety, "shall surely live." Furthermore, the wicked man who turns from his wickedness shall live, for God has no pleasure in the death of the wicked. On the other hand, the righteous man who turns away from righteousness and commits evil will die in his sins. The chapter ends with an assertion of the justice of Yahweh and a plea for repentance. "Cast away from you all your transgressions, whereby ye have transgressed; and make you a new heart and a new spirit: for why will ye die, O house of Israel?"

Miscellaneous Laments, Oracles, and Prophecies 19:1-24:14.

In two dirges in which Israel is compared to a lioness and to a vine, the fates of Jehoahaz, Jehoiachin, and Zedekiah are lamented. In an oracle which is addressed to the elders of Israel in exile, he speaks of the unfaithfulness of the people in Egypt, in the wilderness, and in Canaan itself. Eventually the people will be purged, pardoned, and restored. After a short oracle against the south (Judah?) follows a series of fascinating prophecies of the sword of Yahweh. The passages are in verse and may have been sung and accompanied by a sword-dance. Yahweh's sword is whetted and polished for slaughter; it is the rod of his wrath, and will come down once, twice, thrice, bringing terror and destruction. The sword is also the sword of the king of Babylon. The hour of the prince of Israel (Zedekiah) has come and the sword of the Ammonites will be sheathed and they will be destroyed.

Three oracles describe Jerusalem as a city of blood, as silver which will be smelted, and as an aggregation of classes — princes, priests, prophets, people — all guilty. Chapter 23 depicts the adulterous wives of Yahweh and part of Ch. 24 pictures Jerusalem under siege as a cauldron boiling on a fire; "woe to the bloody city, to the pot whose scum is thereon ... I will ever make the pile for fire great."

Death of Ezekiel's Wife and Fall of Jerusalem 24:15-27.

This is almost the only fact we know about the prophet's personal life. Yahweh tells him he is to lose his wife, the delight of his eyes; yet he is not to mourn, perhaps as a sign to the exiles that they should not lament the unbearable news of the fall of Jerusalem, which will reach them shortly. This concludes the first part of the book: events and oracles up to the fall of Jerusalem.

Oracles against Pagan Nations 25:1-32:32.

These form the second part of the Book of Ezekiel as it now stands. There are similar collections of oracles against foreign nations in Amos, Isaiah, and Jeremiah. While some are original with the prophet and some are actually earlier than 587, some have been added at later times. As post-exile ideas of the return developed, it was often believed that the surrounding nations, which had despised Israel and her God, would be punished and defeated and forced to recognize Yahweh. (See above on Second Isaiah.)

Israel's old enemies, Ammon, Moab, Edom, and the Philistines are attacked first. They will be punished, and says Yahweh, "They shall know that I am the Lord." Next a series of dirges and oracles tell of the coming destruction of Tyre and its descent into Sheol. There is also an oracle against Tyre's companion city, Sidon. The group of poems ends with the promise that these countries will be the object of Yahweh's vengeance and with the prophecy that the scattered peoples of the house of Israel will be gathered together and will live securely in their own land again. Next comes a series of seven oracles against Egypt and the pharaohs, some in the form of dirges. The great sea dragon (AT crocodile) which lies in the Egyptian waters is complacent, but Yahweh will draw it out with hooks and cast it into the desert, so that all Egypt will know that Yahweh is Lord of creation. Yahweh's sword will descend on Egypt and her strength shall fail her. She will become the slave of Nebuchadrezzar. Several short oracles along the same lines follow. In Ch. 31 Egypt is likened to a great cedar tree which reaches to the sky and draws its nourishment from the great deep. The birds build their nests in it and under its branches the animals bear their young. Even the trees of the Garden of Eden cannot surpass it. Yet it will be cut down by the Babylonians, doomed to go down into the underworld and lie with the pagans who have been slain by the sword. A dirge for Pharaoh, who will be destroyed by Yahweh, and one for the teeming multitudes of Egypt conclude this section.

Prophet as Watchman and Fall of Jerusalem 33:1-33.

From here through Ch. 39, the book is concerned with the restoration of Israel. It seems as if once Jerusalem had fallen, Ezekiel took heart and was able to plan for the future; however, it must be remembered that there may be large editorial passages here. The first chapters deal with the responsibilities of prophet and people.

Again addressing the prophet as "son of man," Yahweh orders Ezekiel to tell his fellow countrymen that he, the prophet, is their watchman. It is his duty to warn the people when danger is at hand; it is the people's duty to heed the warning. If the prophet does not blow the warning trumpet and one of the people is lost, his blood is the prophet's responsibility; but if wicked man does not heed the warning, the responsibility is his. "As I live, saith the Lord God, I have no pleasure in the death of the wicked; but that the wicked turn from his way and live; turn ye, turn ye from your evil ways; for why will ye die, O house of Israel?" Again Yahweh repeats the warning that the righteous man who finally sins will die for his sins, whereas the wicked man who turns from his sin will surely live

and not die, "O ye house of Israel," Yahweh concludes, "I will judge you every one after his ways."

When a fugitive brings the news that Jerusalem has fallen, Ezekiel is released from the muteness that came upon him the evening before. Once again he speaks for Yahweh, threatening punishment for the abominations the people left in Judah have committed. But the people are indifferent: Ezekiel is regarded merely as a singer of love-songs.

Israel's Shepherds and Their Sheep: Restoration of Israel 34:1-36:38.

While the prophet is the watchman of his people, the leaders are their shepherds and are responsible for them. But they have often failed in their task: the sheep have been scattered and the shepherds have often looked out merely for themselves. Yahweh now promises to seek out his scattered sheep himself, to gather them in from the various countries, to restore them to good pasture in the mountains of Israel, to be their shepherd and protect them, to send down showers of blessings on them and to see that they dwell in safety, to raise up a Davidic (Messianic?) king for them, and to make with them a covenant of peace. (Much of this passage is probably editorial.) After an oracle against Mount Seir, promising destruction to Israel's ancient enemies, the Edomites, there follows an address to the mountains of Israel: "But ye, O mountains of Israel, ye shall shoot forth your branches, and yield your fruit to my people of Israel; for they are at hand to come." The cities shall be inhabited again and man and beast shall multiply. Yahweh was angry with his people, because they defiled the land by their ways and profaned his name in the midst of the heathen. But now to vindicate his own holiness, he will cleanse them and restore the land. "A new heart also will I give you, and a new spirit will I put within you: and I will take away the stony heart out of your flesh, and I will give you a heart of flesh. And I will put my Spirit within you, and cause you to walk in my statues, and ye shall keep my judgments, and do them. And ye shall dwell in the land that I gave to your fathers; and ye shall be my people, and I will be your God." Yahweh's people and his honor will be vindicated in the sight of all onlookers, "And they shall say, this land that was desolate is become like the garden of Eden."

Valley of Dry Bones and Allegory of the Sticks 37:1-28. The Lord set Ezekiel down in a valley which was full of dry bones and asked. "Son of man, can these bones live?" And the prophet answered, "O Lord God, thou knowest." And Yahweh ordered him to prophesy over the bones and to say "O ye dry bones, hear the word of the Lord." Then the prophet tells of the miracle that only Yahweh could bring about: "So I prophesied as I was commanded: and as I prophesied, there was a noise, and behold a shaking, and the bones came together, bone to his bone. And when I beheld, lo, the sinews and the flesh came up upon them, and the skin covered them above: but there was no breath in them. Then said he unto me, Prophesy unto the wind, prophesy, son of man, and say to the wind, Thus saith the Lord God; Come from the four winds, O breath, and breathe upon these slain, that they may live. So I prophesied as he commanded me, and the breath came into them, and they lived, and stood up upon their feet, an exceeding great army. Then he said unto me, Son of man, these bones are the whole house of Israel ... "

The Lord promises to restore his people to their land (it is this and not a physical resurrection from the grave that is meant); and promises "[I] shall put my Spirit in you, and ye shall live, and I shall place you in your own land: then shall ye know that I the Lord have spoken it, and performed it ..." (The emphasis on Yahweh's self-vindication is characteristic of this book.)

In a brief allegory, the prophet is told to take two sticks and label them "for Judah and for the children of Israel his companions" and "for Joseph, the stick of Ephraim and for all the house of Israel his companions." The two were to become one stick, symbolizing the reunification of the southern and northern kingdoms.

Gog and Magog 38:1-39:29. *These puzzling and almost inexplicable chapters (probably not by Ezekiel) contain many repetitions and inconsistencies.* The author says that Yahweh is bringing Gog from the land of Magog. Yahweh's anger will be aroused at his coming and he will summon the forces of storm and rain against him. Gog and his forces will be destroyed on the mountains of Israel and their bodies given to the birds and animals as a sacrifice. The weapons will be burned as fuel and the bones of the dead buried. Yahweh's holiness will be vindicated. The author seems to regard these events as fulfilling the prophesies of Jeremiah and others. Perhaps he did not intend to picture an ordinary historical war, but some kind of cosmological conflict with Gog representing the forces of dark and evil. This curious narrative closes the third part of the book.

Restored Temple 40:1-44:31. The last nine chapters of the book describe the restored community: Jerusalem. Perhaps Ezekiel laid the foundations for these plans, but many passages here are later than his time; certainly the accounts of the Sacred Calendar in Chs. 45 and 46, and the directions for divisions of land and the rebuilding of Jerusalem in Ch. 48. In fact, a number of scholars think we have nothing from Ezekiel himself after 43:12.

From Babylon the prophet is transported to Mount Zion, where a supernatural being carrying a measuring rod takes him on a tour of the visionary Temple and city. They inspect and sometimes measure the outer and inner courts, the place of sacrifice, the vestibule, nave, and chambers of the Temple, and the priests' chambers. Before the fall of Jerusalem, Ezekiel had seen in a vision the glory of Yahweh leave the Temple. Now he sees the glory once more fill the Temple and hears Yahweh speak, promising to dwell in the midst of a purified Israel forever. The Temple is to be a place set apart and holy. No foreigner or uncircumcised person is to enter it and only "the sons of Zadok," a priestly family, are to serve in it.

Sacred District; Various Regulations 45:1-46:24. The sacred district surrounding the Temple where the priests and Levites are to live is next described, and regulations about weights and measures, the prince's offerings, the sacrifices, cooking arrangements, and other matters are set forth.

Sacred River 47:1-12. From below the threshold of the Temple rises a sacred river which blows toward the Dead Sea, deepening as it goes and freshening the sea's salt waters. It is a source of life, abundance, and healing. Fish live in it in abundance and on its bank grow trees which will bear fresh fruit every month. "The fruit thereof will be for meat and the leaf thereof for medicine." (There is an Eden-like quality about this imagined stream.)

Allotment of Land 47:13-48:35. The boundaries of the new nation are described. Only the land west of the Jordan is included. The land is to be distributed evenly among the tribes. Not only natives but aliens are to have a share. The tribal territories are arranged north and south of the sacred area and the prince's lands which adjoin it. Dan, Asher, Naphtali, Manasseh, Ephraim, Reuben, and Judah are to the north and Benjamin, Simeon, Issachar, Zebulun, and Gad to the south. Finally, the measurements of Jerusalem are given and the gates, called after the twelve tribes, are named. In the renewed community Jerusalem has a special place, and in recognition of this she will be given a new name, Yahweh-Shammah, "the Lord is there."

Daniel

Introduction. The Book of Daniel is not really a book of prophecy at all in the sense that Amos or Isaiah are books of prophecy. However, as it claimed to have been written by someone living in Babylon early in the exile who foretold in it the history of the next five centuries, it was placed with the prophets in the Greek Bible and subsequently in the Latin and English translations. In the Hebrew Bible it stands, more appropriately, with the Writings. The book is in two parts, six chapters recounting heroic stories of Daniel and his three friends in the Babylonian court and six describing Daniel's bizarre visions which purport to predict fates of kings and kingdoms down to the villain of the book, Antiochus Epiphanes, who ruled Palestine in the second century B.C. However, it is clear from both internal and external evidence that the author's knowledge of the Babylonian and other early periods he describes is extremely hazy, while his knowledge of later periods is sound and detailed. It is certain, in fact, that the book was written during the Maccabean Revolt in the second century B.C., probably in the year 164, and that its message was intended for those stirring times. The historical background of the book is the struggle of one body of Jews to maintain their religious integrity against foreign influence and persecution. During the fourth and third centuries, a process of Hellenization had begun to transform parts of the Near East. The Jews of the Diaspora were profoundly affected by this process and even the Jews of Palestine were influenced by it. Many Jews began to read Greek literature and philosophy, wear Greek clothes, interest themselves in democratic forms of government, build gymnasiums and banqueting halls after Greek models, and even develop a taste for Greek cooking, so far as the dietary laws permitted. Even Greek funeral customs were copied. The Torah itself may have first been translated into Greek at this time. Naturally there were some Jews who resented this Hellenizing process and tried to resist it. Among them were the Hasidim ("the pious"), who struggled to retain their traditions and who preached loyalty to the Torah (the Law) at all costs. The Book of Daniel in all probability issued from this circle of conservative and devoted Jews. The struggle between this group and the Hellenizers came to a head in the reign of the Seleucid monarch Antiochus IV, called Epiphanes. A power struggle over who should be the high priest in Jerusalem evidently convinced Antiochus that peace would best be served by a rigorous enforcement of Hellenism on the people and an equally rigorous

attack on what in his eyes was an unimportant local sect. His troops were allowed to plunder and kill in Jerusalem and the city walls were pulled down. The Books of the Law were destroyed and possession of them was made a capital offense. The Temple was the next object of attack. Treasure was taken away and the offering of sacrifice was forbidden. But the worst was to come. A symbol of the pagan god of heaven (equivalent to the Greek Zeus) was set up and a pig, abhorrent to the Jews, sacrificed to it. This was evidently "the abomination of desolation" mentioned in Daniel 11:31. All over the country Jews were ordered to make sacrifices on pagan altars and Antiochus' soldiers were sent to see that they did so

Many people did sacrifice, but in 168 at the little Judaean village of Modein an elderly priest named Mattathias refused. He killed the officer sent to enforce the king's command and also killed a renegade Jew who made the sacrifice as ordered. Then Mattathias and his five sons took to the hills where, joined by other zealots, they started a guerilla campaign against Antiochus. Thus began the heroic Maccabean Revolt, so named after Mattathias' son Judas Maccabus (which may mean "hammerer") who took over when his father died. The success of this heroic band of men was astonishing. They managed to defeat the professional troops of Antiochus and to retake Jerusalem, all but the citadel. Three years from the date of the "abomination of desolation," in the month Kislev (our December 25) they cleansed the Temple and rededicated it. The Feast of Lights of Hanukkah (rededication) celebrates this event.

It seems most probable that the Book of Daniel was written by one of the Hasidim at about this point — after the success of Jerusalem, but when people might be wondering whether victory would be permanent, or whether a time of further persecution, suffering, and testing might follow. The writer seems to have feared the latter, for his purpose is to encourage heroic resistance to persecution, zeal for the Law, and faith in God and his ultimate rule over history. As he wanted his book to be taken seriously by the people, he issued it under the name of an ancient hero, perhaps the Daniel mentioned in Ezekiel and in the Ras Shamra tablets. This was not then considered a dishonest practice, as we should think it, but a legitimate means of getting a hearing for a pious message. The circumstances of the book's composition also explain the "apocalyptic" nature of the last six books. This term comes from a Greek word meaning "to uncover, to disclose." In actual fact, apocalyptic writings "disclose" their meaning only to a circle already informed, for the style is typically obscure and cryptic, purposely so, since the message is not intended to reach the enemy. Apocalyptic is also characterized by extraordinary visions, bizarre symbols, and supernatural revelations, and is capable of weird and extravagant interpretations so that even in our own day contemporary meanings have been read into the book and into the New Testament Apocalypse, the Book of Revelation. In spite of its bizarre quality, Daniel in its day served a noble cause and still has some historical interest because of its religious ideas. For one thing, the writer's conception of angels is more developed than anywhere else in the Bible, though it was to be developed still more by the Pharisees. Here the angel, Michael, has a name and a function in God's scheme of things. Even more striking is the writer's "eschatology," that is, he is concerned with the "end" of history. While he believes that God has a detailed masterplan for his-

tory, and that everything that happens is part of that plan, he believes that the history of the world, as we understand history, will soon come to an end, that the earthly kingdoms will pass away, and that their place will be taken by an eternal spiritual kingdom. This will happen, he thinks, very soon, shortly after the death of Antiochus Epiphanes. In connection with this eschatological belief, the author asserts a doctrine of the resurrection of the dead. Not all the dead, according to his thinking, will be resurrected (that belief belongs to a later period); only the most pure and the most wicked (see 12:2). The pure and the wise, including doubtless the Hasidim, will share in the spiritual kingdom, the consummation of God's victory. In that faith the victims of persecution should stand firm, wait, and hope.

Note: Part of Daniel, 2:4b to 7:28, is written in Aramaic, a language closely related to Hebrew and one which had for some time begun to supplant it in Palestine. It is not certain why these passages were so translated — possibly to make them more widely available.

An account of the additions to the Book of Daniel will be found in the section on "The Apocrypha."

Summary of Book of Daniel

Daniel and his Friends at Court of Nebuchadrezzar 1:1-6:28. Some of the Jewish exiles in Babylon are chosen to be trained for service in the court of Nebuchadrezzar. Among these are Daniel and his three friends, Hananiah, Mishael, and Azariah, better known by their Babylonian names Shadrach, Meshach, and Abednego. Faithful to the dietary rules of the Torah, they live on vegetables and water, but nevertheless are endowed by God with wisdom which exceeds that of the Babylonian sages and magicians. When Nebuchadrezzar has a dream which he cannot recall, it is not the Babylonian wise men, but Daniel, inspired by God, who is able to tell it and interpret it. The strange image with the golden head, breast, and arms of silver, belly of bronze, legs of iron, and feet partly of clay prefigures the kingdoms which will succeed Nebuchadrezzar. Impressed, the ruler prostrates himself and acknowledges Daniel's God. In the next test of virtue, the three friends refuse to worship the golden idol set up by Nebuchadrezzar, but survive unharmed the burning fiery furnace into which they are cast. Once more the king is impressed and promotes the three exiles. Next, Nebuchadrezzar dreams of a huge tree which is chopped down by an angel. Daniel explains that the king will lose his mind and be like an animal. Just so, a year later the king becomes insane and eats grass like an ox. When he recovers, he once more acknowledges Daniel's God.

Belshazzar, Nebuchadrezzar's successor (he was not, as Ch. 5 says, his son), holds a great feast for a thousand of his nobles. They drink from the sacred vessels taken by Nebuchadrezzar from the Temple of Jerusalem. But as a mysterious hand writes "Mene, Mene, Tekel, and Parsin" (RSV) on the walls, the king grows pale and sends for Daniel to explain the strange words. Daniel says that Belshazzar's kingdom will be given to the Medes and Persians. Daniel is clothed in fine purple and a chain of gold, but Belshazzar is killed that very night and Darius the Mede succeeds him. (This Darius is a figure of the story, not a real historical figure. The author is probably thinking of Darius I, who conquered Babylon twenty years later. Cyrus and Cambyses actually followed Belshazzar.) Darius gives Daniel high office, but jealous officials plot against him. Disregarding an edict againt praying to anyone but the king, Daniel prays to God and is punished by being cast into the lions' den. Again he survives unharmed, and again the word goes out that the God of Daniel is to be reverenced. Daniel prospers during his reign and during the reign of Cyrus.

Visions of Daniel 7:1-12:13. In the first vision (Ch. 7) Daniel sees four strange beasts who, as he learns from the cryptic comments of an angelic interpreter, symbolize the four great kingdoms of recent history. The lion with eagle's wings represents Babylon, the bear with ribs in its mouth the Medes, the leopard with four heads and four wings Persia, and the ten-horned beast with iron teeth the Seleucid (Hellenistic) Empire. The little horn with eyes and a mouth which springs up in the fourth beast and destroys three other horns represents Antiochus Epiphanes. (Daniel does not say so, but contemporaries would recognize the description.) The "Ancient of Days," that is, God sitting in judgment, sentences the fourth kingdom to destruction and spares the others for a season. "With the clouds of heaven" comes "one like the Son of man," (literally like a mortal man) who represents "the saints of the Most High," the holy community of Israel who are to inherit the everlasting kingdom which is to come (the cryptic reference to time in vs. 25 is meant to point to the time of Antiochus' persecution of the Jews 167-164 B.C.). In the second vision (Ch. 8) a ram with two horns (the empire of the Medes and Persians) is challenged by a goat (the Greeks) with a single large horn (Alexander the Great). When the large horn is broken, i.e., after Alexander's death, four horns appear, which stand for the four kingdoms of that era. From them springs a little horn, who sets himself against the host of heaven and its prince (i.e., God), profanes the Temple, interrupts the sacrifice, and casts down truth. Again, the writer's contemporaries would recognize that this was a description of Antiochus Epiphanes. The passage hints that the Temple will be restored in three years and two months (vs. 14).

In the third vision (Ch. 9) Daniel puzzles over the prophecy in Jeremiah that the desolation of Jerusalem would last seventy years. He works it out as "seventy weeks of years," i.e., 490 years, which are divided into three periods of seven weeks, sixty-two weeks, and one week. By the end of this period the Jews will have atoned for their sins and the desolation of Jerusalem will be over. Though attempts to figure this all out arithmetically do not work out exactly, probably what is meant is the 49 years from Zedekiah to the priest Joshua, 435 years from Joshua to the priest Onias III, and the period between his assassination and the Maccabean world and the coming of the eternal kingdom.

The final vision (Chs. 10-12) takes place after Daniel has been fasting and mourning for 21 days. A man clothed in linen and girded with gold promises him a vision of the distant future. What is revealed is a cryptic but detailed history of events in Near Eastern history from the Persians to Antiochus Epiphanes. Most of the references can be worked out (see for example the *Interpreter's Bible*, VI, pp. 347-8), but are too numerous to summarize here. The history is carried down to the point where it tells how a "vile person" (Antiochus Epiphanes again) will crush "the prince of the covenant" (probably the high priest who was killed during the dispute which preceded the persecution), set up an abomination in the Temple, and magnify himself above God. However, the writer comes to grief when he tries to predict the future, for he prophesies that Antiochus will meet his doom between the Mediterranean and Jerusalem, with no one to help him, whereas Antiochus actually died (in 163 B.C.) in Persia. In the epilogue to the book it is said that the archangel Michael will come to deliver the Jews from their suffering, and "many of them that sleep in the dust of the earth shall awake, some to everlasting life and some to shame and everlasting contempt." The pure will become more pure and the wicked will remain in their wickedness. Daniel is told to go his way and rest until the end comes. "When the end of the days" comes he will arise to enjoy his share in the kingdom.

Hosea

Hosea's preaching mission followed soon after that of Amos, and should be studied with it. The two are often contrasted. Amos is said to be the prophet of justice and Hosea of mercy. This is an oversimplification, as Amos feels deeply for Israel and is never detached or heartless, whereas Hosea, like Amos, is deeply concerned for the demands of righteousness. However, Hosea does emphasize the divine compassion of Yahweh and believes that he will ultimately save his people.

We know nothing about Hosea except what we can learn from his book. He preached in Israel in the last years of Jeroboam II and afterward. The political situation was very unstable, particularly after the death of Jeroboam, and Israel showed a tendency, deplored by Hosea, to drift into alliance with either Assyria or Egypt. The religious situation was disquieting.

The mass of the people seemed to have forgotten their covenant obligations and were attracted to the local Baalism of Canaan. The Baals were the gods of fertility cults which were characterized by the worship of images, the setting up of many shrines, and by great agricultural festivals which were the occasion of drunkenness and other excesses. At such festivals ritual marriages were often enacted, which were supposed to ensure fertility during the coming year. Cultic prostitution seems to have been common. It was this situation which Hosea tried to deal with.

The book consists of oracles, biography, and what appears to be an autobiographical passage. It is confusing to read, partly because Hosea's deeply emotional style is sometimes difficult to follow and partly because the manuscript was reedited, perhaps several times, to make it applicable to a somewhat later situation in Judah. The text is corrupt and the authorship of several passages is questioned.

Title 1:1. Hosea certainly began his mission before the end of the reign of Jeroboam, and continued it until the time of the Syro-Ephraimitic War of 734-733 B.C. There is no internal evidence that his ministry was longer than this and the name of the other kings may have been added later.

Hosea's Marriage 1:2-3:5. *Here is one of the most puzzling passages in the whole of prophetic literature, yet it is important to try to understand it, since it lies at the heart of Hosea's message.*

In Chapter 1 we hear that Yahweh told Hosea to take a harlotrous wife and harlotrous children, because Israel herself had committed harlotry in forsaking her God. Accordingly Hosea took Gomer as his wife and she bore him (literally "to him") a son. At Yahweh's direction the child was called Jezreel, as a sign that as a condemnation of Jehu and Jezebel, Yahweh would demand the blood of Jezreel. (The fact that this prophecy was not fulfilled does not seem to have troubled Hosea's disciples or editors, who let the prophecy stand.) Gomer conceived again—this time the sentence is not framed so that one is absolutely sure whether the child is Hosea's own or not—and the infant (a girl) is named Lo-ruhamah, which means "Not pitied" or perhaps "Loveless." This name seems to imply that Yahweh's pity and patience are exhausted. The name of the third child, a boy, is Lo-ammi, "Not my people." This name seems to indicate that Yahweh has broken the convenant and rejected Israel. (The authenticity of 1:10-2:1 is disputed.) Next, while the children are told to plead for their mother (i.e., Israel) to put away her harlotry, lest she be destroyed, and to abandon her lovers who, she says, "Give me my bread and my water, my wool and my flax, mine oil and my drink," she thinks the Baals, the fertility gods of Canaan, give her these things, and does not recognize that these are the gifts of Yahweh. He will punish her for following the Baals and offering them sacrifices. Yet the prophet, who sees the analogy between his domestic situation and the relationship between Yahweh and Israel, says he will try to speak persuasively and tenderly to her, so that she will not confuse him with the Baals. She will no longer call him Baal, but husband and, says Yahweh, I will betroth thee unto me in righteousness, and in judgment, and in loving-kindness, and in mercies. I will even betroth thee unto me in faithfulness: and thou shalt know the Lord...and I will say unto them which were not my people, thou art my people, and they shall say, thou art my God."

Ch. 3, written in the first person, seems to recount a somewhat similar experience. Yahweh says, "go again, love a woman who is beloved of a paramour and is a adultress even as the Lord loves the people of Israel" (RSV). The prophet apparently obeys, for he says he has bought the woman and proposes to help her in a kind of probationary isolation, so that she will give up harlotry. Similarly, the children of Israel should be denied some of the externals of religion, until they learn to seek Yahweh and fear him.

What do these narratives mean and what is the relationship between them? Are these real events? Do Chs. 1 and 3 refer to the same events or different ones? If the latter, in what order should we consider them? There are scores, perhaps hundreds, of answers to these questions. Many commentators, especially in medieval times, were troubled by the involvement of a prophet with a prostitute and tried to read the whole episode as an allegory. But there are many details which cannot be allegorized and the difficulty cannot really be solved this way. It is better to recognize that the story is in some sense literal. In this case, does all of Chs. 1 and 3 give different accounts of the same events? It would seem not, since the details are different. Or does Ch. 3 represent an earlier stage, Ch. 1 a later? Probably it is simplest to take the narratives in the order given, to suppose, as the Hebrew wording would suggest, that Gomer's "harlotry" was at first only potential, but became actual after the marriage, indeed perhaps only after the birth of the first child. (There are linguistic arguments against the suggestion that Gomer was a cult prostitute.) Hosea at some point reclaimed her, apparently hoping to rehabilitate her by his faithfulness and love.

What is clear is that through this personal experience of disappointment and disillusion, Hosea gained an insight into Yahweh's love for Israel and his disappointment in her apostasy. He was the first to use marriage as an image of the covenant relationship between Yahweh and people. The loyalty and affection he felt for Gomer helped him to understand Yahweh's "steadfast love" (RSV) for Israel. In Martin Buber's words, Yahweh said to him, "continue loving, thou art allowed to love her, thou must love her; even so do I love Israel." (*The Prophetic Faith*, New York: Macmillan, 1949, p. 113.)

Israel's Unfaithfulness 4:1-13:16.

The prophet speaks of Israel's apostasy and wickedness. There is no fidelity, no knowledge of God, and in consequence cursing, lying, murder, theft, and adultery flourish. Drunkenness prevents understanding, people seek counsel of wooden idols, harlotries multiply. "A people without insight must come to ruin" (AT). Both Israel and Judah will be punished. They think that Yahweh will heal and will revive them, but he tells them their shallow repentance is like a cloud or a mist which soon vanishes, "for I desired mercy and not sacrifices: and the knowledge of God is more than burnt offerings." (Note the frequent expression of this idea in Hosea: if the people really knew Yahweh — the word conveys a close, intimate relationship — they would love and serve him.) The prophet is also troubled about Israel's flirtations with foreign powers. Ephraim (Israel), he says scornfully, is like a half-baked cake, like a silly dove, toying first with Egypt, then with Assyria. In

Yahweh's name, he sneers at the sacred bull of Samaria: "the workman made it; therefore it is not God." Punishment will come upon the land, "for they have sown the wind, and they shall reap the whirlwind." They will go into exile, to Assyria or to Egypt, and nettles will possess the land. Because they have not listened to Yahweh, they will become wanderers among the nations, and will wish the hills and mountains would fall upon them. "Sow to yourselves in righteousness, reap in mercy; break up your fallow ground; for it is time to seek the Lord, till he come and rain righteousness upon you."

Yet (Ch. 11) Yahweh cannot help but recall the covenant relationship with his people. "When Israel was a child, then I loved him, and called my son out of Egypt." He remembers how he guided the infant nation: "I led them with cords of compassion, with the bands of love" (RSV). "How can I give you up O Ephraim," he cries. "How can I hand you over, O Israel? ... I will not carry out my fierce anger; nor will I again destroy Ephraim; for I am God and not man" (AT). Yet once more with a sudden change of mood he thinks of the faithlessness of Israel and Judah and urges them to return to him. They have forgotten him and the words of his prophets, and will therefore be destroyed. They have sacrificed to idols, kissed man-made calves; therefore they shall vanish like a cloud, like chaff above the threshing floor, or like smoke. They have forgotten all that God has done for them, they have taken unto themselves kings and princes. They have rebelled against God and will perish by the sword.

Call to Return and Promise of Forgiveness 14:1-9. Again there is a sudden change of mood (suggesting to some critics that this passage may be spurious), as Yahweh calls Israel to repentance. No longer will the people worship man-made idols. Yahweh promises: "I will heal their backsliding, I will love them freely; for mine anger is turned away from him. I will be as the dew unto Israel: he shall grow as the lily, and cast forth his roots as Lebanon."

Joel

Introduction. The Book of Joel describes the invasion of a plague of locusts which relentlessly strip the countryside and then turn their attention to the city. The devastation is described in vivid poetry. Observers of locust plagues in Palestine in 1915 and 1928 attest to the exactness of the descriptions, both of the swift advance of the locusts and of their terrible effects on the morale of the people. To the poet the scourge suggests that the Day of Yahweh is at hand, when the repentant faithful will be delivered and their enemies punished. The book is clearly post-exilic, but an exact date cannot be established. Somewhere between 450 and 350 B.C., is probable.

Title 1:1. "The word of the Lord that came to Joel ..." — a common superscription.

Plague of Locusts and Drought 1:2-2:29. The prophet calls the whole community, including old men and drunks, to see the locusts: "What the cutting locust left, the swarming locust has eaten. What the swarming locust has left, the hopping locust has eaten, and what the hopping locust left, the destroying locust has eaten" (RSV). With their powerful teeth, the locusts have nibbled the vine and fig trees, stripping off the bark and leaving the branches white. Because the grain and wine and oil have failed, there can be no sacrifices. Pomegranate, palm, and apple are withered. The prophet begs the priests to call a solemn assembly to pray for deliverance from the locusts and from the drought which is making the seeds shrivel in the pods and devouring the fields, so that even the beasts are suffering. He urges the priests to blow the trumpet in Zion, for now the locusts are attacking the city; the day of the Lord is coming, a day of darkness and gloom. The locusts leave behind them only a wilderness. They attack with the speed and order of an army. Since "the day of the Lord is great and very terrible," the speaker urges repentance: "Rend your heart and not your garments." Once more the prophet begs the priests to proclaim an assembly and fast to which all, even the nursing babe and the bride, should come to implore Yahweh's help, or the heathen will say, "Where is their God?" Yahweh's response is gracious. He promises grain, wine, and oil, the removal of the "northerner" (the locusts), rain, fruitfulness, and the return of "the years that the locust have eaten." There will

also be a spiritual gift: "I will pour out my Spirit upon all flesh; and your sons and your daughters shall prophesy, your old men shall dream dreams, your young men shall see visions." Even the servants will prophesy.

Day of the Lord and Future Greatness of Yahweh 2:30-3:21. But the promise that the Spirit will come is a prelude to the announcement that the day of Yahweh is at hand: "The sun shall be turned into darkness, and the moon into blood, before the great and terrible day of the Lord come." Yahweh will gather the nations into the valley of Jehoshaphat where he will punish them for their cruelties to the Jews. Tyre and Sidon will be punished in kind for looting and for enslaving God's people. In a passage which reverses Isaiah and Micah (Isa. 2:4; Mic. 3:3), the nations are urged. "Beat your plowshares into swords, and your pruning hooks into spears..." Yahweh will judge the heathen, while "the sun and the moon shall be darkened, and the stars shall withdraw their shining" and "the heavens and the earth shall shake." But the Lord will protect his own people and give them great prosperity: "The mountains shall drop down new wine, and the hills shall flow with milk, and all the rivers of Judah shall flow with waters, and a fountain shall come forth of the house of the Lord and shall water the valley of Shittim." Edom and Egypt, the enemies of Israel, will be destroyed, but Judah and Jerusalem will remain forever.

Amos

Introduction. Amos was by his own account not a professional prophet but a shepherd from the hills of Tekoa, a few miles south

of Jerusalem. He also did seasonal work as a "dresser of sycamore trees" (RSV), the fig-like fruits which needed special treatment if they were to ripen properly. He evidently kept his eyes open on his travels, as his shrewd and penetrating comments show. He preached about the middle of the eighth century B.C. in the reign of Jeroboam II, at the great shrine of Bethel — that is, though a southerner from Judah, he preached in Israel, the northern kingdom. In Chapter 7, the priest Amaziah tells him substantially to go back where he came from.

Israel at this time was relatively prosperous. Assyria had temporarily withdrawn its attacks because of dissension at home. A flourishing international trade brought wealth to Israel. This wealth, however, became concentrated in relatively few hands, small holdings gave way to large estates, and the gulf between the very rich and the very poor widened. Social injustice was often accompanied by corruption in the courts. There was a great deal of religious activity at the numerous shrines, accompanied by complacency and optimism, but often not accompanied by high ethical standards. It is this false and superficial religion which Amos attacks. The book consists of oracles, visions, and short biographical passages. Note the vividness and imaginative power of his poetry and the penetrating exactness of his criticisms.

Titles and Motto 1:1-2. The first verse is an editorial title to the whole book and tells us that Amos spoke in the time of King Uzziah of Judah and King Jeroboam of Israel. His opening motto declares that "the Lord will roar from Zion," i.e., that Yahweh is about to speak.

Oracles against Surrounding Nations and against Israel 1:3-2:16. In the name of Yahweh, Amos attacks the enemies of Israel. Yahweh will punish Damascus for barbarously attacking Gilead, Gaza (i.e., Philistia) and Tyre for taking other nations into captivity, Edom for warring on his brother Israel, Ammon for greed and barbarity in war, and Moab for desecrating the remains of the king of Edom. (The attack on Judah for breaking God's laws was probably added later.) Each stanza is similarly constructed, beginning "For three transgressions of — and for four, I will not turn away the punishment..." Then the crime in each case is stated and the punishment announced in specific and vivid terms. This repetition has a powerful cumulative effect on the listeners, and they wait as each enemy is named to hear its crimes and fate proclaimed. Suddenly, when their emotions are thoroughly aroused against their enemies, Amos astonishes them by turning the attack on Israel. Israel, too, is guilty in Yahweh's eyes. She has sold the innocent for silver and the needy for a pair of sandals, she has committed moral and religious profanation. Yahweh's inescapable punishment awaits all classes of the nation.

Oracles on Israel's Doom 3:1-5:17. Again Amos speaks for Yahweh, reminding Israel that she will be punished, as she has not acted as the chosen of Yahweh should act. Election involves responsibility: "You only have I known of all the families of the earth: therefore I will punish you for all your iniquities." In a series of analogies, the prophet shows that it is imperative that he prophesy. "Will a lion roar in the forest, when he hath no prey?... The Lord God hath spoken, who can but prophesy?" Because Israel has done wrong, her enemies will overcome her, and there will be no more of her left than the fragments a shepherd rescues from the mouth of a lion — two bones and a piece of ear.

The prophet addresses the rich women of Samaria (i.e., Israel) as cows of Bashan, who oppress the poor indirectly by urging their husbands to exploit the needy in order to have more money for luxuries. They will be dragged away with hooks and cast on the refuse heap. Ironically Amos bids the people gather at the sacred shrines: "Come to Bethel — and transgress; at Gilgal multiply transgressions." He implies that worship without justice is sacrilege. Yahweh has warned his people with many chastisements—famine, drought, blight, plague, and earthquake, but she has not returned to him.

The prophet sings a formal lament for the fallen nation: "The virgin... Israel is fallen, she shall no more rise; she is forsaken upon her land; there is none to raise her up." He begs Israel "Seek the Lord, and ye shall live," but he knows that the people do not want to hear the word of Yahweh; they oppress the innocent, take bribes, and deny justice to the needy. Only if they seek good and not evil will even a remnant be saved.

Day of the Lord 5:18-6:14. The prophet speaks next to those who look forward to a future day when Yahweh will enter into human history, overthrow Israel's enemies, and give her victory and power. The day of the Lord will be, he says, a day of darkness and destruction, not of light. Once again, in one of the most striking and famous passages in the Bible, he speaks in the person of Yahweh, reminding the people that ceremony and sacrifices mean nothing when they are divorced from justice and righteousness: "I hate, I despise your feast days, and I will not smell (i.e., the sacrifices) in your solemn assemblies. ... Take thou away from me the noise of thy songs. ... But let judgment run down as waters and righteousness as a mighty stream." Amos goes on to paint a satirical pre-

tense of the rich who do not care, who are at ease in Zion, "who lie on ivory couches" eating, drinking, and singing, and are not heart-sick over the state of the nation, "are not grieved for the affliction of Joseph." They shall be the first to go into captivity, for ruin and destruction are at hand.

Three Visions of Judgment 7:1-9. Now Amos speaks in his own person of visions or perhaps actual events which seem to relate to Israel's relationship with Yahweh. First he sees Yahweh creating a great swarm of locusts — a symbol of destruction, for locusts are dangerous to the crops. He feels a moment of pity for Israel, and pleads, "O Lord God, forgive... by when shall Jacob (i.e., Israel) arise? for he is small." Yahweh seems to relent, but then comes a second vision, this time of a fire which devours the great deep (i.e., the primeval abyss of the creation story) and the land. Once again Amos pleads for Israel and once again Yahweh relents. But the third vision is stern and final. Yahweh stands with a plumbline in his hand, ready to test the nation. Israel does not meet the test, and Yahweh promises destruction to the sacred places and sanctuaries, destruction to the house of Jeroboam.

Amos and Amaziah 7:10-17. Now the visions are interrupted (for there are two others) by a narrative in the third person, apparently an extract from a longer account. Amaziah, the priest of Bethel, reports to the king (Jeroboam II) that the prophet has been conspiring against him and has even prophesied his death and the captivity of Israel. Amaziah tells Amos to go back to Judah, "there eat bread, and prophesy there," i.e., make your living by prophesying in your own country. In reply Amos denies that he is a regular prophet or a member of a prophetic order. He is a shepherd and dresser of sycamores. (The sycamore was a kind of fig tree, the "dressing" process either making strategic cuts to allow the best fruit to ripen or pricking the fruit to assist it in ripening.) Yahweh seized upon him one day and told him to prophesy to Israel.

Basket of Summer Fruit and Injustice in Israel 8:1-14. The basket of summer fruit is the fourth vision. By a play on words — the word for fruit and the word for end sound alike in Hebrew — the prophet passes immediately to the thought that the end is about to come to Israel. Once again he lashes out at those who trample on the needy and long for the religious celebrations to be over so that they can sell their grain; who falsify their weights and measures, and sell the refuse of their wheat. Suffering and destruction will be the consequences.

Final Destruction of Israel 9:1-8a. In the fifth and final vision, Amos sees God standing on an altar and ordering the destruction of the sanctuary. (Perhaps Amos has Bethel itself in mind.) If any worshipers are left, they will die, slain by the sword. None shall escape.

Epilogue: Restoration of Israel 9:8b-15. This final passage seems to have been added by some later writer who perhaps felt that if Amos reconsidered, he might see hope for Israel. The optimism of this writer is in striking contrast to the sternness and pessimism of Amos. The writer begins indeed pessimistically, saying that Yahweh will shake the house of Israel as one shakes a sieve, but he pronounces the promise of Yahweh to raise up the house of David, restore the fortunes of Israel, and replant his people on their own land. The restoration is unconditional; the favor of God is not, as elsewhere in the book, conditional on just and righteous conduct. For this reason and because of certain linguistic considerations, this part of the book is usually attributed to a post-exilic writer who believed that Yahweh as the Lord of history would secure the ultimate restoration of Israel.

Obadiah

Introduction. The Edomites were supposed to be descended from Esau and therefore kinsmen of the house of Jacob. It was therefore resented deeply when the Edomites actually took part in the siege of Jerusalem and after its fall in 587 used the opportunity to occupy some of the lands of Judah. Obadiah expresses this resentment and desire for revenge. The vengeful spirit of the book, though understandable, can hardly be admired. Vengeance did, in fact, as Obadiah hoped, fall upon them, for the Edomites suffered from attacks of Arabs in the fifth century. The book is commonly dated in the latter part of the century.

Title 1:1a. The title gives the prophet's name and claims that his message concerning Edom is from God.

Judgment against Edom 1:1b-14. A messenger urges the nations to rise up against Edom. Yahweh addresses Edom, telling her he will make her small and despised and bring her down from her lofty and rocky fortresses. Esau's (i.e., Edom's) treasures have been looted and she has been conquered by her previous allies. Even the wise men will be destroyed and every man from the Mount of Esau will be slaughtered. This punishment will be just retribution for the fact that the Edomites actually took part in the attack on Jerusalem. "For thy violence against thy brother Jacob shame shall cover thee, and thou shall be cut off for ever. In the day that thou stoodest on the other side, in the day that the strangers carried away captive his forces, and foreigners entered into his gates, and cast lots upon Jerusalem, even thou was as one of them." This was a violation of the blood ties between Judah and Edom. Edom should not have gloated over his brother in his distress, or looted his possessions, or cut off his fugitives.

The Day of the Lord 1:15-21. The day of the Lord's is close for the heathen nations, of which Edom is one. Retribution is due. "As thou hast done it, it shall be done to thee." The heathen will be judged and must drink the cup of God's wrath and "shall be as though they had not been." But some of the house of Jacob will survive and will return to Mount Zion, the holy place, and will renew the attack on Edom. "And the house of Jacob shall be a fire, and the house of Joseph a flame, and the house of Esau for stubble, and they shall kindle in them, and devour them; and there shall not be any remaining of the house of Esau; for the Lord hath spoken it." Judah and Israel will reunite and will push back the Edomites to the south, the west, the north and the east. Delivers will go up "to Mount Zion to judge the Mount of Esau, and the kingdom shall be the Lord's."

Jonah

Introduction. This little book is one of the most delightful in the Bible, yet its message is a serious and lofty one. Its point is lost if it is treated as history. It is not history or an ordinary book of prophecy at all, but a story whose exaggerations, absurdities, and sudden turns of fate are part of the author's purpose. We might even call it a parable, since it is designed, like some of Jesus' parables, to make the hearer view a situation in a fresh light — ultimately, to look at himself.

The situation the author has in mind was a point in the post-exilic history when nationalistic feeling and particularism were stronger than the universalism preached by Second Isaiah (see above). Israel had suffered so many cruelties, dis-

appointments, and disillusions that often her only feeling toward foreigners was hatred and a desire for revenge. These feelings are expressd in Obadiah and Esther and in part of Joel and Ezekiel. They are understandable, but the author of Jonah felt that such feelings were a violation of Israel's highest beliefs about God. In his story he tries to show that Jonah is actually repudiating his own image of God. He *knows* that God is "gracious and merciful, slow to anger and of great kindness," but this does not make it any easier for him to preach to the hateful Ninevites and he is furious when they repent and earn God's forgiveness. He cannot accept the fact that God cares for the ignorant heathen, too. The pettiness and absurdity of his position is made clear when he is upset over the destruction of the plant which gave him shade, but becomes angry because God forgives thousands of helpless people who have shown every sign of repentance and sincerity.

Perhaps the author meant to go a step further, to show not only the absurdity and cruelty of bigotry, but the shortcomings of Israel in her role in history. The heathen among whom Jonah moves are not unreceptive to his religion. The sailors pray to his God and the Ninevites accept his prophetic message. The name Jonah means "dove," the symbol of Israel. Was the author trying to remind his countrymen that the chosen people were intended to be a light to the gentiles?

Summary of Jonah

Divine Command 1:1-2. The book begins as any prophetic book might, by asserting that God spoke directly to Jonah. He has heard of the wickedness of Nineveh and orders Jonah to preach to the Ninevites.

Jonah's Flight from God 1:3-2:10. The author doubtless chose the Assyrian as the object of Jonah's mission just because they were the people most hated and feared by Israel, who had suffered so much from their cruel attacks. Jonah does not in the least want to preach to the Ninevites, so at Joppa he takes a ship to Tarshish (probably Tartessos, a Phoenician colony in Spain) in an effort to get as far away as possible, "away from the presence of the Lord" (RSV). But the Lord sets in motion a mighty tempest, which so frightens the mariners that they pray, each to his own god, and toss some of the cargo overboard. Meanwhile Jonah is comfortably asleep in the ship's hold. There the captain awakens him and bids him pray to his god, who might be the very one who

could save them. (The captain's outlook is polytheistic; he assumes the storm is caused by the whim of some god who perhaps can be placated, if he can be identified.) When they cast lots to find whose presence is the reason for the storm, the lot falls on Jonah. He admits that he is the cause of the storm and declares his willingness to be cast into the sea. The good hearted soldiers make a valiant attempt to bring the ship in without having recourse to this desperate remedy, but eventually are obliged to carry it out. Jonah is cast into the sea, which immediately ceases from its raging. The sailors, who have prayed to Jonah's God, now offer him vows and a sacrifice.

Meanwhile a great fish which God has assigned to the task, swallows Jonah up and he remains in the fish's belly for three days and three nights. At this point a pious editor, evidently thinking that Jonah in these dire straights should pray, inserted a prayer which he thought appropriate, probably because of the words "the water compassed me about." It is not really appropriate, being a thanksgiving for deliverance, whereas Jonah is not really delivered until vs. 10, when the fish vomits him out on dry land.

"The Reluctant Missionary" 3:1-4:11. (The phrase is J. D. Smart's, see *IB*, VI, 888). Once again the word of the Lord comes to Jonah. He is to preach in Nineveh. Grudgingly he makes his way to the great city, so wide that it takes three days to cross it. His prophecy is a simple one: "Yet forty days and Nineveh shall be overthrown." Success is instantaneous. The people believe in God, proclaim a fast, and put on sackcloth. Even the king himself lays aside his royal robe, rules that all, even the animals, are to share the fast and the sackcloth. He urges prayer, hoping that the anger of God will be turned away, if the people change their evil ways. God is impressed with the transformation that has taken place and decides not to destroy the city.

This makes Jonah very angry. He seems bitterly disappointed that Nineveh is not going to be destroyed after all. He wishes he were dead. God asks him, "Doest thou well to be angry?" Jonah does not answer, but sulkily goes out to the east side of the city, where he makes a little booth and waits, perhaps still hoping for the city's destruction.

Next God orders a large gourd to grow up and shade Jonah's head. Jonah is delighted, but the next day God sends a worm which destroys the plant and a burning east wind which makes Jonah faint.

Once more he wishes he were dead. Once again God asks him, "Doest thou well to be angry for the gourd?" Jonah replies that he is angry enough to die.

Gently God rebukes him and points the lesson: "Thou hast had pity on the gourd, for the which thou hast not laboured, neither madest it grow; which came up in a night, and perishes in a night: And should not I spare Nineveh, that great city, wherein are more than sixscore thousand persons that cannot discern between their right hand and their left hand [i.e., ordinary, ignorant people], and also much cattle?" Jonah was deeply emotional about a plant which grew up and died in a day, yet he was enraged at God's pity for the helpless and repentant Ninevites.

Micah

Introduction. Micah was a native of Moresheth, a little village in the Philistine Plain. He was a contemporary of Hosea and Isaiah, but seems to have been influenced most by Amos whose home, Tekoa, was only about twenty miles from Moresheth. Like Amos, he denounced the social injustice of the cities. He was also deeply dismayed by the ambitions of the Assyrians, who had already conquered Syria and Israel, leaving Judah an unprotected and helpless state between the Assyrian empire and Egypt. Micah seems to have felt that the corruption and social injustice in Judah would justify an Assyrian attack, and this is one argument he uses in trying to arrest the moral decay he saw all around him.

Although the superscription says he prophesied under three kings, it is usually believed that his ministry took place in the last quarter

of the eighth century, perhaps from 725 on. His ministry apparently had some success, for the Book of Jeremiah (26:17-10) credits him with powerful influence for good over King Hezekiah, who destroyed the pagan images on the high places and kept the law of Moses.

The text of Micah has been carefully preserved, but editors have introduced much post-exilic material to balance Micah's rather gloomy outlook.

Superscription. The heading tells us that Micah was from Moresheth and that he focused his attention on Samaria and Jerusalem. It is thought that his ministry was confined to the reign of Hezekiah.

Danger from Assyria 1:2-16. (A short eschatological psalm, vss. 2-4, has been inserted as an introduction.) To call attention to his prophecy, Micah says he will walk about the city naked, crying out his indictment to fix attention on the big cities, Samaria and Jerusalem, as the sources of corruption. However, the cumulative list of towns suggests that he repeated his message in all the places he passed through. He warns the people that Jerusalem is in danger and a conqueror is coming who may take their children into exile.

Evils of Jerusalem and Judah 2:1-3:12.

Micah first directs his wrath against the wealthy men of Jerusalem who lie awake at night devising new plans for seizing their lands and homes of the poor. In the future their captors (i.e., the Assyrians) may take over and divide up their fields, but at present they do not want to listen to any criticism of their exploitation. Micah claims the right to criticize, for the Spirit of the Lord should not be restricted. (Another short passage describing the restoration of the remnant has been inserted here, vss. 12-13).

Next Micah addresses the leaders, the "heads of Jacob" who "hate the good and love the evil," who tear the flesh of the people like butchers. He speaks to the prophets, who "cry Peace when they have something to eat, but declare war against him who puts nothing in their mouths" (RSV). Such false prophets will dwell in darkness. He condemns the leaders who "build up Zion with blood," for "the heads thereof judge for reward, and the priests thereof teach for hire, and the prophets thereof divine for money ..." Because of their iniquity, Jerusalem will become a heap of ruins.

Future of Israel 4:1-5:15.

There is wide agreement that these chapters are not by Micah, but belong to a later period. Two somewhat contradictory poems seem to have been combined. One written somewhat in the spirit of Second Isaiah looks forward to the "last days," after the reform from the Babylonian exile, when many nations will turn to Jerusalem and to the God of Jacob for law and for judgment. It contains the famous and beautiful passage "And he shall judge among many people, and rebuke strong nations afar off; and they shall beat their swords into plowshares, and their spears into pruning hooks: nation shall not lift up a sword against nation, neither shall they learn war any more." The other poem seems to be a hymn of hate, announcing that Zion will "beat in pieces many peoples" and annihilate their enemies. It closes with threats from Yahweh that he will purge the remnant by destroying their armies, cities, fortresses, and heathen symbols.

True Religion 6:1-8.

This famous passage is sometimes ascribed to an anonymous prophet in the reign of Manasseh, but the arguments against Micah's authorship seem less cogent than in the case of the previous section. In any case the poem is well worth studying carefully. It takes the form of a court trial, the case of Yahweh against Israel. The mountains are called as witnesses as the prophet in the name of the Lord summons Israel to present her case. He reminds Israel what God has done for her since he brought her out of Egypt and gave her Moses as her leader, implying that she has forgotten that the covenant relationship involves righteous acts on her side, too. Israel stands ashamed, with no case to plead: "Wherewith shall I come before the Lord, and bow myself before the high God? shall I come before him with burnt offerings, with calves of a year old? Will the Lord be pleased with thousands of rams, or with ten thousands of rivers of oil? shall I give my firstborn for my transgression, the fruit of my body for the sin of my soul? He hath showed thee, O man, what is good; and what doth the Lord require of thee, but to do justly, and to love mercy and to walk humbly with thy God?" It is often said that this summary of prophetic religion recalls Amos' dedication to justice, Hosea's affirmation of steadfast love, and Isaiah's insistence on tranquility in faith.

Jerusalem's Sin and Punishment 6:9-16. In the name of the Lord the prophet accuses the men of the city of dishonesty. Their measures, scales, and weights are designed to cheat the customers. For this Yahweh will punish them; they will sow, but not have time to reap. "You shall eat, but not be satisfied, and there shall be hunger in your inward parts" (RSV). Because they have been as evil as the house of Omri, they will be scorned and despised by other nations.

Prophets Despair 7:1-6. This poem may continue the thoughts of the last chapter. The prophet looks for a godly man, but it is like looking for fruit after it has all been gathered. All men are wicked: "they all lie in wait for blood, they hunt every man his brother with a net." Princes and judges take bribes and great men utter "mischievous desire." The best of them is like a briar or a thorn hedge. The passage concludes with a warning not to trust friends or neighbors, for even the members of a family can turn against each other.

A Psalm of Hope 7:7-20. To conclude the book on a more cheerful note, some editor added a postexilic psalm of hope which shows the influence both of Psalm 137 and of Second Isaiah. The speaker looks forward to the day when God will overthrow his enemies, trample them like mud, and restore the walls of Jerusalem, to which the dispersed Jews will return. God will be the shepherd of his people. The other nations will be ashamed of their power and will lick the dust and turn to God in fear. To the remnant of his chosen people, God will manifest his love and compassion as he promised in the days of old.

Nahum

Introduction. For centuries the Near East had suffered from the Assyrians, whose cruelties were proverbial. Their power was extended even into Egypt, where Asshurbanipal conquered Thebes in 663 (the incident is referred to in Nah. 3:8-10). But in 612 B.C. Nineveh, the Assyrian capital, fell before a coalition of Babylonians, Medes, and Scythians. The prophet Nahum celebrates the fall of the city in this bloodthirsty hymn of revenge, notable for its intensity and its brilliant use of realistic detail. One can hardly call religious the spirit of hatred and vengeance which infuses the poem, but its literary power is of high quality and it must be remembered that Israel had suffered deeply at the hands of the Assyrians. It is not certain whether the book was written before or just after the siege.

Title 1:1. The first verse contains the title of Nahum's poem and also the title of the acrostic poem which precedes it.

Acrostic Oracle against Nineveh 1:2-10. This alphabetical acrostic, imperfectly recalled, was inserted by a much later editor to serve as an introduction. Some lines of it were woven into the passage which follows. For a reconstruction, see *IB*, VI, 995-6. The speaker reminds his hearers that Yahweh is a jealous God, whose power may be experienced in whirlwind and storm, in drought, in earthquake, and in volcanic disturbances. He will take vengeance on his enemies.

Fall of Nineveh 1:11-2:12. Did not Nineveh plot evil against the Lord? Therefore she will be cut off, for "he that dasheth in pieces" (i.e., the coalition of Babylonians and Medes) has come up against her. The prophet pictures the preparation for the attack: "Man the ramparts; watch the road, gird your loins; collect all your strength" (RSV). The war chariots rush back and forth. The officers stumble as they hurry to the walls. The iron gates are opened. Those who live in the palace are terrified. Nineveh is like a pool whose waters are draining away, her treasure is being looted. "She is empty, and void, and waste; and the heart melteth, and the knees smite together, and much pain is in all loins, and the faces of them all gather blackness." Yahweh vows that he will burn her chariots in smoke and devour her lions (a favorite Assyrian symbol).

Ruin of Nineveh 3:1-19. "Woe to the bloody city!" cries the poet, "It is all full of lies and robbery." We hear "the noise of a whip, and the noise of the rattling of the wheels, and of the prancing horses, and of the jumping chariots." We see "the horseman lifteth up both the bright sword and the glittering spear: and there is a multitude slain . . ." The shame of the harlot will be exposed. Ironically the prophet asks. "Are you better than Thebes?" (RSV) — i.e., "Are you better than the city which one of your rulers captured?" — implying that Nineveh in her turn will be captured. The city will be dazed and drunken, as her fortifications fall like ripe figs and her gates lie open to the enemies. In mockery of Nineveh's helplessness, the speaker urges her, "Draw thee strongholds," make brick in vain, for, as he says, "There shall the fire devour thee, the sword shall cut thee off." The Assyrian leaders are useless: "Thy shepherds slumber, O king of Assyria, thy nobles shall dwell in the dust: thy people is scattered upon the mountains and no man gathereth them." The wound given to Nineveh is grievous (literally "festering") and all who hear rejoice, for all have suffered from the wickedness of Assyria.

Habakkuk

Introduction. The reference to the Chaldeans in 1:6 would seem to date the work of Habakkuk in the end of the seventh century after the rise of Nabopolassar in 626 but before the fall of Jerusalem in 587. In the text, as we have it, the book's reply to the prophet's query about destruction and violence implies that the Chaldeans are an instrument of his chastisement, as much as the Assyrians were according to Isaiah 5:26-29. However, some editors think two separate poems have been interwoven here and would separate 1:5-11, 12b, 14-

17, which deals with the Chaldeans, from the prophet's meditation on the problem of evil, 1:2-4, 12a, 13, 2:1-4. The psalm which rounds off the book was almost certainly added later. It is not in the Dead Sea manuscript of Habakkuk, which probably dates from the first century B.C.

The poet's struggle with the problem of evil should be compared to Job's.

Title 1:1. The title gives the prophet's name (of Assyrian origin) and says his oracle came from God.

Habakkuk's Question 1:2-4. "O Lord, how long shall I cry, and thou wilt not hear! even cry unto thee of violence and thou wilt not save!" The prophet addresses God directly. He sees destruction and violence in the world. Justice and the law are violated.

Oracles on the Bitter and Hasty Nation 1:5-11. In the present text, this seems to be God's reply to the prophet's question. "For, lo, I raise up the Chaldeans, that bitter and hasty nation, which shall march through the breadth of the land, to possess the dwelling places that are not theirs." The Chaldeans, whose horses are swift and fierce, are dreadful, terrible, and violent; they take numberless captives, scoff at kings, laugh at fortresses.

Habakkuk Renews his Questioning 1-12-17. "Art thou not from everlasting: O Lord my God, mine Holy One?.... Thou art of purer eyes than to behold evil, and canst not look on iniquity: wherefore lookest thou upon them that deal treacherously, and holdest thy tongue when the wicked devoureth the man that is more righteous than he?" How can God tolerate treachery and wickedness and look on in silence when evil men swallow up good? Men are like fish or crawling things, leaderless, ready to be caught by hook and net.

The Watchtower 2:1-4. The prophet decides to station himself on a watchtower to see what God will say in reply. God tells him to write down the answer plainly, so that anyone going by "on the run" can read it. The reply is as follows: the wicked who is not upright shall fail, but the righteous man shall live by his faithfulness.

The Woes 2:5-20. The prophet makes five pronouncements connected with tyranny. (All are given in the RSV translation.) (1) "Woe to him who heaps up what is not his own," for rebellion will be the result. (2) "Woe to him who gets evil gain for his house," for it will not win him safety. (3) "Woe to him who builds a town with blood." (4) "Woe to him who makes his neighbors drink" and gazes on his shame. (5) "Woe to him who says to a wooden thing, Awake; to a dumb stone, Arise!" — i.e., to him who worships idols of wood and stone. At the end of the chapter, Habakkuk returns to the idea with which he started, that he will wait in silence before God: "But the Lord is in his holy temple: let all the earth keep silence before him."

Habakkuk's Prayer 3. The Book of Habakkuk concludes with a prayer of the prophet that resembles a psalm. It tells of a vision he has had of the Lord. In this vision the Lord appears as a figure of anger and wrath. He strides through the world and the entire creation trembles with fear. The Lord has come to smite the wicked and raise up his people. The prayer concludes on a note of joy: "The Lord God is my strength ... he will make me walk upon mine high places."

Zephaniah

Introduction. During the long reign of Manasseh (697-643) paganism had gained much ground in Judah. Manasseh imitated the Assyrians by worshiping the heavenly bodies as gods. He revived the worship of Canaanite Baals, believed in witchcraft and the cult of the dead, and possibly even practiced infant sacrifice. But after the death of Manasseh's son Amon came the reforming king Josiah (641-609). It is thought that Zephaniah's work, which certainly attacks the syncretism favored by Manasseh, falls in the early years of Josiah's reign, perhaps about 626 B.C. Most of his warnings are not new, but he may have helped to prepare the ground for Josiah's reform of 623/22. His graphic picture of the day of Yahweh (1:14-16) lingered long in Judaeo-Christian memory and inspired the fine medieval Latin hymn *"Dies Irae."* The eschatological predictions of the last chapter, particularly vss. 14-20, probably come from a later period.

Title 1:1. The unusually long opening statement traces the prophet's ancestry back four generations to (apparently) King Hezekiah. If correct, this would make Zephaniah a cousin of King Josiah.

Judgments against Jerusalem and Judah 1:2-18. Chapter 1 is disorganized and the opening verses, with their picture of total destruction, may have been added later. Then a genuine passage from Zephaniah attacks the worship of Baal, those who worship heavenly bodies, the Ammonite cult of Malcham (a variant of Moloch), those who have adopted foreign clothes, and those who leap over the Temple threshold so as not to step on it (a pagan Philistine custom). Yahweh is represented as searching Jerusalem with lamps, ready to punish men who are complacent, "thick" like wine which has not been properly stirred up, who assume that God will do nothing, who say to themselves "The Lord will not do good, neither will he do evil." The day of the Lord, a day of wrath, suffering, desolation, and gloom is at hand, when even strong men will weep.

Judgments against the Nations 2:1-15. The wrath of God is invoked against a "shameless nation" (RSV)—Judah?—and against the Philistine cities. (Plea for humility in verse 3 may be editorial.) Oracles follow against Moab and the Ammonites, who will become as Sodom and Gomorrah, and against the Ethiopians, who will be slain by the sword. Assyria, too, is warned. Nineveh will become a desolation and a wilderness.

Denunciations and Promises 3:1-20. If any of this chapter is genuine, it is the opening attack, vss. 1-7, on Jerusalem's rebelliousness and on the sins of the ruling classes. Her officials and judges prey on the people like animals, her prophets are untrustworthy, her priests blasphemous and lawless. Repeated warnings to the city have been disregarded. Yahweh will first assemble the nations to pour out his anger on them, but later will give them the gift of pure speech so that they may praise him and serve him with one accord. The proud will be removed and the humble remnant which is left will do no wrong, "for they shall feed and lie down and none shall make them afraid."

The book closes with a confident hope for a golden age. "Sing, O daughter of Zion, shout, O Israel," bids the prophet, "The Lord hath taken away thy judgments, he hath cast out thine enemy: the king of Israel, even the Lord, is in the midst of thee: thou shalt not see evil any more." God will "rejoice over thee with joy; he will rest in his love, he will joy over thee with singing. Sorrow will flee away, the lame and the outcast will be gathered in, the people will be gathered together, and will be "a name and a praise among all people of the earth."

Haggai

Introduction. Both Haggai and Zechariah throw light on the year 520 and after, when the rebuilding of the Temple was commenced. Haggai was shocked to find that nearly twenty years after Cyrus had allowed the exiles to return, the Temple was still in a ruined state. His description of the poverty of the community (1:6) suggests that the people were too occupied in scraping a bare living to be concerned about it. They used the foundations for sacrifice anyway and were used to seeing them in their burned-out and damaged state. Haggai, however, felt that if they made the effort to rebuild the Temple, Yahweh would reward them with the fruits of the earth and with prosperity. He evidently convinced them, for the work of reconstruction was actually begun. Haggai is characteristic of post-exile Judaism both in seeing the Temple as the center of the community's life and in objecting to mingling with the Samaritans.

Superscription 1:1. The opening sentence dates the first prophecy and declares that it came to Zerubbabel, governor of Judah, and to Joshua, the high priest.

Call to Rebuild 1:2-15. The people are unwilling or unready to rebuild the Temple, for they live in great poverty, lacking sufficient food and clothes. Haggai tells them that the Lord wants them to rebuild it, so that he can appear there in glory.

In his displeasure, he has withheld rain, grain, wine, and oil. Under the leadership of Zerubbabel and Joshua, the remnant of the people set to work. (Many editors consider 2:15-19 the second message and would place it here.)

Old Temple and New 2:1-9. People who remember are urged to take courage, Yahweh's spirit is among them and he promises that the latter splendor of his house will be even greater than the former.

The Unclean 2:10-14. The meaning of this passage is uncertain. Does Haggai mean that the people are unclean because they have not rebuilt the Temple? Or because they have sacrificed without a Temple? Or because they have mixed with the Samaritans? At any rate, for one of these reasons, Haggai considers that the offerings being made are unclean.

Fruitfulness 2:15-19. Haggai here reverts to the theme that the fruitfulness of the earth is dependent on the restoration of the Temple. Many editors would move this passage to the end of Chapter 1.

Zerubbabel, The Choice of Yahweh 2:20-23. Yahweh says he is about to shake the heavens and the earth and overthrow kingdoms, apparently to remove obstacles to the rule of Zerubbabel, who is to be Yahweh's servant to whom the heathen will surrender their powers.

Zechariah

Introduction. Zechariah's oracles are dated in the years 520-18. His ministry overlaps slightly with Haggai's. Like Haggai, he is concerned with the rebuilding of the Temple, the leadership of Zerubbabel and the priest Joshua, and the coming of the Messianic age. Both writers are hostile to the Samaritans and anxious about ritual purity. Zechariah has touches of universalism which recall Second Isaiah.

The last six chapters of the book are not really the work of Zechariah, but a collection of oracles from various hands, probably from the Greek period.

Superscription 1:1. The superscription gives Zechariah's ancestry and dates his first prophecy in 520 B.C., the "second year of Darius."

Call to Repent 1:2-6. Zechariah reports that Yahweh is angry with the ancestors of the people who did not turn away from their evil deeds. He calls on the present generation to carry out God's laws.

Zechariah's Visions 1:7-6:8. Zechariah sees a series of visions which are explained by an angelic interpreter. Four horsemen who have been riding about the earth report that all is peaceful. Four horses which represent enemies of Israel (Assyrians, Babylonians, Medes, Persians?) are frightened by four smiths who will cast them down. A man (angel?) with a measuring line is told that he need not be concerned about the walls of Jerusalem, for it will outgrow its walls and Yahweh will surround it with a wall of fire. The visions are now interrupted by an appeal to the Babylonian exiles to re-turn home. Next Zechariah beholds Joshua confronted with "the Satan" (here means "the accuser"). However, Joshua's filthy garments, a symbol of (ritual?) impurity, are taken away, and he is clothed with fresh garments and a clean turban, and promised that he will have charge of the Lord's courts. A lampstand with seven lamps and near it two olive trees next appear, but the meaning of this vision is not very clear. Does it mean that the trees (Zerubbabel and Joshua) will supply oil (grace) for the lamp (Israel)? Or that the lamps signify Yahweh who enlightens the two anointed leaders? An enormous scroll about thirty by fifteen feet is inscribed with a curse on thieves and liars. A woman sitting in an ephah (a grain measure) represents wickedness. Finally, four chariots drawn by red, black, white and gray horses ride out from between two bronze mountains and go to the four points of the compass. Those who go to the north are to wreak Yahweh's anger on Babylon.

Zerubbabel Crowned 6:9-15. The prophet is told to take gold and silver and make crowns for Joshua. *This passage seems to have been altered.* Originally it perhaps provided crowns for both Zerubbabel and Joshua, as the use of the plural indicates. If, as is sometimes supposed, Zerubbabel led a rebellion which failed, the passage may have been altered after that event. At present it is obscure.

Inquiry About Fasts 7:1-8:23. A deputation from Bethel asks whether the customary fasts should be continued. Zechariah replies that Yahweh prefers good moral standards to ritual. "Execute true judgment and show mercy and compassion every man to his brother. And oppress not the widow, nor the fatherless, the stranger, nor the poor; and let none of you imagine evil against his brother in your heart." A series of sayings relate to the coming happiness of Jerusalem. Yahweh is "jealous for Zion," and will return and dwell in her. Old men and women will sit happily in the street while children play. Yahweh does not seem to doubt Zerubbabel's success (though apparently some people did). The nation will be saved from Babylon and from Egypt and from internal strife. But when these happy days come, men must do right. "Speak ye every man the truth to his neighbor; execute the judgment of truth and peace in your gates: And let none of you imagine evil in your hearts against his neighbor; and love no false oath: for all these are things that I hate, saith the Lord." Then the fasts will be times of "joy and gladness and cheerful feasts," and people of all nations will turn to the Jews. They will say, "We will go with you: for we have heard that God is with you."

Miscellaneous Oracles 9:1-14:21.

These oracles are anonymous and of uncertain date. The first (9:1-12) pictures the victory of a Messianic king. It may refer to the siege of Tyre by Alexander the Great in 322 B.C. The prophet thinks the siege presages the coming of the Messiah. The more belligerent end of the chapter (vss. 13-17) may express Israel's disappointment when this expectation was not fulfilled. A brief petition from a time of drought (10:1-2) speaks scornfully of those who try to make rain come by appealing to idols and diviners, and directs the people to "ask rain from the Lord," who alone can send it. The next three oracles probably date from the Ptolemaic period. A prophecy of war against tyrants (10:3-12)

foretells the return of the Jews from the Diaspora. An ironic lament for the tyrants (11:1-3) compares their destruction to the fall of great cedars and oaks. A puzzling allegory (11:4-14), in which the prophet says he is a shepherd of a flock doomed to perish, seems to lay the blame for Israel's troubles at home and abroad on their disloyalty to God. Details of the allegory are obscure and scholars do not agree on their interpretation. The last few verses of the chapters (15-17) speak of an evil governor, a "worthless shepherd," who "does not care for the perishing, or seek the wandering, or heal the maimed, or nourish the sound . . ." (RVS). The last are apocalyptic and eschatological in character. The writer of the oracle in 12:1-13:9 expects that when the heathen nations rise to destroy God's people, God himself will strike panic into their hearts, terrorizing horse and rider alike. Judah will be a blazing fire and Jerusalem, protected by God's shield, will stand secure. Its inhabitants will wash themselves in a cleansing fountain and the nation will be purged, only one-third surviving as a faithful remnant. In Ch. 14, another writer gives a different picture of the last days of Jerusalem. He says that after the city has been ravaged and half the population exiled, God in person will appear on the Mount of Olives, which will split in half, while the whole land becomes a plain. A terrible, rotting plague will afflict both people and beasts. If the nations who survive do not worship the Lord and keep the Feast of the Tabernacles (booths), they will be afflicted with terrible droughts. In that day Jerusalem will be so holy that pots to cook the sacrificial meals will have to be as large as ceremonial bowls, and, as a token of holiness, even the horses' bells will be inscribed "Holiness unto the Lord."

Malachi

Introduction. The book of Malachi belongs to the period just before the governorship of Nehemiah, who, in fact, corrected some of the abuses which are mentioned, such as mixed marriages and improperly carried out rituals. Malachi wrote at a time when both priests and people were depressed and discouraged by the realities which faced them after the return to Judah. They had come with high hopes but had had many disappointments. The land was poor and hardly offered a bare living. The nation was a powerless and unimportant little unit in the vast Persian Empire. Where were the glories of the return promised them by Second Isaiah? If they were really God's chosen, people asked, why was not their lot a happier one? Rewards and punishments seem to be very unevenly meted out. The people wanted to know why evil seemed to be rewarded and good not rewarded. They asked "Where is the God of justice?" The prophet attempts to give some answers to this question.

Superscription 1:1. This states that the oracle is addressed to Israel by Yahweh's *messenger* — for that, literally, is what Malachi means.

Downfall of Edom 1:2-5. The prophet explains that the downfall of Edom is one way in which Yahweh has demonstrated his love for Israel: "Yet I have loved Jacob but hated Esau" (RSV). The Edomites will not be able to rebuild the ruins. They are "the people against whom the Lord hath indignation forever."

Various Abuses 1:6-2:17. Priests and people are guilty of sins before the Lord. This is one cause of their present suffering. The priests offer imperfect animals as sacrifices. They are not living up to their high calling because they have not kept the Lord's ways. Faithlessness in marriage and divorce are an offense to Yahweh.

Future Times 3:1-4:3. Yahweh will send his messenger who will purify the priests and people until they make the right offerings. Sorcery and adultery, perjury, and oppression of the helpless — the hireling, the widow, and the orphan — will be done away with. Now the people are robbing God by not paying proper tithes. But if they bring full tithes, he will send them blessings, so that the land and the vines shall bear fruit. The Lord keeps in his book of remembrance the names of those who fear him, and they shall be his special possession. The day will come when the evildoers will be burned up like stubble and "the Sun of righteousness shall rise with healing in his wings," and the faithful shall tread down the wicked. This is the third point at which the prophet tries to answer the question, "Where is the God of justice?"

Epilogue to Book of the Twelve 4:4-5. "Remember ye the law of Moses my servant, which I commanded unto him in Horeb for all Israel, with the statutes and judgments. Behold, I will send you Elijah the prophet before the coming of the great and dreadful day of the Lord." He will turn the hearts of the fathers and the children toward each other, or the land will be cursed.

THE APOCRYPHA

As the introductory section on "The Canon of the Old Testament" explained, the Septuagint (the Greek version) included fourteen books not found in the Hebrew Canon. There was some doubt as to which of these books should be accepted, and this is reflected in the word "apocrypha," which means "secret" or "obscure." While Jerome was inclined to regard these works as secondary, Augustine thought they were important and ought to be included in the Bible. He was probably right. I and II Maccabees and the so-called Wisdom of Solomon are both of the greatest historical interest, while among the stories, Tobit, Judith, and Susanna each has its special charm. Though they were not included in the Jewish Canon, most of the apocryphal books are inserted in appropriate places in Roman Catholic Bibles. In the King James Version, the apocryphal books were originally printed between the Old and the New Testaments, but were gradually dropped out. Since some of them are of general interest, a short account of them is included here.

I and II Esdras. I Esdras (the Greek form of Ezra) is an account of the fall of Jerusalem and the Exile. It is taken with variations from parts of Chronicles, Ezra, and Nehemiah, adding a story of three guards at Darius' court. Most of II Esdras is entirely different and separate. In seven revelations to Ezra, and supposedly related by him, the author tries to foretell the future of Israel up to the fall of Jerusalem in 70 A.D. He is concerned, like the author of Job, with the problem of evil and with the small number who will be saved. Portions of the book, Chs. 1-2 and 15-16, are of Christian origin, but not of any special interest.

Tobit. *Passages in the Dead Sea Scrolls show that this book was known in the first century B.C.* The author knew the latter part of II Kings, the stories of the wooing of Rebecca and Rachel in Genesis, an Aramaic romance, the book of Psalms and the book of Job. As in the case of Job, the author is troubled by the problem of evil. The folk motifs, the bride whose husbands all die and the grateful ghost who gives useful information in return for proper burial, are also used. Out of these sources, and his own imagination, the author has concocted an endearing story of the trials of a pious exile, Tobit, and the adventures of his son Tobias.

The book is written in the first person. Tobit tells how as an exile in Babylon he serves the Assyrian rulers. He is generous in almsgiving and shows a proper respect for the dead of his race by giving them a decent burial. Unfortunately, he loses his position and wealth and eventually becomes blind. Though he wishes he were dead, he never loses his faith in God.

Meanwhile, his kinsman Sarah, far away in Media, is contemplating suicide, because she has married seven times and each time the husband has died before the marriage has been consummated. These deaths were caused by a demon. *(The belief in demons and angels is thought to have been borrowed from the Persians. The existence of these beings is assumed in New Testament literature.)*

Tobit, remembering that he has money in Media, sends a son Tobias to collect it, reminding him to obey God, give alms, beware of harlots, and avoid a foreign marriage. They hire a guide for Tobias, not knowing that it is the angel Raphael in disguise. Tobias' dog goes along. *This is the only instance in the Bible where a dog is spoken of as a companion!* At the River Tigris, Tobias catches a large fish and preserves its organs, as advised by Raphael, who tells him how to use them to frighten away the demon who is killing Sarah's husbands. "The devil shall smell it, and flee away, and never come again." Moreover, Sarah is appointed by God to be Tobias' wife. There is an emotional meeting with Sarah and her pious parents, the smell does indeed scare the demon away, and the pair are married. The parents are still nervous and are relieved to find the young man still alive in the morning.

They all return to Nineveh, where Tobias uses the gall of the fish to cure his father's blindness. Raphael explains that he has been sent by God to look after the pious Tobit and his family and so the story ends happily. *(A psalm of praise by Tobit and a prophecy of the fall of Nineveh seem to have been added later.)*

Judith. Judith reminds many readers of the book of Esther, as it is a tale, set in a pseudo-historical background, in which a brave and beautiful Jewish woman saves her people in a time of great danger. The book may have been written in the mood of patriotism which accompanied the Maccabean revolt.

The narrative begins with a quarrel between Nebuchadrezzar, king of the Assyrians, and the Medes. Since most readers would know that Nebuchadrezzar was king of Babylon, they would real-

ize the book was fiction and would see the king as a representative of a contemporary persecutor, perhaps, Antiochus Epiphanes.

At the order of the king, his general Holofernes wages war on the countries who refuse to worship Nebuchadrezzar and his gods. Having "wasted their countries" and killed all their young men, Holofernes finally comes to Judea. The people prepare to defend themselves, but are "troubled for Jerusalem and for the temple of the Lord." They pray in sackcloth and ashes for deliverance, and fortify the mountain villages. Achior, the captain of the Ammonites, explains to Holofernes that the children of Israel have great pride in their religion and loyalty to their God. "Whilst they sinned not before their God, they prospered," but when they disobeyed, they were defeated. Achior advises Holofernes not to interfere with them, for fear their God should defend them. Holofernes is clever enough to turn Achior over to the Jews, hoping he will be discredited. He is handed over at Bethulia (perhaps Shechem), where the Jews praise him and feast him.

Meanwhile, Holofernes besieges Bethulia. Idumeans (the Edomites, ancient enemies of the Israelites) suggest to Holofernes that he cut off the water supply, and the defenders are ready to give in rather than die of thirst.

Now Judith, the heroine, is introduced rather late into the story (Ch. 8). She is a beautiful and wealthy widow, who numbers among her ancestors Joseph, Gideon, and Elijah, whose courage and intelligence she inherits. To the elders of the city she argues that they should not "test" God by threatening to surrender. She implores God to help her, but herself takes action. Taking off her widow's garments, she bathes (the author has forgotten the water shortage), anoints herself with precious ointment, puts on fresh attire, dresses her hair attractively, and decks herself with jewels "to allure the eyes of all men who should see her." She takes wine, oil, corn, figs and bread, and watched by the astonished citizens, goes with her maid to the camp of Holofernes. There she gets in by pretending that she will tell the general how to overcome the Jews.

Holofernes, lying on his bed beneath his bejewelled canopy, is immensely struck with Judith's beauty and believes her when she tells him that the Jews are about to sin by eating cattle which are really due to the priests. She and Holofernes exchange elaborate speeches. She is careful to make a point of leaving the camp with her maid and carrying her bag every night to pray — this makes her later escape plausible. Though the general invites her to eat with him, she prepares her own kosher food; on the fourth day, she does attend his banquet and at last agrees to drink with him, saying, "I will drink, now, my lord, because my life is magnified in me this day." Judith, of course, is thinking of the deed she intends, whereas Holofernes takes her speech as a piece of flattery and drinks more than usual. As he lies drunk on his bed, she prays for strength and with two blows strikes off his head. Putting it and the canopy (to identify him) into her bag, she and her maid leave the camp as normally, but go straight back to Bethulia, where Judith displays the head and praises God. In the morning the Hebrews go down to attack the army, an easy task, as the soldiers flee in terror when the headless trunk of their general is found. Judith is given his tent, and decked with olive branches, she leads the victory dance. She dedicates the canopy and tent to the Lord and is honored all her long life by her people.

Additions to Esther. In the LXX six passages are added to the book of Esther. When Jerome was working on the Vulgate (translating from the Hebrew), he noted where each of these passages in Greek should go, but his notes were ignored by careless scribes, who copied the additions as if they were continuous. The order can, of course, be reconstructed. There are some duplications of the Hebrew. *The purpose of the additions was to make the book more religious and more interesting.*

A dream of Mordecai contrasts the forces of good and evil and foretells the survival of the Jews. Prayers by Mordecai and Esther are inserted at appropriate points. Esther is made to protest marrying or even eating with a gentile, in accord with Maccabean orthodoxy. Documents purporting to be the edict against the Jews and the edict counteracting it are presented but they disagree in some details with the Hebrew text. *Perhaps the most dramatic addition is a longer account of Esther's approach to Ahasuerus intended to replace Esther 5:1-12.* The king at first is very angry, Esther faints from terror, and he relents. *The story of Esther is made more orthodox and more melodramatic by these additions.*

The Wisdom of Solomon. This important work, *the first to attempt a fusion of Greek and Hebrew thought,* was almost certainly written in Alexandria about the middle of the first century B.C. The object of the author (the name Solomon was merely a bid for authority) was to counteract the skepticism of the book of Ecclesiastes, the chief ideas of which are summarized in Ch. 2. He freely uses Greek concepts and terms to defend what he views as the orthodox Hebrew position and in doing so *he initiates a new tradition, Hellenistic Judaism,* which was continued by the philosopher Philo, by St. Paul and by the theologians Origen and Clement. The author believes in the immortality of the soul, the devil as the source of evil and death, and wisdom (who is highly personified) as God's counselor and agent in creation — all important doctrines in late Judaism and early Christianity.

First the righteous and the ungodly are contrasted. The righteous seek wisdom, which comes from "the spirit of the Lord." Man, made in God's image, was meant to be immortal. The devil (here first identified with the serpent of Gen. 3) brought death and sin into the world, but the righteous will gain immortality and live in God's presence. The ungodly will suffer eternal death. They may indeed live long but it will not profit them. At the Judgment the wicked will recognize how much better true wisdom is.

In Chs. 6-9 the author praises wisdom, at first in the conventional terms familiar in the book of Proverbs, later using Greek terms and concepts. For example, the Socratic and Stoic virtues, "temperance, prudence, justice and fortitude" are praised, and the Greek word "logos" or world soul is used (cf. Jn. 1:1). The last part of the book shows how God has guided and protected Israel since the beginning. The darkness in which the Egyptians move is contrasted with the light given to Israel. At the end God is compared to a harpist harmonizing all the elements of the universe.

Ecclesiasticus. Ecclesiasticus (roughly "the church book") was written in Hebrew c. 180 B.C. by Jeshua ben Sira (Jesus son of Sirach in Greek). His grandson translated the work into Greek. Like Proverbs and other wisdom books, Ecclesiasticus praises wisdom as the source of happiness and long life, and teaches a doctrine of

retribution. However, unlike traditional wisdom teachers, ben Sira equates wisdom with the law and emphasizes the need for constant study and interpretation of it.

All wisdom is the fear of the Lord,
And in all wisdom is the fulfillment of the law.

There are a very large number of verse couplets as in proverbs, but these are often grouped together under topics such as humility and friendship. Interspersed are prose passages, hymns, eulogies, and short maxims.

The first part of the book describes how wisdom comes from God and explains its applications to human life. For example, respect for parents, almsgiving, loyalty in friendship, and the proper attitude to riches are all examined in considerable detail. There are interesting warnings against spoiling children and against imprudent and hasty acceptance of advice. Traveling is praised, as it contributes to a man's wisdom. A physician should always be honored "for of the most high cometh healing." Moreover, "the skill of the physician shall lift up his head."

The second part begins, "Let us now praise famous men, and our fathers that begat us." Ben Sira reviews the history of Israel from Enoch and Noah down through the patriarchs, kings and prophets to Simon the Just, a high priest who lived perhaps a quarter of a century before the book was written. An appendix includes prayers of thanksgiving and an acrostic poem.

Additions to Daniel. There are four short additions to the book of Daniel; the Prayer of Azariah, the Song of the three young men, and two stories, Susanna and Bel and the Dragon. They were written only a little later than the book of Daniel, during the reign of

Antiochus Epiphanes. It is thought that they circulated independently before being added to the Daniel narrative.

Azariath is the Hebrew name of Abednego, one of the three young men who according to the book of Daniel were thrown into the burning fiery furnace for refusing to worship the golden image set up by Nebuchadrezzar. *The prayer is spoken "from the fire," literally from the furnace fire, allegorically from the desperate times in which the writer lived.* The unjust king mentioned in vs. 9 is Antiochus Epiphanes. Even in adversity, Azariath blesses God and praises him for his justice and mercy. A contrite heart is the truest sacrifice.

The Song of the Three Young Men is also connected with the Daniel story, for the young men are Shadrach, Meshach, and Abednego, who sing "in the burning fiery furnace," i.e., in times of suffering. This beautiful canticle is one of the better known passages of the Apocrypha, since vss. 35-65 are often sung as part of the morning service in the various branches of the Anglican Church, including the Episcopal Church. It calls on all creation, sun and moon, dews and frosts, ice and snow, mountains and hills to bless the Lord, to "praise him and magnify him forever." It concludes

O ye Spirits and souls of the righteous, bless ye the Lord:
Praise him and magnify him for ever.
O ye holy and humble men of heart, bless ye the Lord:
Praise him and magnify him for ever.

Susanna is usually placed after Ch. 12 in Daniel, but sometimes before Ch. 1. The latter is logical as Daniel is described in this story as a youth. Susanna (the name means "lily"), the daughter of righteous parents and the wife of an honorable man, is known as one who fears the Lord, i.e., tries to live by the law. In her daily walks in the garden, she attracts the attention of two hypocritical elders, who lust after her and plan her undoing. They hide in the garden as she prepares to bathe on a hot day, and when the garden doors are shut, they rush out and threaten her. If she will not submit to them, they will testify that they caught her in the act of adultery with a young man. Susanna is in a terrible position: "If I do this thing, it is death unto me, and if I do it not, I cannot escape your hands." Either way, she will be accused of adultery, which is punishable by stoning (cf. Jn. 8:1-11).

Next day the two elders come, "full of mischievous imagination," ready to accuse Susanna. Her family, friends, and servants are all much distressed. The elders make her unveil her face (in itself humiliating) and describe how they caught her with the fictitious young man. The assembly condemns her to death. She cries out with a loud voice, "O everlasting God ... Thou knowest that they have borne false witness against me, and behold I must die." The Lord inspires the youth Daniel, who cross-examines the elders separately. (His name means "God is judge.") Their evidence is conflicting for one says he saw the couple under a mastic tree, a small evergreen with aromatic resin; while the other says it was a holm oak, a much larger tree. The assembly turns on the elders and they are put to death for giving false testimony. The family all praise Susanna and Daniel is known for his wisdom from that day on.

The story stresses the importance of chastity, and, perhaps, advocates a more careful examination of witnesses.

Bel and the Dragon contains two separate stories. Like Susanna, the story of Bel has a certain detective interest. The priests daily supply their idol, Bel with great quantities of bread, meat, and wine. Daniel refuses to worship Bel on the grounds that he is "but clay within and brass without, and did never eat or drink anything." Suspense is kept up, as Daniel does not reveal the secret until later. Meanwhile, the angry king calls on the priests for proof that Bel really does devour the supplies. When the proof is forthcoming, Daniel will die.

The priests have the king set out the feast himself and seal the doors with his own signet. But Daniel has his servants scatter ashes on the temple floor in the king's presence. In the morning when they unseal the doors, the food is gone and the king cries, "Great art thou, O Bel, and with thee is no deceit at all." But, laughing, Daniel prevents the king from going in until he sees in the ashes the footsteps of the priests, their wives, and their children. The priests are obliged to reveal the secret doors by which they came in to eat the food. The king has the priests killed and gives Bel and his temple over to Daniel, who destroys them.

The Dragon is another deity worshiped by the Babylonians. Daniel admits that this monster is alive, but denies that he is immortal. He manages to poison the beast with cakes made of hair and pitch. A number of enraged courtiers insist that he be punished, and he is thrown into a lion's den (as in Dan. 6), where an angel brings Habakkuk to comfort him. After seven days he emerges unharmed and the king has the courtiers thrown in instead.

I Maccabees. After the death of Alexander the Great in 323, the two chief powers in the Near East were Syria and Egypt. Egypt at first controlled Palestine, but later this control passed to Syria, ruled by the Seleucid dynasty from Antioch. Antiochus Epiphanes began a policy of uniting his subjects by insisting on religious uniformity. Judah Maccabee (Judas Maccabeus, i.e., "the Hammerer") revolted against this policy. I Maccabees, written by a Palestinian writing in Hebrew, tells the story of this revolt and the subsequent history of the Maccabean house for the next forty years down to the death of Simon Maccabeus in 134 B.C. The style is clear, functional, and graphic. *The date of writing is uncertain, perhaps a little after 104 B.C. when John Hyrcanus died, though some critics would place it earlier.*

After a short account of Alexander the Great, the author describes the sufferings of devout Jews under Antiochus Epiphanes (means "illustrious"), including the desecration of the temple and the slaying of women who had had their children circumcised. Mattathias and his five sons revolt, flee to the mountains, and are joined by others loyal to the cause. The old man dies (166 B.C.) telling his sons to "be zealous for the law." Judas is given command of the holy war and wins an initial victory. At the command of Antiochus, Lycias sends out a large army led by Nicanor and Gorgias and accompanied by a number of elephants. Judas and his small force win a double victory over this army and acquire rich spoils. Eventually his army fights its way into Jerusalem and rededicates the temple, a triumph celebrated today in the Jewish festival of Hanukkah, or the Feast of Lights. After victories in Trans-Jordan and Galilee, part of the army is defeated at Jamnis. Antiochus dies (163 B.C.) and Lycias, now regent, makes terms with the rebels. They are to leave the citadel, but they are permitted to obey the law, keep the Sabbath, and practice circumcision. But soon the war continues. Judas, through representatives who go to Rome, makes a pact of "Amnity and confederacy" with the Romans. Judas is slain in battle and is mourned by his brothers. He is succeeded by Jonathan. He and his brother Simon divide their troops and force the enemy to retire and there is peace of a sort for five years. Jonathan, now high priest, is in a strong position, so much so that rival rulers try to win his support. He makes an agreement with Alexander, the son of Antiochus, and later with Dimitrius II. However, eventually he is deceived by a third ally, Trypho, through whom he is taken prisoner and murdered.

The last brother, Simon, now takes over. "All my brothers are slain for Israel's sake, and I am left alone." His courageous speech raises the spirits of the people, and they fortify the walls of Jerusalem. Dimitrius proposes a peace. Taxes and tributes to Antioch are to cease, though young men must still serve in the army. The Jews believe that at last they are independent of the Seleucids: "Thus the yoke of the heathen was taken away from Israel." The treaty is consolidated by Simon's capture of the citadel in Jerusalem. Simon is generous to the foreign soldiers, taking no revenge, but cleansing the area after they have left. Dimitrius confirms him as a ruler, commander, and high priest. He is praised for his achievements and the people "till their ground in peace."

For every man sat under his
vine and his fig tree,
And there was none to fray
them.

But soon intrigues and fighting begin again. Demetrius is jealous of Roman alliance. Simon is old now. He has three sons, John, Judas, and Mattathias. He tells Judas and John (whom he has had especially trained for leadership) that they must take over the fight against the enemies of Israel. He and two of his sons are treacherously slain, but John, called Hyrcanus, survives to succeed (134 B.C.). The author refers us to the "chronicles of his priesthood" for further knowledge of the "worthy deeds" of John. He conquers most of Palestine, once more achieves independence for Israel, and dies in 104 B.C.

II Maccabees. This is a partial account of the Maccabean revolt with quite different emphasis. The author focuses on Judas Maccabeus, concluding his account with the victory over Nicanor and avoiding all mention of his hero's final defeat and death. He wrote in Greek and probably in Alexandria, making an abridgement of a five-volume history by Jason of Cyrene. The condensation is curiously done, some events being out of order. The style is very different from that of I Macc., florid, rhetorical, and emotional, rather than factual and straightforward. The author has a taste for the supernatural (dreams, angels, etc.) and for grisly martyrdoms. He emphasizes physical resurrection, prayers for the dead, and obedience to the law — all characteristic of the Pharisees.

At the beginning of the book are two letters *of doubtful authenticity*. They urge the Jews of Egypt to celebrate the Feast of the Dedication of the Temple. The first story relates to a period earlier than Antiochus Epiphanes. It was included to show that God always protects the Temple. Through a treacherous Jew named Simon, the king, Seleucus IV, learns of the great wealth in the Temple and appoints his vizier Heliodorus to confiscate it. The priests prostrate themselves before the altar and pray for deliverance. God sends "a horse with a terrible rider" (an angel) and two other heavenly beings who beat Heliodorus until he is unconscious.

Judas Maccabeus is introduced in Ch. 5, when he and a few followers escape a massacre of Jews in Jerusalem ordered by Antiochus Epiphanes. This ruler also forbids all Jewish religious practices, turns the Temple into a temple of Zeus, and tries to Hellenize the Jews completely. Two stories of martyrdom are told: an aged man and a mother and her seven sons are tortured and killed. The scenes are described in grisly detail. The martyrs expect their reward in resurrection, but there is to be no resurrection for the ungodly. Judas and his soldiers put the Greek commander, Nicanor, and his army to flight, but do not pursue them because they have to observe the Sabbath.

Antiochus tries to rob the Temple, but is punished by a horrid disease and a fall from his horse. He repents and promises to return the loot and to become a Jew. *This is certainly fiction.* After his death, the Temple is rededicated and his little son's regent, Lycias, is defeated. (In I Macc. both the dedication and the defeat take place before Antiochus' death.) After attacks on Joppa and Jamnia, Judas is involved in battle with the Idumeans. Some Jews who have died in battle have been carrying religious articles associated with foreign cults. Judas has sacrifices and prayer offered for them. Next there is another account of a battle with Lycias similar to the one in which elephants were used described in I Macc. Philip becomes regent and makes peace with the Jews. Dimitrius, the older brother of Antiochus Epiphanes, who has been in Rome, returns, seizes the throne, and kills Lycias and the young king. Nicanor (who perhaps has been in Rome with Dimitrius) first pretends to be friendly with Judas, then threatens to desecrate the temple if Judas does not give himself up. After the prophet Jeremiah and the high priest Onias appear to him in dreams, Judas encourages his troops to fight their best. They win the battle, decapitate Nicanor, and celebrate their victory on the feast of Purim. In the midst of this account, the author has paused to tell of the persecution and suicide of a pious Jew, Razis, interesting because suicide is unusual in the Old Testament. The book ends with Jerusalem in the hands of the Jews.

THE BIBLE IN ENGLISH LITERATURE

Several of the Genesis stories were dramatized in the mystery cycles, including Adam and Eve in Eden, the rivalry of Cain and Abel, and Noah's escape from the flood. In the Noah story, some humor is used at the expense of Noah's "crabbed" and cantankerous wife, who refuses to go into the ark unless she has her "gossips (cronies) — every one." The York cycle has two simple but effective plays about Adam and Eve, but perhaps of more interest to the student is the Norwich Paradise play which was rewritten in line with Protestant theology. *Abraham's sacrifice of Isaac was a favorite topic because the sacrifice of Isaac was thought to prefigure the sacrifice of Christ.* Among the mystery plays, the most artistic treatment is the Brome "Abraham and Isaac," in itself a little masterpiece. The Protestant theologian Theodore Beza wrote a very popular play on the same subject, which was translated into English in Elizabeth's reign. The Wakefield Cycle has a separate play about Jacob. The Elizabethan *Jacob and Esau*, author unknown, makes use of Roman comedy devices, particularly the contrast of the two brothers, and is amusing for its rather absurd attempt to make the story a proof-test for the doctrine of predestination.

The greatest poem treating Adam and Eve is Milton's epic, *Paradise Lost.* There are references to Adam and Eve and to patriarchs in the poems of Edward Taylor, James Agee, and Phyllis McGinley and the novels of Herman Melville (*Billy Budd* especially), John Steinbeck (*East of Eden*) and William Faulkner. Perhaps the most attractive of modern American poems on Genesis themes is James Weldon Johnson's beautiful "Creation." In the same book, *God's Trombones*, is "Noah Built the Ark."

In modern drama, Bernard Shaw's *Back to Methuselah*, Thornton Wilder's *Skin of Our Teeth*, and Clifford Odet's *Flowering Pearl* all use the Genesis material more or less freely. Marc Connelly's *The Green Pastures* treats the main events in Genesis up to the drunkenness of Noah, placing them in a Negro community in Louisiana.

The Exodus narrative was not as popular with mystery play writers as Genesis. Where the York Cycle has nine plays using Genesis stories, it only has one play on Exodus, which includes the plagues and the crossing of the Red Sea. The Wakefield Cycle likewise has one play.

Curiously, Exodus does not seem to be the source for any important work until American Negroes, with their memories of slavery, seized on the story of the escape of the Hebrew slaves as their own and produced spirituals such as "I Wish I Had Died in Egypt's Land," "Tryin' to Cross the Red Sea," and the unforgettable "Go Down Moses." James Weldon Johnson has a version of the story, "Let My People Go," in *God's Trombones* and Connelly devotes two scenes to it in *The Green Pastures.* Christopher Fry's *The First Born* is a rather slight poetic dramatization of the Exodus.

There is little in the rest of the Pentateuch to attract the writer, except the story of Balaam and his ass, the subject of a play in the Chester cycle.

Joshua's siege of Jericho inspired one of the most exultant of the spirituals, "Joshua Fit de Battle of Jericho." In the book of Judges, the story of Jephthah's sacrifice of his daughter attracted interest in the Renaissance because of its resemblance to the sacrifice of Iphigenia, the subject of two plays by Euripides. However, the humanist writers who chose this subject thought the classical languages more appropriate for what they viewed as a classical subject. George Buchanan, the Scottish humanist, wrote in Latin and John Christopherson of Cambridge wrote the sole surviving Biblical play in Greek from the Tudor period. Both have been translated. The last "judge" provided the subject for the greatest dramatic poem in English, *Samson Agonistes*, Byron's "Song of Saul" is one of several poems which show his interest in the Bible. Browning's "Saul" is one of the few good Victorian poems on a Biblical figure.

The David story has attracted writers of many periods. Thomas Watson, Christopherson's contemporary at Cambridge, was attracted by the revenge theme in the Absalom episodes and outdid Seneca in his melodramatic *Absalom*. George Peele, Shakespeare's contemporary, did include Absalom's revolt, but emphasized the romantic love of Bathsheba and Nathan's parable in his *David and Bathsheba*. Dryden's best satire, on Shaftsbury and other politicians, is *Absalom and Achitophel*. The eighteenth century Christopher Smart's "Song of David" is a hymn of praise rather than a narrative. In more recent times, besides the spiritual "Little David Play on Your Harp," there are James Barrie's *"The Boy David,"* Faulkner's *Absalom, Absalom* and Gladys Schmidt's *David the King*.

In the book of Kings, the notorious Jezebel has been the subject of several plays, including one by Masefield. Clemence Dane's *Naboth's Vineyard* is effective. The mysterious death of Sennacherib's host (II Kgs. 19) is the subject of perhaps the best Romantic poem on a Biblical subject, Byron's "Destruction of Sennacherib."

The dramatic story of Esther was the subject of two Tudor plays, *Godly Queen Hester*, a satire on Wolsey (in the person of Haimon), and *Queen Esther and Proud Haimon*, a version which makes Esther appear ever more pious and heroic than in the original story.

The agony of Job has attracted several modern writers. Thornton Wilder has it in mind both in *The Skin of Our Teeth* and *Hast Thou Considered My Servant Job?* Frost's *Masque of Reason* is a brief version. The most important treatment is Archibald MacLeish's *JB*.

Translations of the psalms into English verse were common in the Renaissance. Besides the Scottish metrical psalms, which are still sung today, Sidney and Milton both wrote verse translations, the best known of which is "Let Us with a Gladsome Mind," a paraphrase of Psalm 136, written while Milton was still in his teens. Spirituals include "The Lord is My Shepherd" and "We Shall Walk Through the Valley of the Shadow of Death."

The Song of Songs was the subject of one of Edward Taylor's sacramental "meditations." There have been several modern attempts to dramatize it, not very successful, because it is really lyrical rather than dramatic.

Though medieval cycles usually include a prophet play, in which the birth of Christ was prophesied, on the whole the form of the prophetic books has not encouraged drama or fiction, though the BBC has done an informative series which tells the stories of Elijah, Amos, Isaiah, and others down to John the Baptist. James Brodie wrote two versions of a Jonah play and the irate prophet is also the subject of Wolf Mankowitz' *It Should Happen to a Dog*. The most exciting work based on a prophetic vision is the spiritual "Ezekiel Saw The Wheel."

The stories in the Apocrypha have attracted some writers. *The Most Virtuous and Godly Susannah* is an attractive early Elizabethan play which stresses family loyalty and piety. James Brodie's *Susannah and the Elders* and *Tobias and the Angel* are appealing.

To name these works based on Biblical stories does not give an adequate impression of the importance of the Bible in English literature. *Its influence is more pervasive as a source of rich allusion and eloquent language.* Shakespeare knew the Bible well, including the Apocrypha ("A Daniel come to judgment"), and his works contain thousands of allusions. Quite aside from his major works, Milton's poetry often assumes a close knowledge of the Bible and cannot be understood without it. Many other seventeenth-century writers are soaked in the language of the KJV, most powerfully John Bunyan and George Herbert. Of the Romantic poets, Blake, although he constructs his own very unorthodox religious philosophy, is steeped in the language of the Bible. In addition to the poems already mentioned, Byron's "Hebrew Melodies" show his interest in creating a kind of Biblical poetry. There are fewer allusions in the poetry of the other Romantics, though S. T. Coleridge and Thomas de Quincey knew the scriptures well and allude to them frenquently in their prose works. Keats thought of the deathless song of the nightingale finding a path "through the the sad heart of Ruth, when sick for home, / She stood in tears amidst the alien corn."

Melville uses Biblical figures such as Ahab, Alijah, Jonah, and Ishmael in *Moby Dick*, and his other novels contain many such allusions. Steinbeck's *East of Eden* uses the Cain and Abel story. Faulkner's short stories refer to familiar figures such as Abraham and Isaac and to the garden of Eden, the land of Canaan, the lion of Judah. Many modern poets make evocative use of Biblical references from T. S. Elliot's *The Waste Land* on. John Masefield's "Guinquerime of Nineveh" is based on a verse describing Solomon's trade in, among other things, "ivory and apes and peacocks."

The works of modern fiction writers as various as Joyce Carey, Graham Greene, Bernard Malamud and Flannery O'Connor contain religious allusions. James Baldwin's title *The Fire Next Time* is an allusion to God's promise never to send another flood, and in *Notes of a Native Son* he makes moving use of Joshua's farewell speech, ending, "But as for me and my house, we will serve the Lord."

It can be safely said that whatever period the student is exploring, from the medieval to the modern, he will find a knowledge of the Bible indispensable.

GLOSSARY

ALLEGORY. A narrative in which abstract qualities are represented as persons to teach a moral or spiritual lesson. The Song of Songs is sometimes interpreted allegorically.

AMPHICTYONY. A league of city-states or tribes, as in Greece or Israel.

ANACHRONISM. A chronological error in which a person or event is (often unconsciously) assigned to a period or date other than the correct one.

ANTHROPOMORPHISM. Representing the deity as man-like in appearance or behavior, as in Gen. 2-3.

ARAMAIC. Semitic language spoken widely over the Near East, especially in Syria, Palestine, and Mesopotamia, c. 300 B.C.-650 A.D.

ASHERAM, pl. ASHERIM. Ancient Semitic goddess (sometimes identified with Astarte and Ashtoreth); sacred pole symbolizing same.

CHARISMA, adj. CHARISMATIC. Divinely conferred gift or power, such as wisdom, prophetic vision, or strength.

CHERUB, pl. CHERUBIM. Celestial being, technically the second order of angels; often represented as a winged child.

DOUBLET. Pair of similar stories, sometimes variants of same original, e.g., the two accounts of David's break with Saul, I. Sam. 19,20.

ETIOLOGICAL STORY. One which explains the origin of some more or less mysterious phenomenon such as human sin or the multiplicity of languages, Gen. 3,11.

EUPHEMISM. The substitution of an inoffensive or mild word for a blunt or harsh one, e.g., KJV "Surely, he covereth his feet," but RSV "He is only relieving himself," Judg. 3:24.

FABLE. A brief, often child-like tale, often involving beasts or plants, and sometimes making a single moral point. Rare in O.T.; see Jotham's fable, Judges 9: 7-21.

HYPOTHESIS. A conjecture put forward to explain some puzzling phenomenon, e.g., the Graf-Wellhausen hypothesis which attempted to explain the discrepancies, contradictions, etc., in the Pentateuch by distinguishing several documents from different historical periods.

LEGEND. A story handed down from earlier times. It is often accepted as historical, and may indeed have historical origins, though it cannot be verified.

MONOTHEISM. The belief that there is only one god.

MYTH. A narrative, usually involving supernatural beings, which tries to explain some natural phenomenon, such as the remains of a great flood.

NAZARITE. A religious devotee who vowed for a period not to take strong drink or cut his hair, or touch a dead body. Not to be confused with **NAZARENE,** a native of Nazareth or a member of an early Christian sect.

PARABLE. A short narrative usually making a single moral or religious point. See Nathan's parable, II Sam. 12:1-23.

POLYTHEISM. Belief in many gods.

SCAPEGOAT. A goat led into the wilderness and let loose after the high priest had laid the sins of the people on his head, see Lev. 16: 8-22; hence one made to take blame for others.

SEPTUAGINT. The most ancient Greek version of the Old Testament, dating from the third century B.C. and later. The word means "seventy," the legend being that 70 (or 72) scholars made the translation.

SERAPH, pl. SERAPHIM. A celestial being, technically the highest order of angels.

SHIBBOLETH. A test word or phrase which characterizes a group or sect. See Judges 12: 4-6.

SYNCRETISM. An attempt to reconcile different or even opposing religious beliefs and practices.

THEOCRACY. A government in which god is looked upon as the supreme civil ruler, his laws being interpreted by the ecclesiastical authorities.

THEOPHANY. A manifestation or appearance of God, as in the burning bush, Ex. 3:2.

WADI. Bed of a stream or river, dry except in the rainy season.

ZIGGURAT. Temple in the form of a pyramid-like tower, in a series of terraces. A broad ramp ascends around the ziggurat. Common among the Babylonians and the Assyrians.

BIBLIOGRAPHY

This bibliography is selective. Readers who need a more extensive reading list will find an excellent one in Bernard Anderson's *Understanding the Old Testament*, Samuel Sandmel's *The Hebrew Scriptures*, or the *Anchor Bibles*. Books marked with asterisks are paperbacks.

TEXTS, COMMENTARIES, ENCYCLOPEDIAS, DICTIONARIES

The Jerusalem Bible. Ed. Alexander Jones. London: Darton, Longman and Todd, 1966. Based on *La Bible de Jérusalem*, issued by the Dominican Bible School in Jerusalem, but the English text was freshly translated from Hebrew and Greek. Has introductions, notes, maps, and an index of themes.

The Oxford Annotated Bible. Ed. Herbert G. May and Bruce M. Metzger. New York: Oxford Univ. Press, 1965. The RSV text with brief but excellent notes, introductions to each book, general articles, and maps. Can be obtained with or without Apocrypha.

The Rabbi's Bible Series. Ed. Morrison Bial and Solomon Simon, 3 vols. New York: Behrman House, 1966. With introduction and clear, helpful notes.

A New Catholic Commentary on the Holy Scriptures. Ed. Reginald C. Fuller, D.D., Leonard Johnston, S.T.L., Conleth Kearns, O.P. London; Nelson, 1969. Uses the RSV text and is, in the words of the editors, "a real contribution to the ecumenical movement fostered by the Second Vatican Council and the World Council of Churches." More extensive and a little more difficult than *The Interpreter's One-Volume Commentary* listed below.

Dictionary of the Bible. Ed. John J. Mckenzie, S.J. Milwaukee: Bruce, 1965.

Encyclopedia of Bible Life. M.S. and J.L. Miller. New York: Harper & Row, 1955.

Harper's Bible Dictionary. Ed. M. S. and J.L. Miller. Revised, New York: Harper & Row, 1973.

The Interpreter's One-Volume Commentary on the Bible. Ed. Charles M. Laymon. Nashville: Abingdon Press, 1971. An excellent work in one volume by an interfaith group of eminent scholars. Has articles on the Canon, Hebrew poetry, the Dead Sea Scrolls, and many other topics. Pictures and chronology.

The Oxford Concordance of the Revised Standard Version. Ed. Bruce M. Metzger and Isobel M. Metzger. New York: Oxford Univ. Press, 1962. Compact concordance for home use.

Any of the above titles could be purchased for home study.

The following larger multi-volume works can be consulted in the library:

The Anchor Bible. Ed. W.F. Albright and David N. Freedman. New York: Doubleday, 1964- Expected to run to at least 58 volumes, 42 of which had been issued by 1974. So far an excellent series. Each book is translated and annotated in detail by a specialist. Comparative readings are given where these are available. Comprehensive introductions, notes, bibliography, various indexes.

Encyclopedia of the Jewish Religion. Ed. R.J.Z. Werblowsky and Geoffrey Wigoder. London: Phoenix House, 1965. Contains many articles on the Bible.

The Interpreter's Bible. Ed. George A. Buttrick. Nashville: Abingdon-Cokesbury, 1952-7. In this twelve-volume work, the KJV and the RSV are printed side by side. Below are extensive exegetical notes and below that exposition of the passages by well-known preachers. The general articles in Vol. I are excellent.

The Interpreter's Dictionary of the Bible. George A. Buttrick *et al.* 4 vols. New York: Abingdon, 1962.

The New Catholic Encyclopedia. Ed. William J. McDonald, 14 volumes. New York: McGraw-Hill, 1967. Includes many articles on aspects of the Bible. Ecumenical in its outlook and distills the results of world scholarship.

Peake's Commentary on the Bible. Ed. Matthew Black and H.H. Rowley. Revised ed. New York: Nelson, 1962. A standard work brought up to date by two eminent scholars.

ATLASES

Grollenberg, L.H., O.P. *Atlas of the Bible,* Trans. J. Reid and H.H. Rowley, New York: Nelson, 1956.

The Westminster Historical Atlas of the Bible. Ed. G. Ernest Wright and Floyd V. Filson. Philadelphia: Westminster Press, 1956.

Both these atlases can be recommended for their excellent maps, clear texts, and well-chosen pictures.

BOOKS ON ARCHAEOLOGY AND NEAR EASTERN TEXTS

The Ancient Near East: Anthology of Texts and Pictures. James B. Pritchard, Princeton: Princeton Univ. Press. Important texts that throw light on the Bible, with superb pictures. For the more experienced student.

Archaeological Encyclopedia of the Holy Land. Ed. Avraham Negev. New York: Putnam, 1972. Contains over 600 articles and covers the subject up to the Byzantine period.

Documents from Old Testament Times. Ed Winton T. Thomas. New York: Harper Torchbooks, 1961. Another collection of Near Eastern documents. There are no pictures, but the book is inexpensive.

Everyday Life in Bible Times. The National Geographic Society. Washington, D.C. Wonderful color pictures of ancient artifacts and modern scenes. Experts such as Father de Vaux, Pritchard, Wright, and Kraeling were consulted.

Landay, Jerry M. *Silent Cities, Sacred Stones.* Wiedenfeld and Nicolson, 1971. A beautiful and illuminating book with fine pictures.

Thompson, J.A. *The Bible and Archaeology.* Grand Rapids, Mich.: Eerdmans, 1972. A good, thorough survey of the field. Pictures.

Vaux, Roland de, O.P. *The Bible and the Ancient Near East,* Tr. Damian McHugh. New York: Doubleday, 1971. A collection of essays which shows how many topics are illuminated by archaeology, e.g., the remnant, the patriarchs, single combat.

Wright, G. Ernest. *Biblical Archaeology.* Revised Ed. Philadelphia: Westminster Press, 1962. Scholarly, thorough, and extremely clear, with good pictures. *There is an abridgment in paperback (no pictures).

INTRODUCTIONS TO THE OLD TESTAMENT

Anderson, Bernhard W. *Understanding the Old Testament*. Englewood Cliffs, N.J.: Prentice-Hall, 1966. An excellent and widely used text, combining history, literature, and religious ideas. Good maps, charts, and pictures.

Bamberger, Bernard, J. *The Bible: A Modern Jewish Approach*. New York: Schocken Books, 1963. A useful, inexpensive introduction.

*Charlier, Celestin. *The Christian Approach to the Bible*. New York: Paulist Press, 1967. Has chapters on texts, historical background, literature of the Bible, etc. Does not deal with the books one by one.

Gordis, Robert. *Poets, Prophets, and Sages*. Bloomington, Indiana: Indiana Univ. Press, 1971. Historical treatment from primitive times to the Qumran community.

Gottwald, Norman, K. *A Light to the Nations*. New York: Harper & Row, 1959. A sound introduction, particularly good on the Old Testament as literature.

Hunt, Ignatius, O.S.B. *Understanding the Bible*. New York: Sheed & Ward, 1962. A straightforward introduction for the layman.

*McKenzie, John L., S.J. *The Two-Edged Sword*. New York: Doubleday Image Books, 1966. A scholarly and beautifully written interpretation.

Moriarty, Frederich L. *Introducing the Old Testament*. Milwaukee: Bruce, 1960. A popularly written book which stresses leading figures in Biblical history.

Napier, Davie. *The Song of the Vineyard*. New York: Harper and Row, 1962. An introduction which emphasizes the development of religious ideas.

*Otwell, John. *A New Approach to the Old Testament*. Nashville: Abingdon, 1967. A clear, sensible introduction for the reader without much previous knowledge.

*Rowley, H.H. *The Growth of the Old Testament*. New York: Harper Torch books, 1961. Short but very compressed and scholarly.

Sandmel, Samuel. *The Hebrew Scriptures: An Introduction to Their Literature and Religious Ideas*. New York: Knopf, 1963. Excellent, thorough, vigorously written. After his introductory chapters, Sandmel treats the O.T. books in their approximate order of composition, beginning with Amos.

Tos, Aldo J. *Approaches to the Bible: The Old Testament*. Englewood Cliffs, N.J.: Prentice-Hall, 1963. An introductory text based on the translation by the Confraternity of Christian Doctrine.

Note: A recent work in several volumes which might be consulted in the library is *The Cambridge History of the Bible* published by the Cambridge University Press, 1970.

MISCELLANEOUS

A few on special topics, several with a literary emphasis, are listed here.

Baly, Denis. *The Geography of the Old Testament*. Revised. New York: Harper & Row, 1972.

Bewer, Julius A. *The Literature of Old Testament*. Revised by Emile G. Kraeling. New York: Columbia University Press, 1962.

Dheilly, Joseph. *The Prophets*. London: Burns and Oates, 1966.

Lowes, John Livingston. *Essays in Appreciation*. Boston: Houghton Mifflin, 1936. Contains "The

Noblest Monument of English Prose," an eloquent appreciation of the KJV.

*The Old Testament and Modern Study. Ed. H.H. Rowley. London: Oxford University Press, 1951. A valuable collection of essays by British and American scholars.

Robinson, Theodore H. The Poetry of the Old Testament. London: Duckworth, 1947.

Russell, David Syme. The Jews from Alexander to Herod. London: Oxford Univ. Press, 1967.

Scott, Robert B.Y. The Relevance of the Prophets. Revised. New York: Macmillan, 1969.

The Way of Wisdom in the Old Testament. New York: Macmillan, 1971.

Van Doren, Mark. In the Beginning, Love. New York: John Day, 1973. Fifteen dialogues between the great teacher and poet and the noted writer and translator, Maurice Samuel, on a variety of topics. Spontaneous and stimulating.